Children *at* Risk

Children at Risk

The Precarious State of
Children's Well-Being
in America

Janice Shaw Crouse

Transaction Publishers
New Brunswick (U.S.A.) and London (U.K.)

This book is printed on acid-free paper that meets the American National Standard for Permanence of Paper for Printed Library Materials.

Library of Congress Catalog Number: 2009018636
ISBN: 978-1-4128-1076-0
Printed in the United States of America

Library of Congress Cataloging-in-Publication Data

Crouse, Janice.
    Children at risk : the precarious state of children's well-being in
    America / Janice Shaw Crouse.
        p. cm.
    Includes bibliographical references and index.
    ISBN 978-1-4128-1076-0 (acid-free paper)
        1. Child welfare—United States. 2. Families—United States.
    3. Child abuse—United States. 4. Children—United States—Social conditions. I. Title.

HV741.C75 2009
362.70973—dc22

                                                    2009018636

Contents

Children are one third of our population and all of our future.
—Select Panel for the Promotion of Child Health, 1981

Introduction

Children's Well-Being and the Nation's Agenda

Since I arrived in Washington, DC nearly two decades ago, my work has centered on analyzing the social science data related to the functioning and well-being of families and children. While working at the U.S. Department of Health and Human Services, then at the White House, and later heading a non-profit think tank, I studied the trends and correlations of a wide array of data series to understand the factors and policies that impact children's well-being. The results of years of analyzing the data have convinced me, beyond all doubt, that the rejection of traditional Judeo-Christian values and morality is at the root of most of the broken relationships that children encounter in American culture. Growing up in *material prosperity* can never compensate for those conditions of *moral poverty* that inevitably produce isolation, despair, and emotional pain.

If we are to change the trajectory of children's living conditions, we must abandon the experimentation with value-free nostrums pushed by those whose *avant-garde* ideas and policies have been so detrimental to the nation's children. When it comes to children, it is really all about the basics of a mother and father within a committed marriage, who establish a family and give their children unconditional love and a solid foundation of nurturing, training, and discipline that will enable them to reach their fullest potential. Such parents are jointly committed to the well-being of their children—to meeting their basic needs for emotional connectedness and sound moral and spiritual development.

The conclusions that I have reached and present in this book have been corroborated by a just-released study in England that is being called a "wake-up call for parents."[1] The study claims that childhood in the United

1

Kingdom is "under threat," "toxic," or "disappearing" and dares to assert that "moral and spiritual values" are a necessary foundation for children. One newspaper summarized the report's findings: "Our children are desperate for love, for time and for affirmation of their fragile self-esteem. Yet we too often substitute toys, TV and Facebook."[2]

Troubled by the increase in emotional and behavioral problems among British children,[3] England's 125 year-old Children's Society issued a clarion "call for evidence" and commissioned interviews with children, parents, and professionals over a two-year period to determine the "barriers to a good childhood." Released on February 5, 2009, the report, *A Good Childhood: Searching for Values in a Competitive Age*, is simply called "The Good Childhood Inquiry."[4] Evidence was contributed by thirty thousand people, including twenty thousand children, through polls, interviews, and focus groups. The bottom line: parents in the United Kingdom put status and success ahead of sacrifice; working mothers and absent fathers have children materially spoiled, but ignored; and children are deprived of moral instruction and left without a spiritual foundation. What is true in the U.K. is certainly true in America.

Ironically, Americans live in a perpetual "year of the baby" with the tabloid magazines repeatedly focusing on pictures of the beautiful people who are expecting a child, usually without benefit of marriage. Numerous celebrities and actresses are pictured with a "bump," current lingo for showing a pregnancy prominently displayed. Given the volume of cover stories and pictures of celebrities like Brooke Shields, Katie Holmes and Tom Cruise, and, especially, Angelina Jolie and Brad Pitt, it is obvious that the public has an insatiable fascination with celebrity pregnancies, adoptions, and births. Supermarket tabloids keep us well informed about the latest flaunting of cultural mores. Social science data reveals that the public is following the example set by the "celebrities" so consistently and publicly showcased by the media.

Listen to the politicians, too, and there is an echoing mantra that this or that policy must be enacted "for our children." With all of the usual concerns about children's well-being stemming from the breakdown of the family and cultural disintegration, it is no wonder that rhetoric about children permeates public discourse. Throw in politics and billions of dollars in federal, foundation, and corporate money and the demagoguery index skyrockets. Every imaginable special interest group with a new project or untested policy, regardless how tenuous the association, pushes its agenda with the claim: "We must do this for the children."

All this being the case, are children really at the heart of the nation's attention and rhetoric? If they are, we need to examine why so many of our children are faring so poorly. With America's material and tangible advantages, the current generation of children should be doing exceptionally well. Instead, all the rhetoric aside, perhaps the truth is that their well-being is often just an afterthought. All too often we see, for example, that children are merely pawns in the struggle between cohabiting partners or divorcing parents. Likewise, we see too often, children rank far below other parental priorities, such as making money, career success, or social advancement. When a single parent is overwhelmed with responsibility and obligations, as is more often than not the case, or when parents are too consumed with their own ambitions or pleasures, children are neglected. Overwhelmingly, children are the ones thrust into poverty when the parents reject marriage. Too many children are emotionally abandoned, abused, ignored, and their needs sacrificed when an immature single mother has to choose between a boyfriend, her addictions, and/or her fun and her children.

Even those children growing up in a prosperous material environment, full of opportunities for positive development unimpeded by obstacles to economic progress, too often have an impoverished emotional and spiritual quality of life. Increasingly, children grow up too fast—having too little time to experience the normal childhood pleasures; seeing too few adult models for healthy relationships and values; and facing too many adult challenges before their reasoning powers have matured.

New adolescent brain research, based on magnetic resonance imaging (MRI) studies, suggests that society is wasting billions of dollars on education and non-directive intervention programs to dissuade teens from dangerous activities, because their immature brains are not yet capable of independently rejecting risky behaviors. The research of Dr. Jay Giedd, chief of brain imaging in the child psychiatry branch at the National Institute of Mental Health, was the cover story for *Newsweek Magazine*[5] and *U.S. News and World Report*.[6] An interview with Dr. Giedd was featured on *Frontline*. His research was featured in *Teachers' Domain*[7] and in *Earth and Sky*.[8] So from popular magazines to scientific and teachers' magazines, his research warns, "It's sort of unfair to expect [teens] to have adult levels of organizational skills or decision-making before their brains are finished being built." The "exuberant growth" of the adolescent brain gives it tremendous potential as an adult. During the teen years, brains are adapting as they prepare for adulthood.[9] Teen activities become "hardwired," making a teen's choices important for his or her future.[10] The challenge is to make sure that the teen, during this volatile period of rapid development, does not make mistakes that will affect the rest of his or her life.[11]

Scores of today's typical emotional and psychological stresses on children were uncommon in the past. Indeed, many children today face a senseless theft of their childhood and their innocence is at risk.

Something about babies and children brings out, in most of us, the adult instinct to protect and cherish. Most adults respond to the vulnerability of children in very predictable ways. Every summer it seems we hear about another adult who drowns while trying to rescue a child in trouble or one who throws caution to the wind to rescue a child, not even their own, who is threatened in some way. We hear numerous stories of adults who risk their own lives in order to save a stranger's child. In a recent incident near my home,[12] an unnamed U.S. Coast Guard petty officer passed a highway crash involving three passenger vehicles and a commercial trash truck. Seeing that the cars were burning and a police officer was working to rescue a woman in one of the cars, "He rushed past several onlookers and, at great personal risk to his own life, reached into the burning vehicle and removed the child." The Fire Chief on duty called the action "absolutely heroic" and noted that the petty officer "placed himself in extreme danger to save a life."

We especially want to protect children's innocence; we reserve the worst censure and penalties for those who harm children. Yet now as always children are threatened by predators who would take advantage of their vulnerability. One only has to look at Northern Ireland or Palestine or any number of other points on the globe to see how tenuous is any communion forged out of adult desires for children's welfare. Even in democratic America the competition of ideas and values about what represents the "good" society in which to raise our children is fierce, as are the differing views about the value of innocence and even life itself. These differing ideas and values affect people's actions even when individual citizens have never reflected on them or have never cared enough to formulate those values into a coherent worldview.

Too often, ideas and values are subconsciously imbibed from the cruder elements of the culture and are cheapened by the activities of those who seek to make a profit without regard for morality or decency; likewise, culture and circumstances are also affected by the era's dominant ideas and values. They interact like a river and its banks. Usually the flow of the river is directed by the banks, but at times, the river shapes the banks, as powerful surges erode and overflow the surrounding territory. A seemingly indestructible boulder in the midst of a river redirects the current; but, let a flood occur and the current of the river can move the obstruction, or over time, reshape the hardest rock. Sometimes cultural ideals and values are as obvious to observers as the dam that blocks the flow of a river; other times they are hidden from view like a riptide under the ocean's surface that only the trained observer can detect even when people are getting caught and swept away.

We like to think we live in an ideal world where differing ideas and values are appreciated and the competition between them is benign, but the clash of values and personal preferences can turn deadly; this has been true since Cain slew Abel. Not all circumstances are imposed; some result from bad choices, which reflect bad ideas and values. Too often we have forgotten the Third Law of Newton's Laws of Motion: "For every action there is an equal and opposite reaction." Ideas and values influence behavior and, thus, have consequences; actions have consequences; decisions have consequences; attitudes have consequences.

Over the past four decades, liberal ideas and values have often prevailed in the competition with traditional values and ideas. This book documents the disastrous consequences suffered by several generations of our nation's children as a result of forty years of policies based on the prevailing liberal ideology and the shift away from Judeo-Christian values as the nation's moral touchstone. One disastrous liberal claim has been that any group of adults can "parent" a child; that the family consisting of a married mother and father in a permanent, lifetime union is passé.

Other defective liberal ideas about the family are clearly evident in political discourse and subsequent policies (such as all for "children," but not for family). The basic problem with a child-centric approach is that children's well-being cannot be considered apart from the well-being of the traditional family. Neither state nor federal programs are ever enough to compensate for society's embrace of moral relativism and the inevitable subsequent breakdown of the family. The body of accumulated data is clear; in particular, it highlights the negative outcomes that tend to be associated with the rapidly increasing numbers of unmarried female heads of household with children. Fathers matter and their absence is a tragic loss to child and mother alike. In fact, the data clearly show linkages between our society's various detrimental trends: out-of-wedlock childbearing rates, marriage rates, abortion rates, divorce rates, etc. The trends make it obvious that liberalism badly ran amuck and produced toxic circumstances for families and children, often with disastrous consequences. Yet for decades, researchers sugarcoated the ill effects of liberal, utopian policies. Now, reality is forcing even many on the left to open their eyes to the obvious fact that family structure does make a difference in children's well-being. As the old saying goes, "Truth will out." And it is not your truth or my truth but "the truth."

The counter-cultural values in the late sixties and early seventies are examples of liberal ideas and policies that negatively affected families and, thus, children. Examples of specific policies include no-fault divorce, the legalization of abortion, and expanding welfare as an "entitlement" with no strings attached even though the mother's lifestyle is dysfunctional (most notably with: alcohol and drug abuse, gambling, indolence, and out-of-wedlock childbearing).

Former President Reagan tried to reform welfare in the early eighties but abandoned the enterprise in the face of the furious response by the leftist advocacy communities. The upsurge in welfare dependency in the early nineties and the growing drug culture helped facilitate a groundswell of demand for change. This was first reflected at the state level as individual states re-designed their welfare programs to impose family caps, stay-in-school provisions, and time limits. Also, this was reflected in public support for welfare reform at the federal level so strongly that former President Bill Clinton, after vetoing welfare reform legislation twice, finally succumbed and signed the congressionally imposed third version. Headlines quoting welfare advocates at the time predicted that welfare reform would put another million children in poverty. Critics declared that an economic recession would bring dire results. That did not happen; child poverty, even in mother-only households, declined by 10 percentage points from 1996 to 2001,[13] key evidence proving that welfare reform has been positive. In fact, welfare caseloads dropped dramatically as women moved from welfare to work.

Child poverty also illustrates how bad ideas and values produce bad policy. Child poverty may be the result of economic circumstances, but those economic circumstances often also reflect bad values, ideas, and the dysfunctional behaviors mentioned earlier. Not all economic circumstances produce the same results in child well-being. Generally, a "poor child" in a married-couple family ends up better off than a "poor child" in a single-mother household. The poverty rates of never-married women are higher than those of divorced women, and the poverty rates of divorced women are higher than those of married women.

A number of organizations and federal agencies produce annual publications with titles like: *Trends in the Well-Being of America's Children and Youth, America's Children: Key National Indicators of Well-Being, or Kids Count Data Book*. These publications provide reams of data about trends affecting children. In fact, we have knowledge overload about children. The nation's scholars and demographers have extensively documented both the problems and the progress related to children's well-being. We have plenty of data; what we need is insight, perception, and wisdom. What is missing is a clear understanding of the sources of the problems and penetrating analyses of the issues underlying those problems. Too often, demographers and scholars miss the forest as they count and label all the trees.

In this book, our purpose is to focus on the major problems facing America's children today: the breakdown of the family, the decline in marriage, negative cultural influences, and the erosion of Judeo-Christian values and morals as the foundation for nurturing children and building a strong society. Our analyses focus on the data, but we probe that data and sift through the research studies in order to understand the extent of the problems and their ramifications for children's well-being. Beyond the presentation of the truths to be found in data and research studies, we believe that insight and wisdom are needed to guide the nation back to the principles that should be the foundation for any specific policies that seek to address children's issues.

In addition, changes in grassroots attitudes and the cultural climate of a nation don't just happen because research data indicates the necessity for such changes. A sustained public effort is required in order to achieve the needed social changes. We can look back at two efforts in America's history that were dramatically successful in producing broad cultural transformations. Both efforts were based on solid research data showing that certain behaviors produced negative health outcomes, especially for pregnant women and their unborn children. Both campaigns for change were public relations efforts that focused on the whole nation and enlisted the efforts of a wide spectrum of opinion leaders, politicians, educators, entertainers, local pastors and religious leaders, celebrities, corporate moguls, journalists, public relations experts, movie and television producers, policymakers, grassroots activists, creative artists, athletes, non-governmental executives, and local community activists. The purpose was to convince women not to smoke or drink alcohol during their pregnancies because of the potential danger to their babies. Subordinate campaigns sought to convince parents that second-hand smoke is damaging to children and that drinking and driving can be deadly.

The results have been dramatic. Now when a young married woman politely demurs at a cocktail party when offered a drink, friends smile, suspecting that the gesture announces her pregnancy.

How did we reach this point when for decades smoking and drinking were considered a mark of sophistication? Looking back on those campaigns is instructive.

In the early 1980s, researchers identified certain alcohol-related birth defects that came to be known as fetal alcohol syndrome (FAS). We learned that FAS is caused by exposure of the fetus to alcohol consumed by the mother and is "characterized by growth deficiencies (or decreased growth), abnormal facial features (specific facial features), and central nervous system (or brain) abnormalities."[14] This finding led to extensive efforts by the government, supported by the media, to educate women of the risks of drinking while pregnant. The public was made to understand that children exposed to alcohol in the womb risk having "deficits in growth, behavior, and neurocognition such as problems in arithmetic, language and memory; visual-spatial abilities; attention; and deficits in speed of information processing."[15]

Likewise in the mid-1980s we saw increased efforts to warn women of the dangers of smoking while pregnant. The Federal Cigarette Labeling and Advertising Act of 1965 was amended in 1984 to require that the health warnings on cigarettes be made more explicit with direct references to the risk posed by smoking while pregnant. The warning on cigarettes included the statements: "Smoking by pregnant women may result in fetal injury, premature birth & low birth weight," or "Smoking Causes Lung Cancer, Heart Disease, Emphysema, And May Complicate Pregnancy." The Surgeon General issued reports couched in technical jargon such as: "Infants born to women who smoke during pregnancy have a lower average birth weight and are more likely to be small for gestational age than infants born to women who do not smoke. Low birth weight is associated with increased risk for neonatal, perinatal, and infant morbidity and mortality."

It remained for others, like the March of Dimes, to bring the cause down to the local level and make explicit: (a) that babies whose mothers smoke while pregnant are more likely to have lungs that do not develop in a normal way, (b) smoking nearly doubles a woman's risk of having a low-birth-weight baby and also increases the risk of a preterm delivery, and (c) that "morbidity" means the likelihood of adverse outcomes in subsequent life, i.e., chronic lifelong disabilities (such as cerebral palsy, mental retardation, and learning problems).[16]

As women's knowledge increased, they understood how their behavior could pose a risk to the priceless infants they carried in their wombs. The effect was to dramatically change the way both women as individuals and the public in general viewed smoking and drinking by pregnant women. Most women who smoked and/or drank made every effort to stop when they became pregnant. Those pregnant women who did not and were seen smoking or drinking were no longer considered sophisticated but were viewed as selfish, self-indulgent, and irresponsible. The researchers' findings coupled with effective public relations efforts changed perceptions and cultural values. Women, seeing the threat to their unborn children, changed their behavior.

The burning question we face today is whether the epidemic of single parenting especially single mothers and fatherless households is likewise amenable to influence by the researchers' findings and whether those who influence public opinion will support the effort to change those attitudes and behaviors that lead to the establishment of single-parent households where children face higher risks.

Other questions are: Will young women and men acknowledge the findings about the harmful effects on children of growing up deprived of the presence and support of a married-couple father and mother? Will married couples care enough about their children's well-being to work out their problems in order to provide a stable family together rather than try to escape by getting a divorce? Knowing the risks that are involved for children living in a household without a married mother and father who love them and who are committed to working together to raise their family, will young, single individuals choose marriage rather than have children out of wedlock and attempt to raise them alone? Is there reason to believe that public attitudes can change on these contemporary issues so important to children's well-being?

Massive advertising campaigns in the early twentieth century convinced people that smoking and alcohol were essential to a sophisticated good life. Massive "free sex" marketing efforts in the 1950s and 1960s were designed to persuade the public, young women in particular, that sexual self-restraint is "prudish" and unhealthy. Several generations embraced the *Playboy*-generated myth: "lose your virginity" as soon as possible in order to enjoy the happiness that is available only through

carefree, uncommitted sexual behavior; don't worry, there are no consequences to meaningless "hook-ups."

For nearly fifty years, opinion leaders, from Hollywood actors and
entertainment celebrities to academic intellectuals and policy makers,
have relentlessly "sold" and modeled a self-indulgent life style that is
supposedly "natural" and completely free of any negative consequences.
Fiction has been labeled fact: narcissistic self-centeredness is the epitome
of glamour, sophistication, and a natural characteristic of the good life.
"Edginess" or "having an attitude" is essential to a "metrosexual" image.
No effort has been spared to promote a rose-colored view of promiscuity.

Researchers of a certain stripe have produced an endless stream of
studies obfuscating the causes of the social problems, problems that
common sense tells us are the natural consequences of self-absorption
and exploitation of women and children. The obvious correlations in the
data were downplayed by raising a caution that those correlations may
only indicate that there is a selection bias rather than a direct linkage.
There was an enormous effort to keep the focus off the clearly evident
negative consequences of the non-traditional lifestyles approved of, no,
advocated by those who had participated in the 1960s sexual revolution
that overthrew the Judeo-Christian foundations of our social order.

Reality, however, cannot be suppressed. An ever-growing body of
research documents the real-life consequences of promiscuous behavior,
and, I believe, the mass of evidence is reaching a tipping point.

Before we go into all the statistics, we need to see the human side
of the numbers. After several days of 4-wheeling through the back
country of the Colorado Rockies, my husband and I rewarded ourselves
with breakfast at the locally renowned Butterhorn Bakery and Cafe in
Frisco, Colorado. The Butterhorn Cafe is one of those places of western
ambiance, located in a rustic, picture-perfect old mining town, the kind
that dot the Colorado mountains. What I remember most, however, was
not the delicious breakfast, but the brief conversation we had with our
waitress.

We had assumed she was a co-ed soon to be headed back to college.
She shocked us by saying that she was twenty-eight; then she cheerfully
volunteered that she had recently moved to Frisco with her boyfriend with
whom she had been living for ten years. They decided, she said, to trade
the beach scene in South Carolina for snowboarding in the Rockies. It's
funny how activists have made privacy such a sacred right, yet people

still want to connect by revealing themselves to others. Our waitress had no idea how much her statement revealed to her customers—two people who analyze the nation's social trends.

While the young woman eagerly anticipated the pleasure of snow-boarding that winter, frankly, we knew that the odds were that she couldn't count on a future with that boyfriend. While she is undoubtedly emotionally bonded to him, she doesn't have a commitment from him. After giving up ten years of her youth, she is unlikely to receive anything but heartbreak in return. Such relationships typically end with the girl being the loser. If and when they get married, it will be the boyfriend who makes the decision, not the girl, and not them together. Typically, she doesn't know that a marriage after living together is more likely to end in divorce than if they had not lived together beforehand. When he decides to "get serious" it will probably be with a fresher, younger girl.

And, her biological clock is ticking; in fact, it's winding down fast. She probably doesn't realize how fast it is going, but at some point she will want a family and children. For many young women in her situa-tion, that realization comes too late. Will her snowboarder boyfriend recognize how significant and full of meaning the life of husband and father is? Will he be willing to give up the life of freedom for one of commitment and responsibility? If she gets pregnant and has the baby, she has no assurance that her boyfriend will stick around and help her change diapers. Many abortions are prompted because the woman has a choice. The boyfriend says, "It's your choice—the baby or me!" And for sure, a baby is an expensive proposition and would certainly hamper their snowboarding.

Explaining her living arrangement was more intimate detail than we expected and we weren't surprised when the waitress abruptly started talking about the freak late summer snowstorm outside. She had called her mom, she said, to tell her about the inch of ice on her car that morn-ing. Her mom. She had called her mom. Not her mom and dad, not her folks, but her mom. There has to be a lot of history behind that simple statement: I called my *mom*. We did not, of course, ask about that his-tory. Whatever it is, it is likely a painful story. But, again, our work with cultural trends provides a likely explanation.

The behavior pattern of our waitress closely fits the profile of thousands of young women raised by unmarried moms who are either divorced or never married. Her mother may have been abandoned by the father of her child or she may have been one of the many who have bought into the myths associated with radical individualism that have become so dominant in our culture. It is a short slide from the *sunum bonum* of this age, self-actualization, to the crass position of "you gotta do your own thing." The problem is that "doing your own thing" ends up affecting many others besides you. Consider for instance, the emptiness felt by children raised in single-parent families whenever they see a friend receiving hugs and affection from *both* father and mother, together.

Anyone with a drug-addicted relative or friend knows firsthand that when an individual does drugs it is the beginning of a long, long road of pain and disappointment to everyone who cares about them. Ditto numerous other social ills so rampant today. Such events cast a shadow over the lives of all of the friends and loved ones connected to those individuals who have chosen those paths.

Even if it were not immoral behavior—an old-fashioned concept these days—cohabitation, by its very nature, is an exercise in foolishness. For the woman, there are the risks to health and personal safety of living with a man not emotionally equipped to make the commitments required of a husband and father. Even if he has good looks and charm, a "nice" guy does not take advantage of the "something-for-nothing" deal that cohabitation entails. A young woman's heart is a delicate, priceless treasure and any male who is a real man—someone worthy to be the father of her children—does not take something of such value unless he is willing to give something of equal worth in exchange, namely, the life-time commitment of marriage.

But that is not the world we live in today, and we are all so very much the poorer. My heart ached that morning as I left the Butterhorn Cafe thinking about our waitress and the millions of other young women like her who are headed down a dead-end road. Theirs is a blighted future. They are forfeiting the priceless joys of marriage to the love of their lives. None of us lives life without some bumps along the way, but a life full of positive and happy times that become cherished memories is possible only in the secure bonds of a firm "till death do us part" commitment—marriage. As I think about all of the young women who have thrown away their virtue—another old-fashioned idea—I am deeply troubled. I like the challenge of "doing our own thing" crossing treacherous Rocky Mountain passes, but I am compelled to accept another, more important, challenge—combating the dangerous trends of today when young people "doing their own thing" end up broken and deserted at the bottom of the treacherous passage from youth to maturity.

This book is an attempt to help young people avoid going off the cliffs of life. In our insights, assessments, and analyses of the research findings, the reader will have an accurate understanding of the risks facing today's children and young people. For too long, America's children and young people have been used as the subjects in alternative life-style experimentation. In these chapters, the reader will discover what actually works for children and youth in contrast to those experimental pipe dreams that have done so much to diminish children's hopes and possibilities for a bright and promising future.

Earlier in this introduction, we mentioned the nation's preoccupation with celebrity pregnancies, adoptions, and births. Sadly, it is important to note that celebrities, viewed as role models by many, often believe that marriage is unnecessary, nothing more than a useless piece of paper. The myth that marriage is unnecessary and even undesirable continues to be popular script for celebrity interviews and features. Worse, this insidious myth has spread throughout American culture.

The indisputable fact is that children, even those with obvious material advantages, need a married mother and father in order to have the best odds of healthy development. Growing up well adjusted—even in a home where the parents' love and commitment are rock solid—is challenge enough for children today.

While there is no question that children need a married mother and father family, it is not enough to promote marriage without a moral foundation. When marriage is a revolving door, children suffer because blended families have many of the same conflicts and problems as single-mother households. Moral boundaries, like the sanctity of life and the sanctity of marriage, are the foundation of a child-friendly society. Moral boundaries, not moral relativism, provide a safe haven for children by preserving their innocence and protecting them from the predators and pedophiles.

Without moral absolutes, children are at risk. When parents and society throw authentic religious faith overboard, children are no longer safe. When there are no underlying moral principles providing a foundation for society, when there are no institutional values unifying the populace, even the best programs and most honorable of intentions are doomed to failure. It is not enough to be well intentioned if, at the same time, you are unrealistic—"bleeding heart," if you will. Our society has suffered grievously from programs and policies that meant well but failed miserably—and on a colossal scale—as is documented by an abundance of data and the obvious social trends in America.

This book is organized into three parts with each successive part having decreasing influence on a child's well-being.[17] Part I: "The Centrality of Marriage" addresses those factors most immediately affecting children: the breakdown of the family through the decline of marriage, the prevalence of single mothers, and the resultant poverty and cohabitation. Part II: "Dangers Facing Children" focuses on those situations that can harm children when the immediate family is not a safe harbor—abortion, childhood sexual exploitation, and child abuse. Part III: "Outside Influences on Children" discusses influences external to the family unit that affect children: media, child care, childhood obesity, foster care, health and safety, and public education. The conclusion stresses the necessity of married-couple families, cultural reinforcement of time-tested values and moral principles as the foundation stones for raising well-adjusted children.

The author would like to express deep appreciation to the Huston Foundation for providing partial funding for the research in this book and to Fieldstead & Company for contributing to the salary for a research assistant. I also want to thank the excellent professional team at Transaction Publishers who made this project a pleasant and rewarding experience; especially Jennifer Nippins, my editor, with her extraordinary attention to detail. All were unfailingly encouraging and supportive.

I especially want to thank Concerned Women for America for their encouragement and support for this project. Brenda Zurita was invaluable in her editorial suggestions; she provided expertise and many hours of research, fact checking, editing, and copy editing. Joan Turrentine, educator and editor as well as my sister, provided professional guidance as she helped to refine and polish the manuscript. George Tryfiates, Ken Ervin, and my husband, Gilbert L. Crouse, Sr., were excellent advisors throughout the writing process. I am responsible for any errors or mistakes that remain in the book.

This book is dedicated to my mother, The Reverend Ruth Baird Shaw, who, in addition to her many other very admirable accomplishments, is first and foremost a wonderful and caring mother. She and our father, The Reverend Charles C. Shaw, who died more than twenty years ago, provided a family heritage from which my six siblings and I have been able to draw strength, inspiration, and encouragement in times of trouble or discouragement. Mother's generosity, unselfish devotion, wise insights, and godly counsel forged bonds of love that frees each of us to pursue our dreams with courage and confidence. Thank you, Mother, not just

for teaching us, but also for being a role model of character and integrity, challenging us to do our very best, encouraging us to serve others and illustrating for us how to live a rich and full life.

Notes

1.   "This is wake-up call for parents," *The Gloucestershire Echo,* February 4, 2009, *HighBeam Research,* http://www.highbeam.com/doc/1P2-19839979.html.
2.   Ibid.
3.   While the U.K. is among the richest of the E.U.'s member states, its children are more engaged in risky behaviors (smoking, drinking, drugs, and sex) and have more emotional problems (poor relationships with parents and peers, anxiety and depression, and poor subjective evaluations of their health and happiness). Further, it is a well-known fact that one-third of England's sixteen-year-olds are living without their fathers, and the U.K. has the highest teen pregnancy rate in Europe.
4.   Richard Layard and Judy Dunn, *A Good Childhood: Searching for Values in a Competitive Age* (London: Penguin Books, February 2009). A book based on the study is available via Amazon. The Executive Summary and the Full Report are available on-line at: http://www.childrenssociety.org.uk/all_about_us/how_we_do_it/the_good_childhood_inquiry/about_the_good_childhood_inquiry/2254.html.
5.   Sharon Begley, "Getting Inside a Teen Brain," *Newsweek,* February 28, 2000, http://www.newsweek.com/id/82963/.
6.   Sharon Jayson, "Expert: Risky Teen Behavior is All in the Brain," *USA Today,* April 4, 2007, http://www.usatoday.com/news/health/2007-04-04-teen-brain_N.htm.
7.   Teachers' Domain, "Dr. Jay Giedd: The Adolescent Brain," September 26, 2003. http://www.teachersdomain.org/resource/tdc02.sci.life.reg.gieddweb/.
8.   Eleanor Imster, "Studying Teens from Inside Out," an interview with Jay Giedd, *Earth & Sky Radio Series,* June 2005, http://www.earthsky.org/article/jay-giedd-interview.
9.   Ibid.
10. Sarah Spinks, "Adolescent Brains are Works in Progress," *Frontline,* Public Broadcasting Service, March 9, 2000, http:/www.pbs.org/wgbh/pages/frontline/shows/teenbrain/work/adolescent.html.
11. "Inside the Teenage Brain," interview with Dr. Jay Giedd, *Frontline,* Public Broadcasting Service, January 31, 2002, http://www.pbs.org/wgbh/pages/frontline/shows/teenbrain/interviews/giedd.html.
12. Peter Hermann, "Child Saved from Accident in Arundel," *The Baltimore Sun,* March 4, 2009, http://weblogs.baltimoresun.com/news/crime/blog/2009/03/child_saved_from_accident_in_a.html.
13. U.S. Bureau of the Census, "Poverty Status of People by Family Relationship, Race, and Hispanic Origin: 1959 to 2007" Current Population Survey Reports: Historical Poverty Tables—People, Table 10, http://www.census.gov/hhes/www/poverty/histpov/histpovtb.html (accessed March 20, 2009).
14. Office of the Surgeon General, "Surgeon General's Advisory on Alcohol Use in Pregnancy" (February 21, 2005), http://www.surgeongeneral.gov/pressreleases/sg02222005.html.
15. Ibid.
16. March of Dimes, "Professionals & Researchers: Smoking During Pregnancy," http://www.marchofdimes.com/professionals/14332_1171.asp.

17.   The author expresses appreciation to Martha Kleder, her colleague at Concerned Women for America, for suggesting this organizational framework for the book.

Part I

The Centrality of Marriage

The first bond of society is marriage.
—Cicero

If you bungle raising your children,
I don't think whatever else you do well matters very much.
—Jacqueline Kennedy Onassis

1

The Decline of Marriage
and the Rise of Divorce

From its founding, marriage has been integral to the American family. As the central institution of society, marriage has contributed to individual and societal well-being. Yet the marriage rate today is less than half the level in 1969; fewer people are getting married and they are waiting longer to get married.[1] The Census Bureau estimates that the median age for women at first marriage has risen from 20.3 years in 1960 to 25.5 years in 2006.[2] *The Washington Post* reported, "In 1940, less than 8 percent of all households consisted of people living alone. Now more than a quarter do."[3]

Marriage used to be the only socially acceptable household structure for couples, and there was general agreement that children needed a married mother and father. When a girl had an out-of-wedlock pregnancy, the couple typically married to provide the child with the protection of a father and the support of the church and community. Ironically, despite a great many of what were referred to in that era as "shot-gun" weddings, the divorce rate in those days was much lower than now. Indeed, the divorce rate is more than 60 percent higher[4] than it was in 1960 and remains high in spite of increased efforts to strengthen marriage as a social and cultural institution.

Likewise, the percentage of children who do not live with both of their own biological parents has increased from about one out of five to two out of five since 1960 (22.3 percent to 39.2 percent[5]). The number of single mothers is at record levels (with some inner city areas having 80 to 90 percent out-of-wedlock births); the number of cohabiting couples is 10 times larger than in 1970, and about 40 percent of these are couples with children.[6]

While many experts argue that these trends are irreversible, others are tackling the problem head on, convinced that success comes from the efforts of many. There are excellent non-governmental organizations devoted to reversing the breakdown of the family. Premier among them is The World Congress of Families,[7] uniting more than 50 pro-life, pro-marriage, and pro-family co-sponsoring organizations in the effort to reverse family breakdown. The World Congress of Families has sponsored 5 international conferences where declarations about the importance of the natural family were issued—1997 in Prague, 1999 in Geneva, 2004 in Mexico City, 2007 in Warsaw and 2009 in Amsterdam. Thousands of delegates from around the world attend these international conferences where plenary and break-out sessions provide a platform for more than 100 world-renowned authorities to speak on various subjects related to strengthening the natural family.

Three major books about marriage have had profound influence on the culture. Linda Waite and Maggie Gallagher's, *The Case for Marriage: Why Married People are Happier, Healthier, and Better Off Financially*, refutes three common arguments against marriage: (1) that marriage is a bad deal for women, (2) that divorce is better for children if the parents are unhappy, and (3) that marriage is essentially a private choice, rather than a public institution. They present convincing arguments that marriage should be the socially preferred household structure and that marriage is the foundation for a healthy and happy society.[8]

A PBS documentary, written by Barbara Defoe Whitehead, narrated by Cokie Roberts, and aired nationally on Valentine's Day 2002, was the impetus for the second book. The documentary, which Whitehead said relied heavily on research published in *Gaining Ground*,[9] provided the outline for the book. Edited by Katherine Anderson, Don Browning, and Brian Boyer, the book, *Marriage: Just a Piece of Paper?*[10] is based on ten years of research and directly addresses the issue of whether marriage is central to the family. The book acknowledges that many people who think that strong families are necessary for a strong society fail to see how marriage is essential for that goal. Social science researchers who participated in the marriage project sought to provide a rationale for marriage as necessary for the family.[11]

The third book, *The Meaning of Marriage,* was edited by Robert P. George and Jean Bethke Elshtain, two outstanding scholars who are both senior fellows of the Witherspoon Institute.[12] George and Elshtain's book seeks to answer the question, "Why is marriage in the public interest?"[13] They bring together the "most eminent authorities on marriage and public policy in the English-speaking world," to make "a case for marriage as a positive institution and ideal that is in the public interest and serves the public good." Starting with the basic premise that the past five decades have "witnessed the erosion of marriage as a public institution," the contributors point out, "All great civilizations have sought to unite, in the institution of marriage, the goods of sexual intimacy, childbearing and childrearing, and life-long love between adults."[14]

A private-sector movement of national organizations joined together to produce a document, "The Marriage Movement: A Statement of Principles,"[15] that stated concisely and without equivocation, "Marriage is not a conservative or liberal idea, not a plaything of passing political ideologies, but a universal human institution." The statement pledged, "in this decade we will turn the tide on marriage and reduce divorce and unmarried childbearing, so that each year more children will grow up protected by their own two happily married parents and more adults' marriage dreams will come true."

"The Marriage Movement: A Statement of Principles" resulted from a consultation of marriage leaders in 2000 sponsored by the Coalition for Marriage, Family and Couples Education, the Institute for American Values, and the Religion, Culture, and Family Project of the University of Chicago Divinity School. The statement was signed by over one hundred leaders, including[16] Don Browning (University of Chicago), Allan Carlson (Howard Center), Jean Bethke Elshtain (University of Chicago), Francis Fukuyama (George Mason University), William Galston (University of Maryland), Mary Ann Glendon (Harvard University), Kay Hymowitz (Manhattan Institute), Michael McManus (Marriage Savers), Steven Nock (University of Virginia), David Popenoe (Rutgers University), and James Q. Wilson (Pepperdine University).

There are numerous faith-based marriage movements, including Marriage Savers,[17] headed by Harriet and Mike McManus, a husband and wife team that works through local churches to hold marriage enrichment weekends and "back from the brink" workshops for couples on the verge of divorce. They have helped establish Community Marriage Policies in more than two hundred cities and towns in forty-three states where divorce rates are down an average of 17.5 percent and cohabitation by one-third.

Several universities have established research centers on marriage issues. Rutgers' National Marriage Project,[18] headed by David Popenoe and Barbara Defoe Whitehead, produces an annual "State of our Unions" report. The University of Chicago Divinity School has launched a project, "The Religion, Culture, and Family Project"[19] led by Don Browning, to rediscover the mainline Protestant marriage tradition, and The University of Virginia has a new scholarly initiative, "The Center for Children, Families, and the Law."[20] The National Institute for Fatherhood[21] is an initiative pointing out the inextricable link between marriage and fatherhood. The federal program, Healthy Marriage Initiative, started projects in dozens of states similar to the ones in Florida and Oklahoma.[22]

In spite of all of these efforts, that nation's marriage-aged young people are still buying into the prevalent myths that "you don't need a piece of paper" for a sexual relationship even when children are involved. According to a Pew survey of over two thousand adults, there is a widening gap between parenthood and marriage.[23] As a result, children are living in a wide variety of household structures, all far less likely to contribute to their well-being than a family that consists of a married father and mother.

The data, however, are clear; and the experts agree: no other household structure comes close to the married-couple family where the father and mother work together to ensure their children's well-being. The natural, traditional family produces the best outcomes for children.

These views are expressed in a manifesto written by Allan C. Carlson and Paul T. Mero, *The Natural Family*.[24] Carlson and Mero call the family the "natural and fundamental" unit of society that is at once an "ideal vision" and a "universal reality." They cogently argue that all the other organizing principles of life become stronger when we base society on the natural family:

> All facets of life are enriched when we choose the natural family as the fundamental unit of society. Our social life is richer—we experience broad diversity within a context of stable familiarity. Our cultural life is richer—we are better able to take advantage of generational experience and the lessons of tradition. Our political life is richer—strong, autonomous families maximize the best functions of democracy. Our economic life is richer—we work with lasting purpose, cooperatively and altruistically, for others and not just for ourselves. And our spiritual life is richer—we are motivated to become our better selves as we give birth and nurturing to the rising generations.[25]

Surprisingly, ordinary people agree with the experts; nearly 70 percent of the general public believes that a child needs both a mother and a father to grow up happily.[26] More than 65 percent of adults think that single motherhood is bad for children and society and nearly 60 percent disapprove of cohabiting couples.[27] The majority of teenagers value marriage: 82 percent of the girls and 70 percent of the boys report that it is "extremely important" to them to have "a good marriage and family life."[28]

Decline of Marriage

Behavior, however, differs from the positive attitudes of teenagers toward marriage. The proportion of American women who are married is a little less than 54 percent, as compared with 67 percent[29] in 1960, and 61 percent of the economically depressed 1930s.[30] The decline among black women has been significantly greater, dropping from 60 percent to 34 percent.[31]

How ironic! Marriage is very important to most Americans and around 90 percent will marry during their lifetime.[32] The two-parent household is still the rule rather than the exception for white America, and 66 percent of the population lives in a married couple family. Yet, the proportion of married Americans continues to decline to levels we've never seen before.

Over the last three decades of the twentieth and into the first decade of the twenty-first century, we saw a dramatic decline in marriage rates—reflecting the powerful influence of ideas in changing values and behavior. This stands in contrast to the first seven decades of the twentieth century, during which we saw numerous fluctuations in marriage rates that were tied—with the possible exception of the roaring twenties—primarily to major exogenous historical events.

By plotting the marriage rate, we can easily identify changes that coincide with particular historic events. We see for example:

1. a drop in the marriage rate at the time of the financial panic of 1907 when the stock market lost about half its value;

2. an even larger drop in 1918 at the time of the influenza pandemic when more than 500,000 persons died from March through November;

3. a modest decrease with the onset of World War I and then a sharp increase attending the demobilization and return to civilian life of the nearly four million men in the armed forces at war's end;

4. the marriage rate declined about 18 percent in the roaring 1920s, prior to the Great Crash of the stock market, and then another 10 percent from 1929 to 1930; the rate continued its decline until 1932 when it finally bottomed out[33];

5.   World War II and the subsequent demobilization and return to civilian life of over eight million enlisted men and women at war's end in 1945 produced enormous gyrations in both marriage and divorce rates;

6.   after the Korean War, there was a small up-tick in marriage rates along with economic expansion; after a subsequent nearly-year-long recession, marriage rates declined further until the onset of the Vietnam War in the mid-1960s.

With two exceptions, we generally see fairly short-term effects associated with these six major episodes. A disturbance of seismic proportions would temporarily cause an increase or decrease in marriage and divorce rates then, within a year or two, the rate would return to within 10 percent of its median value rate of 77.1 per thousand unmarried women age fifteen and older. The Great Depression and the aftermath of World War II are exceptions to the general tendency in that the deviations afterward persisted for four and six years respectively.

The last thirty years of the twentieth century are a different matter all together. The 1960s were a period of unprecedented social and cultural upheaval, though one might argue that the roaring twenties were something of a small preview. With access to the birth control pill, women—particularly college-age women—began to engage in sexual activity outside marriage in ever increasing numbers. Sexual freedom, along with growing economic independence, lessened ties to marriage; men didn't "need" to marry to engage in sexual activity. These new freedoms were a part of a growing sense of entitlement that encouraged a "me-centered" preoccupation with personal fulfillment rather than individual responsibility and obligations to others—including children, a husband, or a wife. Adults were able to engage in irresponsible behavior without seeming to be irresponsible; they were, instead, admired for becoming self-confident, self-sufficient, and emotionally independent.

The feminist movement, which became the dominant force over the "free-love" sexual revolution[34] and the "me-centered" preoccupation of the 1960s counterculture profoundly changed people's attitudes toward marriage. As women embraced feminist ideas, they exchanged fulfillment in motherhood for success in the workplace; as they brought in paychecks and became economically independent, they felt that they didn't "need" to be dependent upon men or marriage.

In time, these attitudes would come to be reflected in the marriage rates. In the mid-1960s, before the adverse effects of these anti-traditionalist ideas took root, however, a countervailing force exerted itself: college enrollment rates[35] and marriage rates rose, fueled by those seeking ways to avoid military service in a very unpopular war. From 1970 onward, we start to see a cumulative effect, now not so much of events, but of the power of ideas and changing values that affected both the behavior of individuals and the formulation of public policy. Added to the feminist's ideologically-driven, direct assaults on marriage, there were several key idea- and values-driven policy changes whose indirect effects on marriage proved to be enormous: most notable was the overturning, in 1960, of the rule that out-of-wedlock childbearing disqualified a woman from receiving welfare benefits, which in 1968 was followed by the ruling in *King vs. Smith* that dismantled the regulations barring a mother from receiving income assistance if she were cohabiting.

Following quickly behind that decision was the rush of states to pass no-fault divorce legislation beginning with California in 1969, which accelerated the rise in divorce rates. Finally, with *Roe vs. Wade* in 1973, the Supreme Court invalided state laws banning abortion.

The combined effect of ideology and policy changes on values and behavior is clearly visible in the sharp drop in marriage rates from seventy-eight per thousand (women fifteen and older) in 1972 to sixty-four per thousand by 1977, just five years later.[36] It can hardly be deemed coincidental that as abortions increased, by forty per thousand during this period, the marriage rate decreased by more than 18 percent. Since then, the marriage rate has continued to decline steadily, albeit at a slower rate, reaching thirty-seven per thousand in 2006,[37] a level less than half the rate of the pre-*Roe vs. Wade* era. Clearly many premarital conceptions that would have precipitated marriage before pro-abortion legislation were aborted after *Roe vs. Wade*.

The large drop in marriage rates in the 1970s may have also been exacerbated somewhat by economic changes that occurred in the mid-1970s as well. The Armed Forces returning from the Vietnam War faced not only strong anti-war sentiments, but the twin economic problems of rising inflation and rising unemployment as the economy slid into a sixteen-month-long recession from November of 1973 to March of 1975.[38] Thereafter, marriage rates have continued to decline both in periods of recession and economic boom to less than one-half the median rate during the first seventy years of the twentieth century with no end to the decline yet in sight. Clearly, the power of ideas and values has exerted far more force over a far longer period than the major historic events of the twentieth century.

Skeptics say that it is too late to reverse this long-standing trend away from marriage. But we must. The decline of marriage means that the nation's children are losing their safe haven as well as the central place where character and values are inculcated. The absence of marriage in the child's home life means that no one is obligated, either by duty or by love, to care for the child.

In his book, *The Marriage Problem*, the eminent political scientist James Q. Wilson[39] questioned why marriage has universally endured. He concluded that marriage is a "reproductive alliance" that people enter into freely because "experience teaches that the marriage relationship is indispensable to the rearing of the young."[40] The hope for marriage rests, in Wilson's analysis, on the fact that "human nature makes people responsive to an overriding concern—child care." Our task then is to design and maintain a culture that will "keep them together in achieving what most want, and when they get it, cherish. Their own child."[41]

The logo of the Children's Defense Fund[42] is a simple line drawing of a small child alone in a boat on a wide-open sea. The image of a defenseless child touches even the most hard-hearted person. Without the marital bond between a husband and wife to provide a safe, defined space for children, they are alone on the sea of life, buffeted by winds of chance and cruelty. Despite all our good intentions, despite our urge to rush in to save all "our" children, the absence of marriage means that the fundamental needs of children are at risk in what is quite often a cold, hostile, and unforgiving world.

Increase in Divorce

Divorce now severs more families each and every year than did all the maternal deaths related to childbirth during the entire twentieth century.[43] Though the number of divorces has been dropping slightly since the early 1980s, still the shrinking number of women who marry face daunting divorce statistics; this is due in part to the fact that an ever-increasing number of them are following the example of celebrities in the entertainment world and having one or more children before marriage. The effect of this choice on their odds of a subsequent successful marriage, however, is often negative. Those who have a first child out of wedlock are twice as likely to end up divorced or separated as those who wait to have a child after marriage (29 percent versus 14 percent after five years of marriage and 50 percent versus 26 percent after ten years).[44] In addition, those couples driving the divorce rate are the less educated, which

tends to be a self-perpetuating trend. Among women who married in 1990, only 16.5 percent of college-educated women were divorced ten years later, but 46 percent of the women who dropped out of high schoo] were later divorced.[35]

Shockingly, the divorce rate is no better in so-called Christian families where marriage generally is considered a sacred covenant. The Barna Research Group found in 1999 (and again in 2004 and 2008) that 27 percent of those who identify themselves as born-again Christians are or previously were, divorced (compared to 24 percent of remaining adults).[46] Statistics like these represent a tidal wave of change during the past century. It should be noted, however, that divorce findings are more positive among those self-identified Christians who attend church regularly.[47] This fact points to the importance of looking to actual behavior instead of relying solely on verbal statements of beliefs.

In her book, *The Unexpected Legacy of Divorce: A 25-year Landmark Study*, Judith Wallerstein documents the long-term effects of divorce. Beginning in 1971, she periodically conducted in-depth interviews with 131 children and their parents from the time of divorce. "We've seriously underestimated the long-term impact of divorce on children [and]...the numerous ways a child's experiences differ when growing up in a divorced family."[48]

Elizabeth Marquardt, an affiliate scholar with the Institute for American Values and author of *Between Two Worlds* surveyed 1500 people age eighteen to thirty-five and found that the one million American children every year whose parents divorce experience inner conflict,[49] they "inhabit a more difficult emotional landscape than those in intact families." One comment was particularly poignant, Ms. Marquardt wrote, "Children of divorce feel less protected by their parents, and they're much less likely to go to their parents for comfort when they are young, or for emotional support when they are older."[50]

Judith Wallerstein noted that often children of divorce lingered longer in the adolescent stage before embracing adulthood than children in married-couple families; they tended to be less socially competent and were more worried, underachieving, and self-deprecating adults.[51] While children with married parents generally feel "emotionally safe,"[52] Andrew Cherlin, a family demographer at Johns Hopkins University, said that even those with very successful lives as adults carry "the residual trauma of their parents' breakup."[53]

Proponents of new family structures accuse pro-family advocates of wanting to return to the supposedly ideal 1950s when marriages were more stable, but the problem of the growth in frequency of divorce began earlier than most people realize. The first doubling of the ratio of divorces to marriage occurred between 1910 and 1930 (the number of divorces per 100 marriages increased from 8.8 to 17.4) and, by the 1950s, there were twenty-five divorces for every one hundred marriages. Even so, the divorce rate didn't begin a steep climb until the end of the 1960s. Then, as states rushed to pass no-fault divorce laws following the example set by California in September of 1969, the upward movement in the divorce rate accelerated.[54] With the high rate of divorce followed by remarriage, by 1990, only 63 percent of all marriages were first marriages.[55]

Before no-fault divorce, the spouse who wanted a divorce had to identify the other spouse as the one "at fault" in the marriage. By moving to "no-fault" divorce, couples were supposedly able to have a "good" divorce where nobody was to blame. The focus was on making the parents happy, and the assessment of the impact on the children, such as it was, has proven to have been deeply flawed. To the degree that the well-being of the children was considered, the general opinion was that children were better off without angry parents stuck in a bitter marriage.

The combination of falling marriage rates and rising divorce rates doubled the ratio of divorces to marriage again from 1960 to 1979 raising the ratio to slightly over fifty divorces per one hundred marriages. Since marriage rates have declined parallel to the decline in the divorce rate since 1979, the trend of ratio of divorces per one hundred marriages for the last twenty years has been flat.[56]

After four decades of a high ratio of divorces to marriage, objective observers have a growing respect for the role of marriage on children's well-being. Marriage counselors, who used to recommend divorce because parental unhappiness led to children's unhappiness, are now returning to their earlier advice that if possible and if abuse is not an issue, couples considering divorce should stay together for the sake of their children. The movement has spawned articles and books teaching couples how to stay together and restore harmony in their marriage. Counselors have found that couples who learn how to work their way through their problems when they are on the verge of divorce end up with happier marriages five years later than they were before they faced their seemingly insurmountable problems.[57]

As empirical evidence of the folly of rejecting marriage and too-easy divorce accumulates, many people have begun to reject attempts by many radical academics that are invested in outdated ideology to relegate marriage to history as an antiquated institution inherently harmful to women. Also, as the number of married-couple households becomes a smaller and smaller proportion of the total variety of family structures, people are noticing that the stabilizing influence of married-couple families in the nation's communities, most particularly within the schools, is diluted.

Rejecting Same-Sex "Marriages"

Likewise, the public is also rejecting the push for so-called same-sex marriage. In all thirty states where the issue has come up for a public vote, the public has overwhelmingly voted to keep marriage as a unique and special designation of the married-couple union of a man and woman. At first, the public was hesitant to appear judgmental, but rationality is prevailing. People are seeing the harm that will come from counterfeit marriages—not just to the individuals involved, but also to children's well-being[58] and, indeed, the nation's well-being if marriage and family, the foundation for society, continue to weaken.

Marriage is a sacred institution, a covenant between a man, woman, and God, that is honored by people across virtually all faith traditions.[59] It is also a legal contract carrying both responsibilities and privileges. Same-sex relationships are notoriously unstable and short-term affairs with few, if any, commitments (this characterization applies in general but somewhat more so among same-sex male couples than with female couples); thus, neither the sacred covenant nor the legal contract tends to carry the same meaning for same-sex couples as marriage has historically for male-female unions. Certainly, marriage has been weakened already by divorce, cohabitation, and the unwillingness of many young people today to make a commitment. To broaden the definition of marriage to include same-sex unions would further undercut the institution that should be the foundation for a strong and vital society. Marriage is the essential foundation for strong families, which, in turn, are vital for democratic government to flourish, providing both stability and the nurturing of the values and beliefs that are essential for democracy.

Conclusion

The promise of the twenty-first century rests on whether America reverses the disintegration of marriage and the family. The restoration of marriage and the family is no longer a luxury that would be nice; it is a necessity for the survival of American civil society. But the social indicator warning signs have too long been ignored, as if champions of the family and traditional values were akin to Chicken Little, the old fable about a chicken who ran through town screaming, "The sky is falling!" so often that people paid no attention to the warning.

But today's young people freely admit that their sky *is* falling. They have been the painful pawns of ugly divorce suits. They've experienced emptiness at the end of meaningless one-night stands. And their self-esteem has plummeted. Their cries for meaning have produced a web of social institutions that try to fill the void of family connections and to reproduce the security and contentment that the family produces. The security, fulfillment, and love that young people seek are found in the affectionate ties of close-knit families.[60] It is past time for us to overturn the negative cultural perceptions about marriage. We must demonstrate by our own personal commitments the value of marriage on both an individual level and at the community/society/national level. We must trumpet the personal rewards of marriage and its community-wide social benefits. We must dispel the cynics' myth that a happy marriage is unattainable, and in the process, give young people the tools to seek and build good marriages.

We need to raise up great legions of ordinary men and women who will speak out about what it means to live and love within the safe and nurturing framework of the natural family. When family life again flourishes, children will be able to thrive from infancy through adolescence and reach adulthood as well-adjusted persons. Further, they will have the internal strength and confidence to become successful in their personal and professional lives as well as prepared and willing to contribute to their communities and nation.

Notes

1.   Janice Shaw Crouse, *Gaining Ground: A Profile of American Women in the 20th Century,* (Washington, DC: The Beverly LaHaye Institute, 2000): 37-42. Concerned Women for America, www.cwfa.org.
2.   U.S. Bureau of the Census, "Median Age at First Marriage for Women: 2005," 2005 American Community Survey, Table 1205, http://factfinder.census.gov/servlet/AF-FAdvSearchGeneralServlet?_lang=en&_sse=on and Jason Fields, "America's Families and Living Arrangements: 2003," Current Population Reports, Series P-20, no. 553 (Washington, DC: U.S. Bureau of the Census, November 2004) and earlier reports, http://www.census.gov/population/www/socdemo/hh-fam.html (accessed February 16, 2009).

3.   D'Vera Cohn, "Married-With-Children Still Fading," *Washington Post*, May 15, 2001.
4.   Vera B. Tejada and Paul D. Sutton, "Births, Marriages, Divorces, and Deaths: Provisional Data for 2007," *National Vital Statistics Reports* 56, no. 21 (July 14, 2008): 1, Table A; and earlier reports, http://www.cdc.gov/nchs/data/nvsr/nvsr56/nvsr56_21.htm#TA (accessed February 16, 2009).
5.   Rose M. Kreider, "Living Arrangements of Children: 2004," Current Population Reports, Series P-70, no.114 (Washington, DC: U.S. Bureau of the Census, 2008): 4, Table 1, http://www.census.gov/prod/2008pubs/p70-114.pdf (accessed February 16, 2009).
6.   U.S. Bureau of the Census, "Unmarried-Couple Households, by Presence of Children: 1960 to Present," Families and Living Arrangements, Historical Time Series: Living Arrangements of Adults, Table UC-1 (Internet release July 2008), http://www.census.gov/population/www/socdemo/hh-fam.html#history (accessed February 16, 2009).
7.   http://worldcongress.org.
8.   Linda J. Waite and Maggie Gallagher, *The Case for Marriage: Why Married People are Happier, Healthier, and Better Off Financially,* (New York: Doubleday, 2000).
9.   Crouse, *Gaining Ground.*
10.   The title came from an article by Janice Shaw Crouse, "Marriage: Is it Just a Piece of Paper?" *The Washington Times*, March 18, 2001.
11.   Katherine Anderson, Don Browning, and Brian Boyer, eds., *Marriage: Just a Piece of Paper?* (Grand Rapids, MI: William B. Eerdmans Publishing Company, 2002).
12.   Robert P. George and Jean Bethke Elshtain, *The Meaning of Marriage,* (Dallas, TX: Spence Publishing Company, 2006).
13.   Ibid., Introduction.
14.   Ibid., Cover Flap.
15.   "The Marriage Movement: A Statement of Principles," Institute for American Values, 2000:1-36, http://www.americanvalues.org/pdfs/marriagemovement.pdf.
16.   Ibid, 24-30.
17.   http://www.marriagesavers.org/sitems/index.htm.
18.   http://marriage.rutgers.edu/.
19.   http://divinity.uchicago.edu/martycenter/research/family.shtml.
20.   http://www.virginia.edu/ccfl/.
21.   http://www.fatherhood.org/.
22.   U.S. Department of Health and Human Services, "Putting Marriage on the Agenda: How Oklahoma Laid the Foundation for Its Marriage Initiative," Office of the Assistant Secretary for Planning and Evaluation, *Research Brief*, July 2008, http://aspe.hhs.gov/hsp/06/OMI/Foundation/rb.shtml.
23.   "As Marriage and Parenthood Drift Apart, Public is Concerned about Social Impact: Generation Gap in Values, Behaviors," Pew Research Center Report, July 1, 2007, Executive Summary.
24.   Allan C. Carlson and Paul Mero, *The Natural Family,* (Dallas, TX: Spence Publishing Company, 2007).
25.   Ibid., 98.
26.   Pew Research Center, "Marriage and Parenthood Drift Apart," 3.
27.   Ibid., 5.
28.   David Popenoe, "The Future of Marriage in America," *The State of our Unions: The Social Health of Marriage in America, 2007,* (Rutgers University: The National Marriage Project, 2007): 33, Figure 15.

29.   U.S. Bureau of the Census, "Marital Status and Living Arrangements: March 1960," Current Population Reports, Series P-20, No. 105 (Washington, D.C.: GPO, November 1960): 7, Table A.

30.   U.S. Bureau of the Census, Series A 160-171, "Marital Status of the Population, by Age and Sex: 1890 to 1970," in *Historical Statistics of the United States: Colonial Times to 1970, Part 1,* (Washington, D.C.: GPO, 1975): 20-21.

31.   U.S. Bureau of the Census, "Marital Status of the Population 15 Years Old and Over, by Sex and Race: 1950 to Present," Families and Living Arrangements, Historical Time Series: Marital Status, Table MS-1 (Internet release July 2008), http://www.census.gov/population/www/socdemo/hh-fam.html#history (accessed February 16, 2009).

32.   Barbara Dafoe Whitehead and David Popenoe, "The Marrying Kind: Which Men Marry and Why," *The State of Our Unions: The Social Health of Marriage in America, 2004,* (Rutgers University: The National Marriage Project, 2004), http://marriage.rutgers.edu/Publications/SOOU/TEXTSOOU2004.htm#Marriage (accessed February 17, 2009).

33.   U.S. Bureau of the Census, *Historical Statistics of the United States,* 20-21. Marriage rates for the intercensal years from 1900-1920 and all years from 1994-2006, computed by the author based on marriage data from the National Center for Health Statistics and population data from the Census Bureau. Number of marriages are from: Raymond I. Eldridge and Paul D. Sutton, "Births, Marriages, Divorces, and Deaths: Provisional Data for December 2006," *National Vital Statistics Reports* 55, no. 20 (August 2007) and earlier reports, http://www.cdc.gov/nchs/products/pubs/pubd/nvsr/nvsr.htm#vol56 (accessed February 16, 2009); Number of women fifteen to forty-four are from: U.S. Bureau of the Census, National Population Estimates—Characteristics, "Annual Estimates of the Population by Sex and Five-Year Age Groups for the United States: April 1, 2000 to July 1, 2007," Table 1, and earlier reports, http://www.census.gov/popest/national/asrh/ (accessed February 16, 2009); Percent of unmarried women fifteen to forty-four are from: U.S. Bureau of the Census, Families and Living Arrangements, "Marital Status of People 15 Years and Over, by Age, Sex, Personal Earnings, Race, and Hispanic Origin, 2006" and earlier reports Current Population Survey Reports: 2006 March CPS, Table A1, http://www.census.gov/population/www/socdemo/hh-fam.html (accessed February 16, 2009).

34.   Allan Bloom, *The Closing of the American Mind,* (New York: Simon and Schuster, 1987).

35.   Thomas D. Snyder and Charlene M. Hoffman, U.S. Department of Education, National Center for Education Statistics, "Table 187—College enrollment rates of high school graduates, by sex: 1960 to 1998," *Digest of Education Statistics, 1999* (Washington, D.C., March 2000): 215, http://nces.ed.gov/Programs/digest/d99/d99t187.asp (accessed February 20, 2009).

36.   Sally C. Clarke, "Advanced Report of Final Marriage Statistics, 1989 and 1990," *Monthly Vital Statistics Report* 43, no. 12 Supplement (July 14, 1995): 7, Table 1, http://www.cdc.gov/nchs/products/pubs/pubd/mvsr/mvsr.htm#vol44s (accessed February 16, 2009).

37.   This marriage rate was computed by the author from number of marriages, female population fifteen and older, and percent of females fifteen and older who are married. Marriage data are from: Eldridge and Sutton, "Births, Marriages, Divorces, and Deaths: Provisional Data for December 2006," and earlier reports, National Center for Health Statistics, http://www.cdc.gov/nchs/products/pubs/pubd/nvsr/nvsr.htm#vol56 (accessed February 16, 2009); Female population data are from

U.S. Bureau of the Census website, "Annual Estimates of the Population by Sex and Five-Year Age Groups for the United States: April 1, 2000 to July 1, 2007 (NC-EST2007-01)," http://www.census.gov/popest/sex.html (accessed February 19, 2009); Percent of unmarried females: U.S. Bureau of the Census website, "America's Families and Living Arrangements: 2006," Table A1, Marital Status of People 15 Years and Over, by Age, Sex, Personal Earnings, Race, and Hispanic Origin, 2006, http://www.census.gov/population/www/socdemo/hh-fam/cps2006. html, (accessed February 19, 2009).

38.   National Bureau of Economic Research, "Business Cycle Expansions and Con-tractions," http://www.nber.org/cycles.html (accessed February 16, 2009).

39.   James Q. Wilson, *The Marriage Problem: How Culture Has Weakened Families* (New York: HarperCollins Publishers, 2002).

40.   Robert P. George, "What's Sex Got to Do With It: Marriage, Morality, and Ratio-nality," Quoting James Q. Wilson in Robert P. George and Jean Bethke Elshtain, *The Meaning of Marriage,* (Dallas, TX: Spence Publishing Company, 2006):142-143.

41.   Ibid., 146.

42.   www.childrensdefense.org.

43.   Computations completed by the author from maternal death rates and number of births. Maternal death rates are from: Donna L. Hoyert, "Maternal Mortality and Related Concepts," National Center for Health Statistics, *Vital Health Statistics* 3, no. 33 (2007): 10, Table 3 and earlier reports, *www.cdc.gov/nchs/data/series/ sr_03/sr03_033.pdf* (accessed February 16, 2009); Births are from: Joyce A. Mar-tin, et. al., "Births: Final Data for 2006," *National Vital Statistics Report* 57, no. 7 (January 2009): 29, Table 1 and earlier reports, http://www.cdc.gov/nchs/births. htm (accessed February 16, 2009).

44.   Matthew D. Bramlett and William D. Mosher, "Cohabitation, Marriage, Divorce and Remarriage in the United States," National Center for Health Statistics, *Vital and Health Statistics* 23, no. 22 (2002): 56, Table 21, http://*www.cdc.gov/nchs/ data/series/sr_23/sr23_022.pdf* (accessed February 16, 2009).

45.   Stephen P. Martin, "Trends in marital dissolution by women's education in the United States," *Demographic Research* 15, no. 20 (2006): 546, Table 1, http://www. demographic-research.org/Volumes/Vol15/20/ (accessed February 16, 2009).

46.   "New Marriage and Divorce Statistics Released," The Barna Group, Ltd., March 31, 2008. This study updates previous studies in 1999 and 2004. Many experts questioned the first findings, (questioning the self-identification of respondents as "Christian," see "Divorce Rates of Christians" an unpublished paper by Brad Wright, Department of Sociology, University of Connecticut (January 24, 2007) found at *brewright.com/Research/Divorce-blogsummary.doc*). The first Barna report is no longer online; a review of the 1999 report found at: http://www. religioustolerance.org/chr_dira.htm. The Barna website is: www.barna.org. The 2004 and 2008 reports are at: http://www.barna.org/FlexPage.aspx?Page=Barna Update&BarnaUpdateID=170 and http://www.barna.org/FlexPage.aspx?Page=B arnaUpdateNarrow&BarnaUpdateID=295.

47.   "Church Attendance and Divorce Rates," Marriage Reformation Blog, October 6, 2007, http://marriagereformation.wordpress.com/2007/10/06/church-attendance-and-divorce-rates/.

48.   Judith Wallerstein, Julia M. Lewis, and Sandra Blakeslee, *The Unexpected Legacy of Divorce: A 25 Year Landmark Study,* (New York: Hyperion Books, 2000): xxvii-xxviii.

49.   Elizabeth Marquardt, "The Children Left Behind," *Los Angeles Times*, November 15, 2005, http://articles.latimes.com/2005/nov/15/opinion/oe-marquardt15.

50.   Tamara Lewin, "Poll Says Even Quiet Divorces Affect Children's Paths," *New York Times,* November 5, 2005.

51.   Karen S. Peterson, "Kids of divorced parents straddle a divided world," *USA Today*, July 12, 2003.

52.   Lewin, "Poll Says Even Quiet Divorces."

53.   Ibid.

54.   National Center for Health Statistics, *Vital Statistics of the United States: Volume III— Marriage and Divorce, 1988,* (Washington: Public Health Service 1996):1, Section 1, Table 1-1 and Section 2, Table 1-1, http://www.cdc.gov/nchs/data/vsus/mgdv88_3.pdf (accessed February 16, 2009).

55.   Clarke, "Advanced Report," 14, Table 8. http://www.cdc.gov/nchs/products/pubs/pubd/mvsr/mvsr.htm#vol44s (accessed February 16, 2009).

56.   Computations of the ratio are by the author from the number of marriages and estimated number of divorces. Marriage data are from: Eldridge and Sutton, "Births, Marriages, Divorces, and Deaths: Provisional Data for December 2006" and earlier reports, National Center for Health Statistics, http://www.cdc.gov/nchs/products/pubs/pubd/nvsr/nvsr.htm#vol56 (accessed February 16, 2009); Divorce data are from: Tejada and Sutton, "Births, Marriages, Divorces, and Deaths: Provisional Data for 2007," and earlier reports, http://www.cdc.gov/nchs/data/nvsr/nvsr56/nvsr56_21.htm#TA (accessed February 16, 2009). Note: The last national estimate of the number of divorces by NCHS was for 1998; from that time forward, the author has estimated the number of divorces assuming the divorce rates NCHS has computed for those states, which continue reporting, is a reasonable estimate of the national rate, including the six non-reporting states.

57.   For instance, Joshua Coleman, *Imperfect Harmony: How to Stay Married for the Sake of your Children and Still be Happy,* (New York: St. Martin's Press, 2003).

58.   Janice Shaw Crouse, "Girls Need a Dad and Boys Need a Mom," Townhall, 2009. http://townhall.com/columnists/JaniceShawCrouse/2009/01/05/girls_need_a_dad_and_boys_need_a_mom.

59.   Dr. Dennis F. Kinlaw, "Who Cares About Homosexual Marriage? God Does!" The Covenant Series, The Francis Asbury Society, 2005, http://www.cwfa.org/articledisplay.asp?id=9249&department=CWA&categoryid=family

60.   Janice Shaw Crouse, "Seeing Marriage Through the Trees," Townhall, 2009, http://townhall.com/columnists/JaniceShawCrouse/2009/04/06/seeing_marriage_through_the_trees?page=2.

The inevitable consequence of poverty is dependence.
—Samuel Johnson

2

Single Mothers and Poverty

The single biggest economic factor related to children's material well-being is that children living in female-headed households with no husband now make up 24 percent of all related children and those living in male-headed households with no wife make up 6 percent, for a combined total of 30 percent of all related children living in single-parent households.[1] Why is this significant? The rate of poverty in 2007 for female householders with children under eighteen and no husband present was 37 percent.[2] The rate of poverty in 2007 for male householders with children under eighteen and no wife present was 17.5 percent. By comparison, the rate of poverty for married-couple families with children under eighteen was only 6.7 percent.[3]

The latest information from the U.S. Census Bureau reports that real median income increased 1.3 percent from 2006 to 2007, the poverty rate was 12.5 percent (not statistically changed from 2006) and the number of uninsured Americans declined by 1.3 million.[4] This is not quite the picture that usually is presented in the media as it relentlessly beats the drum for expanding government's role in and control over our families and communities all in the name of providing assistance for the benefit of children. The census estimates there to be about thirty-seven million Americans who are "poor," i.e., below the federal poverty thresholds.[5] The number of poor has held relatively steady for several years, and the poverty rate has remained close to 12.5 percent of the population for the last five years.[6]

In the simplest terms: The poverty rate of single mothers with children is 5 times higher than the rate for married couples with children, and

35

the rate for single fathers is more than 2.5 times the married-couple rate. That information is sobering enough, but to grasp the magnitude of the problem it is important to see the discrepancy between the total numbers of children in the two different categories. While children in single-parent households with no spouse present comprise three out of ten children (i.e., they are 21.8 million out of 72.8 million), the poor children in single-parent households constitute almost two-thirds of all poor children (i.e., nearly 8.5 million out of the 12.8 million poor children or 66 percent). In 1960 before liberal social welfare policy was greatly expanded and radical feminist ideology infected the culture, poor children in single-parent families comprised only 25 percent of all poor children.[7]

It is instructive to analyze this situation further by breaking the rates out by the children's age. Of the nearly four million single mothers with children under age six, the poverty rate is 49.9 percent. Among the 1.1 million single mothers with two or more children under six, the poverty rate jumps to 63.8 percent.[8] The clear and unequivocal message from the data about American children living in poverty is undeniable. There is no way to address poverty in America without addressing the problem of single mothers and absent fathers.

If the family structure of the population had been the same in 2007 as it was in pre-*Roe vs. Wade* 1972, the poverty rate for all families, instead of increasing from 11.8 percent in 1972 to 15 percent in 2007, would have a been lower (10.7 percent) in 2007 than it had been in 1972.[9]

The two problems, poverty and fatherless families, are inextricably linked; yet as a nation we continue, for the most part, to operate our anti-poverty programs in a manner that implicitly assumes little connection to family structure. In fact, we have so-called experts (particularly the theoreticians in academia who are far removed from the realities that anyone can plainly see just driving through the mean streets of the ghettos of our large cities) constantly peddling the myth that one kind of family structure is as good as another. Some experts go so far as to try and sell the idea, especially to impressionable young people who are the ones most likely to start a family, that we should celebrate the variety of family structures in America.

Also, opinion leaders push the false idea to young women that casual sex is natural, even healthy, and has no negative consequences as long as those involved are "careful" and always "use a condom." The young women are not given a clear picture of the pressure they will face to skip the condom, since unprotected sex is so much more intimate and so very much more pleasurable; nor are they fully informed about how frequently and easily condoms fail (in real world situations as opposed to in the testing lab) for one reason or another. It borders on cruelty to young people when supposed experts imply that a condom will protect them from sexually transmitted diseases and pregnancy, not to mention heartbreak and emotions they are ill prepared to handle.

It is tragic enough that so many young people are skeptical about marriage because of their own parents' divorces. Many of them are also convinced by the entertainment world's campaign that all a couple needs is passionate sex; they do not need a "piece of paper" to prove their love. Most of them have not reckoned with the fact that having a baby out of wedlock means a 50-50 chance that they will end up in poverty. Few of them understand that having two babies out of wedlock means that the possibility of poverty goes up to more than 60 percent.

It is no surprise, given the volume of misinformation that was injected into our culture in the last four decades of the twentieth century, that most young women also do not understand that raising their children in a fatherless family is likely to seriously limit their children's future as well as their own. After decades of mindless talk by ideologues asserting the interchangeability of male and female parents and the superfluity of marriage, the problems arising in our schools and on the streets of our communities (if an inner city ghetto can be called a community) have grown to the point that it has forced researchers to face the realities their data show about the differential impact of family structure on childrearing.

Finally, social scientists—from both the ideological left and right—are willing to admit that children need to be in a married-mom-and-dad family. The effects on children growing up in alternative family structures have been documented conclusively and a consensus has been reached: growing up in a single-mother home is associated with substantially higher risk of negative consequences for children. For example, Harper and McLanahan found those youths in father-absent households had significantly higher odds of incarceration (2 to 3 times greater likelihood) than those in mother-father families even after controlling for education and poverty.[10]

Obviously, many children who grow up in a mother-only family do well, and many single mothers are heroic. Even so, we have forty years of social science data detailing the higher frequency of adverse child development outcomes for children raised in single-mother households.

Dr. Wade Horn, former Assistant Secretary for Children and Families, U. S. Department of Health and Human Services, summarized the situation this way:

> Nearly four out of ten children in America are being raised in homes without their fathers and soon it may be six out of ten. How did this happen? Why are so many of our nation's children growing up without a full-time father? It is because our culture has accepted the idea that fathers are superfluous—in other words, they are not necessary in the "modern" family. Supposedly, their contributions to the well-being of children can easily be performed by the state, which disburses welfare checks, subsidizes midnight basketball leagues, and establishes child-care facilities.

> Ideas, of course, have consequences. And the consequences of this idea have been as profound as they have been disastrous. Almost 75 percent of American children living in fatherless households will experience poverty before the age of eleven, compared to only 20 percent of those raised by two parents. Children living in homes where fathers are absent are far more likely to be expelled from or drop out of school, develop emotional or behavioral problems, commit suicide, and fall victim to child abuse or neglect. The males are also far more likely to become violent criminals. As a matter of fact, men who grew up without dads currently represent 70 percent of the prison population serving long-term sentences.

> Undeniably, fathers are important for the wellbeing of children. So, too, are traditional families. They ensure the continuity of civilization by propagating the species and socializing children.[11]

For decades when liberals, progressives, feminists, and welfare advocates tried to get to the bottom of the problem posed by the triad of out-of-wedlock childbearing, single motherhood, and child poverty, they typically asserted that: (1) either the below-par public education in the young woman's poor neighborhood failed to adequately explain sex and conception, or (2) poverty is the source, rather than the result, of the problem. The solution to the problem, in their eyes then, is to provide abortion-on-demand and higher welfare benefits. From their point of view, there are only two options to avoid inflicting the hardship of poverty on an unmarried woman's child. Either she should (1) terminate the pregnancy—no child, no child poverty—or (2) the government must give her the funds she needs for the necessities of life both for herself and her child. In turn, the government is supposed to search for the father and extract from him part of his earnings for reimbursement. That is to say, in their view a single mother needs guaranteed access to government-funded *abortion* or government-provided *income assistance*.

These assumptions constitute the prevailing, indisputable "truth" among the liberal experts who study poverty. The very existence of poverty and an underclass equates to an ironclad demand, a moral imperative if you will, for legal, government-funded abortion as well as generous income assistance (cash, food stamps, housing, and medical care) provided, of course, by tax dollars. Though they may admit that there is two-way causality at work, they formulate policy proposals as if the problem to be solved is how to deal with poverty as the dominant factor leading to unwed teen childbearing.

What is abundantly clear is that teens having sex, getting pregnant, and dropping out of high school to have babies clearly leads to more poverty. It is foolish to think that handing out condoms, providing government-funded abortions when contraception fails, and finally doling out cash assistance when the baby arrives will break that vicious cycle or solve the problems of single-parent childrearing. It is not enough to address such serious problems with socially acceptable bromides. Instead, we must address the root causes of the problem: the absence of personal discipline in the lives of the individuals and the lack of commitment to each other of the couple. Nor will it be sufficient for policymakers and those who implement policies and programs at the grassroots level to focus simply on secondary problems, like limited job opportunities for unwed fathers and mothers, racial discrimination, and the temptation to make easy money by dealing drugs. Too many of our poverty experts take the easy road and address the derivative problems that are socially acceptable rather than tackle the thorny, controversial issues.

But, we do well to pause and consider the old axiom: "The problem is not what we don't know, but what we *think* we know that *just isn't so.*" Experience has shown that the relationship between unwed teen pregnancy and poverty is more than a one-way street running from poverty to pregnancy, but a two-way thoroughfare leading both ways.

Moreover, the policy that will break the vicious cycle between unwed childbearing and poverty is anything but more government-funded condom distribution, abortion, and income assistance. More than forty years of failed policies have shown that when the wrong solution is applied to a bad situation, increases in funding simply magnify the problem.

Even the Brookings Institution, no hotbed of conservative thinking, issued a report acknowledging that the over $580 billion spent in 2004 by the government on means-tested programs designed to assist the poor (4 times that spent in 1968) has failed to address and has even made worse the main causes of poverty. To their credit, the first item in their list of causes is the breakdown of the family; but when they move to listing their new generation of anti-poverty policy proposals, the number one element is the more politically correct one—requiring and rewarding work.[12]

Plotting the trends of poverty rates and unwed birthrates is very revealing. First, it is clear that, contrary to the underlying assumption of the conventional wisdom of the last forty years, the trends in poverty and unwed childbearing have often moved in opposite directions. Second, since 1991 we have witnessed an unprecedented decrease in unwed-teen childbearing, particularly among black teens, both when poverty rates were increasing and when they were decreasing. In 1991, the unwed birthrate for black teens was 107.8 per thousand unmarried fifteen through nineteen year olds, but in 2006 the rate was only 63.5 per thousand.[13]

The 41 percent drop in black unwed-teen childbearing did not occur because of an increase in the availability of abortions. To the dismay of Planned Parenthood, the opposite has happened, and the number of abortion providers declined by 25 percent from 1992 to 2005.[14] The facts that explain this decline in the unwed black teen birthrate are completely contrary to the expectations of liberals; the Centers for Disease Control reported, "During 1991-2007, the percentage of U.S. high school students who ever had sexual intercourse and the percentage that had multiple sex partners decreased." For female black teens, the percent ever having sexual intercourse dropped from 81 percent in 1991 to 61 percent in 2007, and the percent currently sexually active declined from 59 percent in 1991 to less than 44 percent in 2007.[15] With sexual activity of teens decreasing, *both* the abortion rate *and* the unwed-teen birthrate have decreased.

With the decline in the unwed black teen birthrate came a leveling off in the growth in the number of black female-headed households with children, which had doubled from 1973 to 1993 and whose poverty rate was never less than 54 percent and had risen as high as 64 percent. The number of black, female-headed families with children has not only stopped growing, but their poverty rate has declined. In the period from 2001 to 2007 that rate has been around 41 to 44 percent.[16]

Still, some die-hards persist in claiming that the abstinence message of self-control is unrealistic. As it turns out, it is the conventional worldview that has proved to be unrealistic. The history of the 1970s and 1980s clearly contradicts the notion that there could ever be enough abortions and welfare benefits to counter the snowballing effects of irresponsible sexual behavior. The tide began to change only as the message of abstinence's promise of a hopeful future took hold and welfare policy was reformed in 1996, removing many of the incentives for teens to have unwed births.

The abstinence message was combined in the mid-1990s with a "realistic" welfare policy that ended public assistance as an entitlement and made government support a temporary *lifeboat* rather than a permanent *lifestyle*. The welfare rolls declined by 60 percent when (1) welfare benefits were limited to five years at a maximum (two years in many states), (2) teen mothers were required to live under adult supervision and stay in school to remain eligible for assistance, and (3) when a child conceived while a mother was on welfare no longer meant a larger welfare check.[17]

Throughout the thirty-five years preceding the passage of the Welfare Reform Act of 1996, because taxpayers were subsidizing out-of-wedlock childbearing and the formation of single-mother households rather than work and responsibility, both conditions soared in number. It is a vivid illustration of the economists' dictum: "You get more of what you subsidize and less of what you tax."

Every year more than one million children are separated from one or the other parent by divorce, and many more are added to that total because their cohabiting, unmarried, biological parents decided to stop living together. Add to these children affected by the separation of their parents all those babies who are born to unmarried mothers (in 2006, there were over 1.6 million non-marital births or 38.5 percent of all births)[18] and it is clear that an unprecedented number of the nation's children are being raised without the presence of their biological fathers (although, of course, some mothers who give birth out of wedlock will eventually marry the father of their children).

Take note of the fact that the above data constitutes a single year's contribution to the swelling mass of children growing up with no opportunity to know or interact with the man who bequeathed his genetic heritage but is not around to guide, protect, and teach his children. It does not take a social scientist to see the impact of the increasing number of children growing up in families where the father is not present, nor involved in parenting. Without the socializing benefits of a responsible, mature male influence—and not just any male, but one whose authority is rooted in fatherhood—there is a serious deficit in self-control. On any trip to a local mall, you'll see at least half a dozen mothers struggling with rambunctious young boys, and no father will be in sight. You'll also see groups of angry, belligerent, pre-teen and teenage boys hanging around looking for mischief. Fatherless girls are more likely to be sexually promiscuous in trying to satisfy their unmet emotional needs. The emotional problems and insecurities of these fatherless boys and girls play out in the larger community, with particularly severe consequences in the public schools and violent streets of the inner cities.

So, where do we look for encouraging news? The reformed system of welfare assistance produced a very significant and positive development: the percentage of all related children under eighteen who are living in mother-only families has stopped growing. The percentage was the same in 2007 as in 1995 (24 percent) and the poverty rate of mother-only families has declined from 50 percent to 43 percent[19]—a level never achieved before the Welfare Reform Act of 1996.

The never-married, mother-only families, however, are another matter. While unwed teen birthrates have declined, those of women twenty to forty-four have increased, driving up the overall percentage of all children born out of wedlock. With this increase has come an increase in both the number and the percentage of children living with a never-married mother. In 1980, only 15 percent of all children living in mother-only families were in households where the mother had never married. In 2007, never-married mothers' share of children in mother-only families had nearly tripled, to 44 percent.[20]

There is yet another dimension of the single-mother trend that needs to be considered—the continuation of high infant mortality rates in the United States. The infant mortality rate decreased dramatically from about 86 per thousand live births in 1920 to less than 12 per thousand by 1981;[21] since then, however, progress has been limited. We still lose seven infants for every thousand born in the United States.[22] Compared to other countries worldwide, the U.S. rate is remarkably high, and our ranking among nations has dropped. In 1960, the United States ranked twelfth in the world for low infant mortality. Today that ranking has slipped to forty-second in the world.[23]

As it turns out, the formidable American medical system is only able to do so much to care for vulnerable babies. The front-line of defense has to be their mothers and their fathers. There has been a long-standing assumption that poverty and lack of health care were the major endangering situations for babies. However, we are indebted to Nicholas Eberstadt for his groundbreaking research that demonstrated conclusively the link between out-of-wedlock childbearing and higher rates of infant mortality.[24] Commenting on America's poor standing compared to other advanced nations, Gopal Singh, of the National Center for Health Statistics (NCHS) (underscoring Eberstadt's research), stated, "The decline in the infant mortality rate would have been greater if not for a rising number of out-of-wedlock births."[25]

Clearly, statisticians are well aware of the fact that infant mortality rates for births to unmarried women are significantly higher than for births to married women; from 1995 through 2005, the infant mortality rates for births to unmarried women were from 78 to 88 percent higher than the rates for births to married women.[26] But, despite their knowledge of these facts, the official NCHS position on the relevance of marriage for infant mortality is hazy: "marital status may be a *marker* [emphasis added] for the presence or absence of social, emotional, and financial resources. The support afforded by such resources may have a positive effect on fetal growth through fostering healthy maternal behaviors."[27] An earlier wording used by the NCHS statisticians makes this faulty thinking even more explicit: "Marital status has been associated with health effects for both the mother and infant, and is seen as a *proxy* [emphasis added] measure of the availability of social and economic support."[28]

The intended implication of their use of the terms "marker" and "proxy" appears to be that marriage *per se* is not the relevant factor. The actual implication is that other more fundamental underlying factors (factors that may be highly associated with marriage but not inextricably a part of it and, hence, separable from marriage) are significant but, unfortunately, not directly measurable. For example, one NCHS demographer attributed the higher risks associated with out-of-wedlock births to the fact that, with these births, there tended to be "less attention and less support" and that "the mothers were more likely to smoke, and the infants were more likely to have a low birthweight."[29]

Now it is entirely reasonable to emphasize the threat of smoking since the facts are clear: "Tobacco use during pregnancy causes the passage of substances such as nicotine, hydrogen cyanide, and carbon monoxide from the placenta into the fetal blood supply. These substances restrict the growing infant's access to oxygen and can lead to adverse pregnancy and birth outcomes such as low birthweight, preterm delivery, intrauterine growth retardation, and infant mortality."[30] Nevertheless, saying that marital status is just a marker for the beneficial conditions that tend to follow from a healthy marriage is a bit like saying that breathing may be associated with health. Everyone knows that breathing is the means of getting oxygen into the blood, just as beneficial conditions flow from sharing life together as husband and wife.

Moreover, if we compare the infant mortality rates of nonsmokers with those of married women, the mortality rate for infants of nonsmokers in the period from 1995 to 2005 ranged from 17 percent to 25 percent higher than for those of married women.[31] Marriage, like breathing, is nature's way of helping adults and children thrive. Marriage is integral to the process of life, not just a marker of an event. There can be no doubt that a heart-lung machine is an imperfect substitute for normal breathing. Just so, other family arrangements can never fully substitute for a healthy marriage.

In the past, the NCHS statisticians presented a more illuminating (though still not entirely adequate) description of the effects of marital status when they said, "Marital status interacts with a wide variety of other factors, such as the degree of economic and social support for the mother and child; whether or not the pregnancy was wanted; as well as maternal age, educational level, and the quantity and quality of prenatal care."[32] It would not be politically correct to point out that marriage has persisted over the millennium precisely because it is the arrangement that has proven to produce beneficial conditions for mother and child to the highest degree and with the greatest consistency.

Accompanying the upward trend in out-of-wedlock births is a little-noted growing threat to babies, infant homicide. From 1979 to 1991—a period of rapidly escalating unwed teen birthrates—the number of infants who died before their first birthdays as a result of intentional homicide more than doubled (increasing from 170 in 1979 to 380 in 1991). Almost four hundred murders a year—that is more than one killing per day on average! No wonder the media is filled with story after story of these precious babies being killed. During the period from 1990 to 2005, the number of deaths has leveled off but at a rate nearly 40 percent higher than in the 1979 to 1985 period.[33]

It is disturbing to see how the natural human instinct of parents to protect their offspring is dulled. Two interlocking insidious influences worked in our culture to produce a loss of sensibility and regard for the sanctity of human life. We denied that human beings are created in the image of God and, thus, have transcendent value. We taught generations of high schools and college students that human beings are the product of random processes, nothing more than material beings. Lacking a soul or significance, we are capable only of deterministic responses to environmental stimuli. Even our houses of worship accept the notion that science is the ultimate arbiter of all truth. This viewpoint (so far divorced from the inalienable right to life in the Declaration of Independence) naturally progresses to a rejection of absolute truth. Moral relativism, then, inevitably leads to the horrendous pronouncements of Peter Singer, the Princeton professor of bioethics who claims that parents should have a trial period after a baby's birth to decide whether to allow their child to live or not.[34] In this impoverished worldview, there is no moral inconsistency then to call the killing of an infant once it is born a "murder" while such an action while the baby is still in the mother's womb, or only partially born, is called a "choice." Words have such huge consequences.

As we have blurred the definition of family by expanding family to include the nebulous and indefinable "families," we have also expanded the number of vulnerable children. Similarly, the more "our" children become viewed as a corporate responsibility; *belonging* to everyone, the more likely the individual child is to be *loved* by no one. What a tragic irony! While it is easy to romanticize children categorically as adorable darlings, the individual child is needy, demanding, and time-consuming often in messy ways. It is only within the teamwork of family that those messes are *endurable*; it is only within the commitment of family life that messes have *eternal* relevance.

We read almost daily of yet another instance where the child protective services provided by the government have either abused their authority or failed in their mission to safeguard the children under their care. However noble the intended purpose might be, government agencies are a poor substitute for a healthy family. Solely bureaucratic approaches to providing for the welfare of the next generation are fundamentally limited in their capacity. There are not enough government programs in the world to counteract the deficits that arise when a society does not have healthy marriages operating effectively to provide for the physical, emotional, and spiritual needs of children. The experience of the past forty years shows that attempting to have government provide for the material needs of children in a negative relational setting—one where the child constantly encounters bad role models and emotionally harmful interactions—which significantly increases the likelihood that the child will not develop a capacity for empathy and responsibility, basic ingredients of our humanity. Without these elements of character to restrain their self-centered impulses, children's capacity for self-indulgence and/or violent, evil behavior towards others knows no limits.

There are lessons we must learn from the data: through better medical technology, we have lowered the infant mortality rate only to see drug addiction and other irresponsible behaviors result in increasing numbers of babies born with low birth weight, drug addiction, or HIV. Tragically, others are born healthy, with all of the potential of their unique life in front of them, only to be beaten senseless and discarded like so much flotsam on the sea by the transitory men who floated through their mother's lives.

Welfare reform's expectation of and demand for responsible behavior from teens and adults alike, as opposed to the old liberal ideas that people are victims helplessly at the mercy of their environment, has brought a new day of hope to the lives of millions. With that hope has come greater personal responsibility and progress; during the heyday of liberal social welfare policy from 1972 to 1995, the child poverty rate for those living in female-headed households averaged 53 percent, but despite the recession of the opening days of this decade, the average rate from 2000 to 2007 declined by one-fifth to 41 percent.[35]

Matt Miller, a columnist for *Fortune Magazine*, wrote in his book, *The Tyranny of Dead Ideas: Letting Go of the Old Ways of Thinking to Unleash a New Prosperity,* about the "distorting influence" of outmoded ideas when a culture becomes hung up on tacit assumptions and trapped in old ways of thinking. Problems arise, he believes, when ingrained instincts that were broadly shared and had traction fifty years ago, become outmoded and are no longer reasonable explanations for a current problem or basis for a solution.[36] Miller describes how axioms percolate "through the culture for decades becoming second nature to many." He says these axioms are often dubious or dead wrong, yet they determine the policies that we consider and the possibilities that we allow ourselves to imagine.[37]

Miller's assessment was meant for the economy or culture, but it applies in other areas in ways that he did not intend. Certainly, in the area of single-mother poverty his words characterize the expert "establishment" where axioms have percolated for years. Perhaps though, this book will contribute to a new perspective—free of the "distorting influences" of "outmoded ideas"—so that parents can rise to the challenge of helping their children navigate the treacherous waters of adolescence and young adulthood to reach their full potential and become contributing citizens and productive adults.

With the rebirth of the American creed of personal responsibility and self-reliance, millions in the so-called "underclass," millions of those written off by liberals as hopelessly in need of a government dole, have found jobs and are recovering the American dream of independence and self-respect. A truly "realistic" worldview, one that sees us all as endowed by our Creator with the possibility of choosing what is right and good, have produced hope for a brighter future for all those previously thought trapped by poverty. Unfortunately, the recession and election of 2008 has brought yet another ill-advised call for a return to the old failed social welfare policies of entitlement and it is distressing to contemplate the lapse back into the old ways of victimhood this seems destined to rekindle.

Notes

1. U.S. Bureau of the Census, "Related Children by Number of Working Family Members and Family Structure: Table for below 100 percent of Poverty, All Races, 2007," Current Population Survey Reports: Annual Social and Economic Supplement (March 2008): POV13, http://pubdb3.census.gov/macro/032008/pov/toc.htm (accessed February 21, 2009).
2. U.S. Bureau of the Census, "Poverty Status of Families, by Type of Family, Presence of Related Children, Race, and Hispanic Origin: 1959 to 2007," Current Population Survey Reports: Historical Poverty Tables–Families, Table 4, http://www.census.gov/hhes/www/poverty/histpov/histpovtb.html (accessed February 21, 2009).
3. Ibid.
4. Carmen DeNavas-Walt, Bernadette D. Proctor, and Jessica C. Smith, "Income, Poverty, and Health Insurance Coverage in the United States: 2007," *Current Population Reports*, Series P60, no. 235 (Washington, DC: GPO, 2008): 1-19, http://www.census.gov/hhes/www/poverty/poverty07.html (accessed February 21, 2009).
5. Ibid., "Families by Age of Householder, Number of Children, and Family Structure: 2007," 3 and 45. Note that an individual is determined to be poor according to income level and size of family. For example, a two-person family (consisting of a householder under sixty-five and one child) the federal poverty threshold level of income in 2007 is $14,291, for a three-person family (with two children), $16,705, and for a four-person family (with two children), it would be $21,027. If the family's income is below that family's poverty threshold, then everyone in that family is counted as being poor (the one exception to this is the case of a cohabiting couple with children where the adult in the household who is not the actual parent is treated as a separate, unrelated individual).
6. U.S. Bureau of the Census, "Poverty Status of People by Family Relationship, Race, and Hispanic Origin: 1959 to 2007," Current Population Survey Reports: Historical Poverty Tables–People, Table 2, http://www.census.gov/hhes/www/poverty/histpov/histpovtb.html (accessed February 21, 2009).
7. U.S. Bureau of the Census, "Related Children by Number of Working Family Members," POV13.
8. U.S. Census Bureau, "Families by Age of Householder, Number of Children, and Family Structure: Table for Below 100 percent of Poverty, All Races, 2007," Current Population Survey Reports: Annual Social and Economic Supplement (March 2008): POV4, http://pubdb3.census.gov/macro/032008/pov/toc.htm (accessed February 21, 2009).
9. Computations by the author for this hypothetical comparison are as follows. In 1973 married-couple families with children under eighteen made up 84.7 percent of all families with children under eighteen and single-parent families with children

under eighteen were 15.3 percent. In 2007, the poverty rate of married-couple families with children was 6.7 percent and the poverty rate of single-parent families was 32.7 percent. If the distribution of families that existed in 1973 had existed in 2007, the poverty rate would have been $10.7 = 6.7 \times 0.847 + 32.7 \times 0.153$. The data come from: U.S. Bureau of the Census, "Poverty Status of Families, by Type of Family, Presence of Related Children, Race, and Hispanic Origin: 1959 to 2007," Current Population Survey Reports: Historical Poverty Tables–Families, Table 4, http://www.census.gov/hhes/www/poverty/histpov/histpovtb.html (accessed February 21, 2009).

10. Cynthia C. Harper and Sara S. McLanahan, "Father Absence and Youth Incarceration," *Journal of Research on Adolescence* 14 (September 2004): 382, Table 2, http://www.gwu.edu/~pad/202/father.pdf (accessed February 25, 2009).

11. Wade F. Horn, "Why There Is No Substitute for Parents," *Imprimis* 26, no. 6 (June 1997): 2, https://www.hillsdale.edu/news/imprimis/archive/issue.asp?year=1997&month=06 (accessed February 21, 2009).

12. Ron Haskins and Isabel V. Sawhill, "Attacking Poverty and Inequality: Reinvigorate the Fight for Greater Opportunity," The Center on Children and Families, The Brookings Institution (February 28, 2007): 1-13, http://www.brookings.edu/~/media/Files/Projects/Opportunity08/PB_Poverty_Haskins_Sawhill2.pdf (accessed February 21, 2009). (For a discussion of the report, see Janice Shaw Crouse, "The Politicizing of Poverty," An opinion editorial on Townhall.Com and www.cwfa.org, March 27, 2007, http://townhall.com/columnists/JaniceShawCrouse/2007/03/27/the_politicizing_of_poverty and http://www.cwfa.org/articles/12665/BLI/dotcommentary/index.htm.

13. Joyce A. Martin, Brady E. Hamilton, Paul D. Sutton, Stephanie J. Ventura, Fay Menacker, Sharon Kirmeyer, and T.J. Matthews, "Births: Final Data for 2006," *National Vital Statistics Reports* 57, no. 7 (January 7, 2009): 55, Table 19, http://www.cdc.gov/nchs/data/nvsr/nvsr57/nvsr57_07.pdf (accessed February 24, 2009).

14. Rachel K. Jones, Mira R.S. Zolna, Stanley K. Henshaw, and Lawrence B. Finer, "Abortion in the United States: Incidence and Access to Services, 2005," *Perspectives on Sexual and Reproductive Health* 40, no. 1 (March 2008): 11, Table 3, http://www.guttmacher.org/pubs/journals/4000608.pdf (accessed February 24, 2009).

15. Danice K. Eaton, Laura Kann, Steve Kinchen, Shari Shanklin, James Ross, Joseph Hawkins, William A. Harris, Richard Lowry, Tim McManus, David Chyen, Connie Lim, Nancy D. Brener, and Howard Wechsler, "Youth Risk Behavior Surveillance—United States, 2007," Centers for Disease Control and Prevention, *MMWR Weekly* 57, no. SS-4 (June 6, 2008): 97 and 99, Tables 61 and 63 and earlier reports, http://www.cdc.gov/mmwr/preview/mmwrhtml/ss5704a1.htm (accessed February 24, 2009).

16. U.S. Bureau of the Census, "Poverty Status of People," Table 4.

17. U.S. Department of Health and Human Services, Office of Family Assistance, "TANF Caseload Data—Number of Families and Recipients, Caseload Data 2000-2007," and earlier reports, http://www.acf.hhs.gov/programs/ofa/data-reports/index.htm, (accessed February 24, 2008).

18. Catharine Paddock, "American Teen and Non-Marital Births Up," *Medical News Today,* December 6, 2007, [Reporting on the *National Vital Statistics Report* 6, no. 6, December 5, 2007], http://www.medicalnewstoday.com/articles/90851.php.

19. U.S. Bureau of the Census, "Related Children in Female Householder Families as a Proportion of All Related Children, by Poverty Status: 1959 to 2007," Current Population Survey Reports: Historical Poverty Tables–Families, Table 10, http://

www.census.gov/hhes/www/poverty/histpov/histpovtb.html (accessed February 24, 2009).

20. U.S. Bureau of the Census, "Children under 18 Years Living with Mother Only, by Marital Status of Mother: 1960 to Present," Current Population Survey Reports: Historical Time Series–Living Arrangements of Children, Table CH-5, http://www.census.gov/population/www/socdemo/hh-fam.html#history (accessed February 24, 2009).

21. T.J. Mathews and Marian F. MacDorman, "Infant Mortality Statistics from the 2005 Period Linked Birth/Infant Death Data Set," *National Vital Statistics Reports* 57, no. 2 (July 30, 2008): 9, and earlier reports, http://www.cdc.gov/nchs/data/nvsr/nvsr57/nvsr57_02.pdf (accessed March 4, 2009)

22. Melonie P. Heron, Donna L. Hoyert, Jiaquan Xu, Chester Scott, and Betzaida Tejada-Vera, "Deaths: Preliminary Data for 2006," *National Vital Statistics Reports* 56, no. 16 (June 11, 2008): 3, Table A, and earlier reports, http://www.cdc.gov/nchs/data/nvsr/nvsr56/nvsr56_16.pdf (accessed February 24, 2009).

23. Central Intelligence Agency, "Rank Order - Infant mortality rate," *The 2008 World Fact Book* (2009 estimate), https://www.cia.gov/library/publications/the-world-factbook/rankorder/2091rank.html (accessed February 26, 20009).

24. Nicholas Eberstadt, *Public Interest* 115 (April 1,1994) cited in Nicholas Eberstadt and Sanders Korenman, "Why Babies Die in D.C.," American Enterprise Institute, January 1, 2000, http://www.aei.org/publications/filter.all,pubID.4101/pub_detail.asp (accessed February 24, 2009)

25. Shankar Vedantam, "Dangers Cited in Teenage Pregnancies / Along with Out-of-Wedlock Births, They Keep Infant Mortality High in the U.S. Other Factors Increase Risk," *The Philadelphia Inquirer*, July 10, 1995.

26. Mathews and MacDorman, "Infant Mortality Statistics from the 2005 Period," 9 and earlier reports.

27. T.J. Mathews and Marian MacDorman, "Infant Mortality Statistics from the 2002 Period Linked Birth/Infant Death Data Set," *National Vital Statistics Reports* 52, no. 10 (November 24, 2004): 7, http://www.cdc.gov/nchs/data/nvsr/nvsr57/nvsr57_02.pdf (accessed March 4, 2009).

28. T.J. Mathews, Marian MacDorman, and Fay Menacker, "Infant Mortality Statistics from the 1999 Period Linked Birth/Infant Death Data Set," *National Vital Statistics Reports* 50, no. 4 (January 30, 2002): 6, http://www.cdc.gov/nchs/data/nvsr/nvsr50/nvsr50_04.pdf (accessed March 4, 2009).

29. Vedantam, "Dangers Cited In Teenage Pregnancies."

30. Mathews and MacDorman, "Infant Mortality Statistics from the 2005 Period," 9 and earlier reports.

31. Ibid. Ratios calculated by the author.

32. T.J. Mathews, Sally C. Curtin, and Marian MacDorman, "Infant Mortality Statistics from the 1998 Period Linked Birth/Infant Death Data Set," *National Vital Statistics Reports* 48, no. 12 (July 20, 2000): 6, http://www.cdc.gov/nchs/data/nvsr/nvsr48/nvs48_12.pdf (accessed March 4, 2009).

33. U.S. Centers for Disease Control and Prevention, "Compressed Mortality File, 1979-1998 and 1999-2005," CDC WONDER online database, http://wonder.cdc.gov/cmf-icd9.html (accessed March 7, 2009).

34. Peter Singer, *Practical Ethics*, 2nd ed. (New York: Cambridge University Press, 1993): 175-217.

35. U.S. Bureau of the Census, "Related Children in Female Householder Families," Table 10; averages calculated by author.

36.   Matt Miller, interview by Renee Montayne and Linda Werthheimer, "Is America Weighed Down by 'Dead Ideas'?" *Morning Edition*, National Public Radio, February 9, 2009.

37.   Ibid.

Children are unpredictable.
You never know what inconsistency
They are going to catch you in next.
—Franklin P. Jones

3

Cohabitation[1]

The number of couples in the United States who are "living together" without marriage has increased nearly 1000 percent since 1970.[2] And over one-third of the resulting households include children. This trend is producing a cultural transformation that has profound ramifications for both people and public policies. Increasingly, too, cohabitation precedes marriage and displaces it as the locus of sexual intimacy. Of American women born from 1954 to 1963 a little less than half (48 percent) experienced premarital sex by age twenty, but among those born from 1994 to 2003 who had had sex before marriage by age twenty, the proportion had risen to nearly 3 out of 4 (74 percent).[2] Clearly, when the prevailing attitude is that having sex is "no big deal" and entailing no commitment, then moving in and living together with no strings becomes that much more likely.

Several facts illustrate the growing importance and phenomenal growth in cohabitation. Researchers report that, by the 1990s, nearly 60 percent of American unions began with cohabitation.[3] There has been a ten-fold increase in the number of cohabiting couples since 1970. In 1970, there were eighty-six married couples for every cohabiting couple, but by the year 2006, there were fewer than eleven married couples for every cohabiting couple. Carried with this growing tide is the number of offspring it inevitably produces who are being exposed to a very uncertain, high-risk environment. From 1970 to 2006 the number of cohabiting couples with children increased on average by about forty-five thousand each year, while the number of married couples with children increased on average by only twelve thousand per year.[4] Thus, in four decades, American family structure had changed, and more than 10 percent of all children shifted from a two-parent home to a single-parent household.[5] Given the welfare implications for cohabitation on children, it is distressing that by 2006 nearly 3.3 million children (4.4 percent of all children), lived in a cohabiting household.[6] The demographic shift from marriage to cohabitation and the increasing number of children thus exposed has significant consequences for the well-being not only of those directly involved but also for the rest of the community in which they reside. Their circumstances and behaviors touch all of today's generation.

Living together has become the "normative experience," with nearly 50 percent of young adults aged twenty to forty cohabiting.[7] Moreover, the percentage of women in their late 30s who said that they had cohabited at least once reached 48 percent in 1995.[8]

One of the most significant indicators of the changes in attitudes toward the role of marriage in family formation and parenting in the United States in the last three decades can be seen in the dramatic increase in the number of nonmarital births (312 percent increase between 1970 and 2006). This drove the overall ratio of out-of-wedlock births to 38.5 percent; among black children, more than two-thirds are born out of wedlock.[9] In that same period, the number of single-parent families increased by 221 percent, and the number of unmarried couples with children went up by 833 percent. Since there has been minimal growth in the number of married-couple families with children (less than 2 percent since 1970),[10] the proportion of cohabiting couples with children (as a percent of all families with children) has risen from less than 1 percent in 1978 to just over 5 percent in 2006.[11]

If current conditions continue, 40 percent of all American children alive today will spend some time in their childhood living in the household of a cohabiting couple. Among children born to a single (i.e., never-married) mother, the proportion likely to see a parent move in with an unmarried partner is 76 percent; in contrast, for children born to married parents, the proportion is 20 percent.[12]

There are those who see no problem with this change in household arrangement and family structure. Some people argue that—now that so many people enjoy affluence—the increase in cohabitation simply reflects peoples' indulgence, individualism, and their preference for independence. Others say that marriage is unnecessary and irrelevant. They argue that the quality of relationships in a household is more important than the "piece of paper" that constitutes, in their minds, the only difference between marriage and cohabitation.[13] Family structure, in other words, is irrelevant in their view.

Certainly, this attitude (that marriage is irrelevant and cohabitation is normal) is prevalent on college campuses. In fact, college textbooks seem to perpetuate the myth that cohabitation is better than marriage. In the book, *Closed Hearts, Closed Minds*, Norval Glenn reported the results of his research study that reviewed twenty college textbooks on marriage and family.[14] These textbooks are used on eight thousand college campuses[15] around the nation as the primary text for courses in marriage and family. None of the twenty books discussed children's well-being or the effects on children of family disintegration.[16] Calling the books a "national embarrassment,"[17] Glenn characterized the textbooks as containing "glaring errors, distortions of research, omissions of important data, and misattributions of scholarship."[18] Further, the books describe marriage pessimistically, as more a problem than a solution for society.[19] Marriage was presented in very bleak terms; one could be forgiven for thinking that marriage exists to perpetuate violence against and oppression of women.[20] In fact, as depicted in the textbooks, marriage is "dangerous"[21] and "psychologically stifling."[22] Cohabitation, same-sex unions, and single parenthood, though, were extolled as "equally acceptable and equally productive adult relationships."[23] Not surprisingly, these textbooks, though filled with unfounded assertions and glaring distortions,[24] are having an impact, since they pander to the younger generation's natural tendency to seek adventure and to want to assert their independence by seeking their own road. Many young people have bought into the myth that cohabitation is a good way to "test the waters" before marriage.

While increasingly common among college students and young professionals, living together without marriage is even more common among the uneducated and poor.[25] More and more young adults, because they have seen too much divorce and too many miserable marriages, do not believe in lasting love or in marriage. Dr. Neil Clark Warren interviewed five hundred individuals asking them to tell him about the marriage they most admired. Nearly half could not recommend even one single healthy, exemplary marriage.[26]

Yet, ancient Rome's great orator and statesman, Cicero, declared that marriage was the "first bond of society." Indeed, throughout history, marriage has been the bedrock of civilized societies, and sexual promiscuity has been destructive to civilization. A Miami University Political Science professor, Reo Christenson, reported on the findings of a Cambridge University professor more than fifty years ago. Dr. J.D. Unwin studied more than eighty early societies and found a strong correlation between sexual restraint and social progress. "Primitive societies with the greatest sexual freedom had made the least cultural advances. Those with stricter limitations had made the greatest progress."[27] Arnold Toynbee, student of world civilizations, also declared that those cultures that postpone rather than stimulate sexual experience are more prone to progress. Will and Ariel Durant, authors of *The Lessons of History*, wrote that it was imperative to for youth to maintain rigorous sexual restraint.[28]

Contemporary research still proves the validity of Cicero and Christenson's remarks. In fact, research findings follow a general pattern regardless of nationality, age of partners, or income of the couple. Across cultures and over time, cohabitation is distinctly different from marriage and it produces distinctly different—and decidedly inferior—outcomes for children. Researchers across the philosophical, ideological, and theological perspectives have come to the same conclusions regarding the family structure that is best for children. As weak as the marriage bond has become in the era of no-fault divorce, on average the harmony, stability, health effects, and longevity of marital unions are still far superior to that of cohabiting couples. The whole truth put simply is this: marriage is not merely best for the mother and father, it is best for the children, too![29]

Many studies show that a household structure not anchored by one's own biological parents is damaging to the future of children[30] and that cohabitation and out-of-wedlock births are associated with increased risks of negative outcomes for the individuals involved and, thus, for society in general.[31] United Families International stressed:

> Stable, traditional marriages produce economic, physical, emotional and psychological benefits for men, women and children that alternative relationships cannot match. As marriage declines, the demand for government intervention and social programs rise. Taxpayers then increasingly foot the bill for the steep costs of poverty, drug addiction, court services, crime, remedial education services, crisis pregnancy, health problems, foster care, child support enforcement, mental health needs and more. Marriage is the vehicle in which every successful society works to channel human sexuality and provide children the attention, love and resources of a mother and a father.[32]

Cohabitation among unmarried couples does not serve the best interests of adults, children, society, or governments. Indeed, substituting cohabitation for marriage ultimately produces a weakened society characterized by unstable homes, children at risk, domestic violence, and poverty. In addition, living together without marriage typically leaves in its wake a trail of shattered emotions and broken relationships.

General agreement in the research community has begun to emerge as more and more data confirm the essential role of stable, healthy marriages. Recent studies show that family instability, measured by transitions into and out of a married-couple household, is strongly associated with negative outcomes for children. With increased cohabitation, there has been a dramatic decline in the well-being of children: children in non-intact families have roughly twice the incidence of social and behavioral problems compared with children in married-parent families.[33]

There has been a dramatic increase in the number of today's children living with problems that researchers identify as associated with broken families: emotional upheaval and struggles with anxiety, depression, eating disorders, and other psychosocial difficulties.[34] These outcomes should not be surprising, given that the parenting role of a cohabiting partner toward the children of the other person is vaguely defined. In addition, other aspects of the cohabiting relationship make the household a high-conflict, unstable, and often volatile living arrangement for children. The cohabiting partner has no legal, financial, parental/custodial rights or obligations relative to the children, and discipline and relationship-building are therefore tenuous at best.[35]

The Urban Institute, a research think tank located in Washington, DC, evaluated the well-being of children living in cohabiting families. They found that all household arrangements are inferior to married biological or adoptive parents in terms of outcomes for children. Less than 8 percent of the children living in a married biological/adoptive family are poor, as compared to poverty rates of nearly 20 to 43 percent for children who are in cohabiting or single-mother households. Children in married-couples families are read to more often than those in other household arrangements (20 percent versus more than 25 percent that are "seldom" read to). Less than 5 percent of children in married families have behavior problems, but the percentage of children with behavior problems in other household structures is at least double and, in some cases, multiplied by five.[36]

The Urban Institute researchers found that older children (six to eleven years of age) exhibited the highest number of behavioral problems living in cohabiting-partner households (16.4 percent); cohabiting-parent households were next highest at 14 percent, with single-parent households at 9 percent, as compared with only 3.5 percent among those living with married parents. For teens, the situation is similar—cohabiting and single-parent households produce several times more behavioral problems in teens than are exhibited in teens living with their married-parent families.[37]

In short, the mass of sociological evidence suggests that cohabitation is an inferior alternative to the married, intact, two-parent family. The data confirms that marriage works best in terms of the well-being of all the persons involved. Clearly, cohabitation is damaging to the social well-being of women and children. Further, cohabitation puts a considerable strain on the agencies of government that deal with social, correctional, and welfare issues.

The first and overwhelming problem with cohabitation is that such relationships contribute little to those inside and certainly little to those outside the arrangement. Cohabitation is a tentative arrangement that lacks stability; no one can depend upon the relationship—not the partners, not the children, not the community, not the society. Cohabiting relationships are experimental in nature, tenuous at best, and tend to dissolve at about twice the rate of marriages; hence, children living in such situations are twice as vulnerable to the anguish and hardships associated with separation from a parent. Further, today the majority of cohabiting relationships do not usually end in marriage. During the 1970s, about 60 percent of cohabiting couples married each other within three years, but this proportion has since declined to less than 40 percent. [38]

Numerous studies of college students have found that men typically cohabit because it is "convenient." Women, on the other hand, expect that "cohabitation will lead to marriage." Obviously such an imbalance of intentions puts women in a disadvantageous, if not perilous, position. Dr. Roland H. Johnson III, now retired, was a college sociology professor who conducted informal surveys in his marriage classes. He discovered that college students viewed cohabitation as a "trial marriage" and the females "really believed that they were going to marry the guy" that they were living with. On the other hand, the men liked cohabitation for the "readily available sex." In his study, Dr. Johnson asked the men directly, "Are you going to marry the girl you are living with?" Their overwhelming response was, "No!" When he asked the women, their response was, "Yes!" When he asked why, their response was "Because we love each other. Because we are learning how to be together." When Professor Johnson asked the men the same question, they responded, "She was that easy for me, how can I trust her to be faithful in marriage?" It's the age-old story—women tend to get serious and men just tend to enjoy what they think is an advantageous situation.[39]

Sometimes couples choose to live together as a substitute for marriage even though they profess love for each other and want a permanent relationship. They explain that if the relationship goes sour, they want to avoid the trouble, expense, and emotional trauma of a divorce. The couple does not understand that without the commitment of marriage, there is little incentive or likelihood that they will work through their problems or that they will maintain the relationship under pressure. It is more likely that one or the other will "cut and run" when conflict arises, since each person's individuality is more likely stronger than their relationship together.[40]

What research shows is that cohabiting relationships in the United States tend to be fragile and relatively short in duration; less than half of cohabiting relationships last five or more years.[41] Typically, they last about eighteen months.[42] Not surprisingly, partners in a cohabiting relationship are more likely to be unfaithful to each other than are married couples. Research conducted at Western Washington University found that there is less sexual fidelity between cohabiting partners with 20 percent of the cohabiting women cheating compared with only 4 percent of the married women.[43] The National Sex Survey (polling 3,500 people) reported that men in cohabiting relationships were 4 times more likely to be unfaithful than husbands and that women in cohabiting relationships were 8 times more likely to cheat than were wives.[44]

Many couples say that they want to live together to see if they are compatible, not realizing that cohabitation is more a preparation for divorce than it is a way to strengthen the likelihood of a successful marriage. A study on premarital cohabitation conducted by researchers from Yale University, Columbia University, and the Institute for Resource Development at Westinghouse revealed that the divorce rates of women who cohabit are nearly 80 percent higher than the rates of those who do not.[45] Reviewing the literature, University of Michigan researcher Pamela Smock concurs concluding that, contrary to common expectations, "premarital cohabitation tends to be associated with lower marital quality and to increase the risk of divorce."[46]

Unstable adult relationships are not healthy, secure places for children. Clearly, children whose mothers cohabit are experiencing unusual amounts of instability in their lives. Yet, living in such arrangements is standard fare for far too many children. Early research established that family transitions are highly stressful for children[47] and further research indicated that the negative effects are cumulative over time and over the various transitions.[48] Researchers found that the average child in the early 1990s could expect to experience 0.63 family changes due to marriage or the dissolution of marriage by age twelve.[49] Children in a cohabiting home experience a completely different reality. Those researchers found that "...ignoring cohabitation obscures a substantial amount of instability." In fact, they concluded "that adding transitions into and out of cohabitation increases...family instability by about 30 percent for white children and over 115 percent for black children."[50]

The instability of cohabiting relationships is an inherent and, hence, an inescapable problem for the couple involved and, especially, for the children living in such households. But these problems spill over and also affect the broader society not only in terms of the direct material costs entailed, but more importantly perhaps by their impact on the community's quality of life and its ability to function harmoniously and productively.

Clearly, the negative impacts of cohabitation on children are both predictable and well documented. Two problems at the top of the list are poverty and health.

Poverty

Compared to children with married parents, 3 and 4 times as many children in cohabiting homes live in poverty depending upon the overall national economic conditions.[51] In 2002, the poverty rate for all children in married-couple families was 8.2 percent, but for children in single-parent families the poverty rate was 4 times higher at 35.2 percent.[52] Thus, poverty is one of the harshest results of the breakdown in traditional marriage and family, with women and children bearing the consequences most severely. Children living with cohabiters are more likely to be poor, less likely to have regular, nutritious meals, are read to infrequently, and exhibit more behavioral problems than children living with married parents.[53]

While cohabitation increases the number of children in poverty across the racial spectrum, it affects black children more than white children.

One researcher estimates that if family structure had not changed (i.e., if there had been no rise in cohabitation with a commensurate decline in marriage) between 1960 and 1998, the black child poverty rate in 1998 would have been 28.4 rather than 45.6 percent, and the white child poverty rate in 1998 would have been 11.4 percent rather than 15.4 percent.[54] Robert Rector of the Heritage Foundation estimates that if family structure had not changed since 1960 (i.e., if there had been no rise in cohabitation with a commensurate decline in marriage) the child poverty rate would have dropped by nearly 30 percent (from 15.7 percent to 11.2 percent). Dr. Robert Lerman of the Urban Institute and two researchers from the Brookings Institution calculated similar drops in the child poverty rate.[55]

And, while both women and children suffer more poverty after a co-habiting relationship breaks up, there is typically an economic imbalance in favor of the man even *within* such relationships when they are intact. Couples who live together say that they plan to share expenses equally, but, more often than not, the women support the men. Studies show that women typically contribute more than 70 percent of the income in a cohabiting relationship. Likewise, the women tend to do more of the cleaning, cooking, and laundry. If they are students facing economic or time constraints requiring a reduction in class load by one partner, it is almost invariably the woman, not the man, who drops a class.[56]

Health

Cohabitation, in contrast to marriage, is also detrimental to the health of those involved in the relationship. A University of California at Los Angeles (UCLA) survey of 130 published empirical studies revealed that marriage was considerably healthier than living together. Marriages preceded by cohabitation were more prone to problems like drug and alcohol use, more permissive sexual relationships, and an "abhorrence of dependence"[57] than were marital relationships that were not preceded by cohabitation. Both alcoholism and problem drinking are more prevalent among the unmarried than the married—70 percent of all chronic problem drinkers are unmarried versus only 15 percent married.[58]

The increase in sexually transmitted diseases tracks the increase in cohabitation. It is no great surprise that about 40 percent of men in cohabiting relationships are unfaithful, thus endangering not just themselves, but also the women who are living with them. In fact, the biggest health risk in cohabitation is sexually transmitted diseases.

The data from the Centers for Disease Control[59] are alarming:

- Nearly 65 percent of sexually transmitted diseases (STDs) appear in people who are under twenty-five years of age and more than 20 percent of all AIDS cases are among college-age people.

- Approximately fifteen million new cases of STDs occur every year in the United States. This is an epidemic that should be producing extreme concern and searching for a remedy, but is barely causing a ripple of concern.

- Not only is the number of cases increasing—they have tripled in just six years—but the types and deadliness are also growing.

- Whereas in 1960 there were only three STDs, currently there are over two dozen STDs that are considered *incurable.*

- The fastest-spreading STD, human papillomavirus—commonly called HPV—causes over 90 percent of cervical cancers, kills about five thousand American women every year and is virtually unaffected by condom use.

- The number of STD cases among cohabiting women is 6 times higher than among married women.

- One doctor has estimated that a woman who has 3 or more sexual partners in a lifetime increases her odds of cervical cancer by 15 times.

In summary, while cohabitation is detrimental to the partners' health, marriage can literally save a husband and wife's life.[60] Unmarried individuals, even when living together, have a higher mortality rate than married couples: 50 percent higher among women and an amazing 250 percent higher among men.[61]

There is also a troubling, but predictable, range of social and behavioral problems that are associated with children living in cohabiting households. It is well documented that children suffer trauma from the disruption, uncertainty, and instability that is typical in the family life of a cohabiting household. Little wonder, then, that decline in children's well-being is so dramatic—children in non-intact families have roughly twice the risk of social and behavioral problems compared with children in married-parent families.[62]

Decreased Academic Achievement

Children who live in cohabiting households are less inclined to care about school and homework performance, and their academic performance tends to be poorer than that of children living with their married biological parents.[63] One study examined the well-being of teens living with their mother and their mother's boyfriend rather than their biological father. White and Hispanic teens were found to be more likely to have emotional and behavioral problems and be suspended or expelled from school than even teens living with a single mother alone. Black teens are no better off in such cohabiting families than they would be living with a single mother.[64]

Compromised Ability to Get Along with Others

Children in cohabiting households tend to have more emotional and behavioral problems, such as contentious relationships with peers, difficulty in concentrating, depression, and feelings of sadness. Among adolescents ages twelve to seventeen, one study found that the percentage of those exhibiting emotional and behavioral problems was 6 times greater in cohabiting stepfamilies than in married biological-parent families.[65]

Early Premarital Sexual Activity

Children from married-couple homes are less likely to engage in early, premarital sex,[66] and they have fewer discipline problems than those who live in unmarried homes.[67]

Adolescent Criminal Activity

A disproportionate number of adolescents convicted of crime come from cohabiting households. Darby, et al. (1998) examined adolescents convicted of homicide in adult court and found that, at the time of the crimes, 43 percent of the convicted adolescents' parents had never been married, 30 percent of such parents were divorced, and 9 percent were separated, combining for 82 percent of such cases.[68] In general, delinquency is more frequent among children from cohabiting couples than from families where the biological parents remain married to each other and the family remains intact. Fagan and Hanks (1997) found that nearly three-fourths of the children involved in criminal activity were living in a cohabiting household at the time of the crime while only one-fourth lived in an intact, married-parents family. [69]

Sex Abuse and Violence

It comes as no surprise that research shows children in cohabiting households are at greater risk for sexual abuse and violence than are children in married families. Aggression is at least twice as common in cohabiting households as it is among married-parent families. One study reported that during a one-year period, about thirty-five out of every one hundred cohabiting couples experienced physical aggression, compared to fifteen out of every one hundred married couples.[70]

The data are very clear and compelling; the accumulating body of research sends an urgent message that family organization is very important for child well-being. Some researchers estimate that child abuse is increasing by more than 10 percent a year. The increase seems clearly related to the changing family structure. There is agreement in the research—the most dangerous living arrangement for a child is a household where the mother is living with a boyfriend rather than the child's biological father—the typical cohabiting household. Rates for serious abuse of children are lowest in the intact family, 6 times higher in stepfamilies, 14 times higher in the always-single-mother family, 20 times higher in cohabiting biological-parent families, and an astonishing 33 times higher when the mother is cohabiting with a boyfriend.[71]

Linda Waite, professor of sociology at the University of Chicago, found that 16 percent of cohabiting women reported arguments with their partners can turn physical, while only 8 percent of married women have had similar experiences. The surveys also showed that 20 percent of cohabiting women reported they had secondary sex partners, while only 4 percent of married women reported they did.[72]

The United States Department of Health and Human Services (1994) reported that unmarried women were 3 to 4 times more likely to be abused by their boyfriends while pregnant than married women by their husbands.[73] Similarly, the Department of Justice estimates that women are 62 times more likely to be assaulted by live-in boyfriends than they are by husbands.[74]

Similarly, Dr. Jan Stets of Washington State University found that aggressive behavior is twice as common among cohabiting partners as among married couples. She found that approximately 14 percent of those who live together admit to hitting, shoving, or throwing things at their partner compared to only 5 percent among married people.[75] Numerous studies from the Family Violence Research Program at the University of New Hampshire duplicate the finding that cohabiting partners are more violent than married couples.[76] The United States Justice Department Victimization Study found that 65 percent of violent crimes against women were committed by a boyfriend or ex-husband, while only 9 percent were committed by husbands.[77] Clearly, cohabiting households are not safe for women.

Children, too, are at risk. Studies report that children are as many as 20 times more likely to be abused when the mother is cohabiting than when she is married to the father of the child. An article in the *Tribune Review* in Pittsburgh, Pennsylvania—typical of what can be found in other cities—noted that during 2007 four children from the area had been abused and killed by boyfriends of their mothers.[78] Dr. Janet Squires, chief of the Child Advocacy Center at Children's Hospital of Pittsburgh said, "There are certain risk facts and recipes for child abuse, and they include having an adult in the home who has poor bonding with the child."[79] This corresponds with the findings of two researchers at Pennsylvania State University who compared cohabiting relationships with marriage and found that couples who live together without marriage are more apt to argue, shout, and hit than married couples.[80]

Conclusion

Ideas can exert a powerful force on behavior. Thus, as the consensus about the detrimental effects of unmarried parenting grows stronger among researchers who study family life, it brings hope that the research data combined with common sense understanding of what is good for children may be taking hold. Certainly, marriage has an "irreplaceable role in childbearing and in generational continuity; it is society's most important institution for protecting child well-being, turning children into good citizens, and fostering good behavior among adults."[81]

In the 1960s, citizens spent the greater part of their life (62 percent) living with a spouse and children; by 1985, the percentage had dropped to 43 percent, the lowest in United States history.[82] Sadly, the latest Census data indicate that the number of cohabiting couples both with and without children continues its steep upward trend in both absolute and relative terms. Only time will tell whether documenting of the true effects of cohabitation will be as effective in changing behavior as has the public relations assault of facts on smoking.

In her book, *Experiments in Living*, Rebecca O'Neill reported:

The social fabric, once considered flexible enough to incorporate all types of lifestyles, has been stretched and strained. Although a good society should tolerate people's right to live as they wish, it must also hold adults responsible for the consequences of their actions. The weight of evidence indicates that the traditional family based upon a married father and mother is still the best environment for raising children, and it forms the soundest basis for the wider society.[83]

G.K. Chesterton wrote, "If we wish to preserve the family, we must revolutionize the nation." Given the seriousness of the decline in marriage, and the ramifications that are so harmful to everyone, including the larger society, it is past time for a fact-fueled revolution to overthrow the pernicious anti-marriage myths that took root in the 1960s and 1970s. The costs of continuing the current trends are simply too high.

Notes

1.   An earlier version of this chapter was published previously in *The Family in the New Millennium, Volume One: The Place of Family in Human Society*, edited by A. Scott Loveless and Thomas B. Holman, (Westport, CT: Praeger Perspectives, 2007).
2.   Lawrence B. Finer, "Trends in Premarital Sex in the United States, 1954-2003," *Public Health Reports* 122 (January-February 2007):76, http://www.publichealthreports.org/userfiles/122_1/12_PHR122-1_73-78.pdf (accessed February 19, 2009).
3.   Larry Bumpass and Hsien-Hen Lu, "Trends in Cohabitation and Implications for Children," *Population Studies* 54, no. 1 (March 2000): 29-41.
4.   U.S.Bureau of the Censuˢ, "Unmarried-Couple Households, by Presence of Children: 1960 to Present," and "Households by Type," Families and Living Arrangements, Historical Time Series: Living Arrangements of Adults, Table UC-1 and Table HH-1 (Internet release July 2008), http://www.census.gov/population/www/socdemo/hh-fam.html#history (accessed February 20, 2009).
5.   Ibid., 2.
6.   U.S. Bureau of the Census, "Living Arrangements of Children Under 18 Years and Marital Status of Parents, by Age, Gender, Race, and Hispanic Origin of the Child for All Children: 2006," *Current Population Survey Reports: 2006 March CPS*, Table C-3 (Internet release date May 24, 2007), http://www.census.gov/population/www/socdemo/hh-fam/cps2006.html (accessed February 20, 2009).
7.   Bumpass and Lu, "Trends in Cohabitation."
8.   Paolo Scommegna, "Increased Cohabitation Changing Children's Family Settings," National Institute of Child Health and Human Development (NICHD), National Institutes of Health, *Today's Issues*, no. 13 (September 2002)· For information enabling comparison in Western Europe: Trends, Issues, and Implications in *Just Living Together: Implications of Cohabitation on Families, Children, and Social Policy,* ed. A. Booth and A.C. Crouter, (Mahwah, NJ: L. Erlbaum Publishers, 2002); and M.F. Brinig and S.L. Nock, "Marry Me Bill: Should Cohabitation be the Legal Default Option?" *Louisiana Law Review* 64, no. 3 (2004): 403-442.
9.   Joyce A. Martin, Brady E. Hamilton, Paul D. Sutton, Stephanie J. Ventura, Fay Menacker, Sharon Kirmeyer, and T.J. Matthews, "Births: Final Data for 2006," *National Vital Statistics Report* 57, no. 7 (January 2009): Table 18 and earlier reports, http://www.cdc.gov/nchs/births.htm (accessed February 16, 2009).

10. U.S. Bureau of the Census, "Families, by Presence of Own Children Under 18: 1950 to Present," Families and Living Arrangements, Historical Time Series: Families, Table FM-1 (Internet release date July 2008), http://www.census.gov/population/www/socdemo/hh-fam.html (accessed February 20, 2009).

11. U.S. Bureau of the Census, "Unmarried-Couple Households," Tables UC-1 and HH-1.

12. "Cohabitation: Trial Marriage or Lack of Commitment?" Family First (copyright 2001), reprinted with permission on Crosswalk.com, www.crosswalk.com/family/marriage/516028.html.

13. Janice Shaw Crouse, "Just a Piece of Paper?" *The Washington Times*, March 18, 2001, available through Concerned Women for America, www.cwfa.org.

14. Norval Glenn, *Closed Hearts, Closed Minds: The Textbook Story of Marriage* (New York: Council on Families, 1997), http://www.americanvalues.org/pdfs/closedhearts.pdf.

15. Ibid., 4.

16. Ibid., 12-15.

17. Ibid., Executive Summary.

18. Ibid.

19. Ibid.

20. Ibid., 10.

21. Ibid., 5.

22. Ibid.

23. Ibid.

24. Ibid., 9.

25. Bumpass and Lu, "Trends in Cohabitation"

26. Dr. Neil Clark Warren, "The Cohabitation Epidemic," *Focus on the Family magazine* (June/July): 10-11, http://www.josh.org/site/c.ddKDIMNtEqG/b.4186681/apps/s/content.asp?ct=5426739.

27. Reo M. Christenson, "Political Scientist calls for Common Sense," *American Family Association Journal* 24, Issue 4 (April 2000): 4, http://www.afajournal.org/archives/24040000352.asp.

28. Ibid.

29. Janice Shaw Crouse, "Unmarried with Children: Has the Upward Trend of Cohabiting with Children Halted?" The Beverly LaHaye Institute, *Data Digest* IV, no. 1 (May 26, 2004), available through Concerned Women for America, www.cwfa.org.

30. Phyllis Bronstein, Golda S. Ginsburg and Ingrid S. Herrera, "Parenting Behavior and Children's Social, Psychological and Academic Adjustment in Diverse Family Structures," *Family Relations* 42, no. 3 (July 1993): 268-276.

31. Alan Booth and Ann C. Crouter, eds., *Just Living Together: Implications of Cohabitation on Families, Children, and Social Policy* (Mahwah, NJ: Lawrence Erlbaum Associates, Inc., Publishers, 2002): 134-136, 142-143.

32. Marcia Barlow, United Families International, "A Guide to Family Issues: Cohabitation vs. Marriage: Part I," Family Issues Guide (May 2007): 9, http://unitedfamilies.org/downloads/Cohabitation_Part_I.pdf.

33. Gregory Acs and Sandi Nelson, "The Kids are Alright? Children's Well Being and the Rise in Cohabitation," *New Federalism: National Survey of America's Families* Series B, no. B-48 (July 2002), http://www.urban.org/url.cfm?ID=310544.

34. Sheela Kennedy and Larry Bumpass, "Cohabitation and Children's Living Arrangements: New Estimates from the United States," *Demographic Research* 19 (December 31, 2008): 1663-1692, http://www.pubmedcentral.nih.gov/articlerender.fcgi?tool=pubmed&pubmedid=19119426.

35.   William Harms, "Research looks at cohabitation's negative effects," *The University of Chicago Chronicle* 19, no. 11 (March 2, 2000) http://chronicle.uchicago.edu/000302/cohabit.shtml.

36.   Gregory Acs and ⁣Sandi Nelson, "The Kids Are Alright? Children's Well-Being and the Rise in Cohabitation," *New Federalism: National Survey of America's Families* Series B, no. B-48 (July 2002): Table 1, http://www.urban.org/url.cfm?ID=310544 (accessed February 20, 2009).

37.   Acs and Nelson, "The Kids Are Alright?"

38.   Larry L. Bumpass, "The Declining Significance of Marriage: Changing Family Life in the United States," (paper presented at the Potsdam International Conference "Changing Families and Childhood," December 14-17, 1994)

39.   Roland L. Johnson III, "Cohabitation (good for him, not for her)," item 7 in the Love and Marriage section, 1996 (updated 2007), on the Church with No Walls website, http://churchwithnowalls.net/L&M.htm.

40.   Bumpass, "Declining Significance."

41.   Child Trends, "Marriage and Children's Well-Being: What the Research Tells Us," April 17, 2002, http://www.childtrends.org/Files//Child_Trends_2002_04_17_FS_Marriage.pdf (accessed February 20, 2009).

42.   Bumpass and Lu, "Trends in Cohabitation"

43.   Jennifer Steinhauer, "No Marriage, No Apologies," *The New York Times*, July 6, 1995, http://query.nytimes.com/gst/fullpage.html?res=990CEFDF1438F935A35754C0A963958260.

44.   Linda J. Waite and Maggie Gallagher, *The Case for Marriage: Why Married People are Happier, Healthier, and Better Off Financially* (New York: Doubleday, 2000): 93.

45.   Neil G. Bennett, Ann Klimas Blanc, and David E. Bloom, "Commitment and the Modern Union: Assessing the Link Between Premarital Cohabitation and Subsequent Marital Stability," *American Sociological Review* 53 (1988): 127-138.

46.   Pamela J. Smock, "Cohabitation in the United States: An Appraisal of Research, Themes, Findings, and Implications," *Annual Review of Sociology* 26 (2000): 6.

47.   Andrea Kane and Daniel T. Lichter, "Reducing Unwed Childbearing: The Missing Link in Efforts to Promote Marriage," The Center for Children and Families, The Brookings Institution, *CCF Briefs*, Number 37 (April, 2006): 5, http://www.brookings.edu/papers/2006/04childrenfamilies_kane.aspx?p=1.

48.   Julie E. Artis and Tait Runnfeldt Medina, "Parental Cohabitation, Family Transitions, and Young Children's Cognitive Development," January 2006 draft, 5, found at AllAcademic Research website, http://www.allacademic.com//meta/p_mla_apa_research_citation/1/0/4/1/4/pages104140/p104140-7.php.

49.   R. Kelly Raley and Elizabeth Wildsmith, "Cohabitation and Children's Family Instability" (working paper, Population Research Center, The University of Texas, January 2, 2006): 12, http://www.prc.utexas.edu/working_papers/wp_pdf/01-02-06.pdf.

50.   Ibid., 13.

51.   Susan L. Brown, "Child Well-Being in Cohabiting Families," in *Just Living Together: Implications of Cohabitation on Families, Children, and Social Policy* (Mahwah, New Jersey : Lawrence Erlbaum Associates, 2002): 173-187

52.   Robert Rector, Kirk A. Johnson and Patrick F. Fagan, "The Effect of Marriage on Child Poverty," The Heritage Foundation, Center for Data Analysis Report #02-04 (April 15, 2002): 1, http://www.heritage.org/research/Family/CDA02-04.cfm.

53.   Acs and Nelson, "The Kids Are Alright?"

54. Adam Thomas and Isabel Sawhill, "For Richer or For Poorer: Marriage as an Anti-poverty Strategy," *Journal of Policy Analysis and Management*, 2002.

55. Rector et al., "The Effect of Marriage on Child Poverty," 7.

56. Raley and Wildsmith, "Cohabitation and Children's Family Instability."

57. The term "abhorrence of dependence" refers to excessive fear of and avoidance of commitment in a relationship because it might lead to a loss of independence.

58. Robert H. Coombs, "Marital Status and Personal Well-Being: A Literature Review," *Family Relations* 40 (1991): 97-102.

59. More information about each of these facts can be found in Janice Shaw Crouse, *Gaining Ground: A Profile of American Women in the Twentieth Century* (Washington, DC: The Beverly LaHaye Institute, 2000), available through Concerned Women for America, http://www.cwfa.org.

60. Waite and Gallagher, *The Case for Marriage*, 47-64.

61. Ibid., 47.

62. Janice Shaw Crouse, "Leaving on a Jet Plane: Illegitimacy Trends and the Nation's Children," *Data Digest*, The Beverly LaHaye Institute, January 2004, available through Concerned Women for America, www.cwfa.org.

63. Brown, "Child Well-Being."

64. Acs and Nelson, "The Kids are Alright?"

65. Brown, "Child Well-Being."

66. Institute for American Values, "Family Structure and Children's Educational Outcomes," Center for Marriage and Families, *Research Brief* No. 1 (November 2005): 4.

67. Ibid., 3.

68. Patrick J. Darby, Wesley D. Allan, Javad H. Kashani, Kenneth L. Hartke and John C. Reid, "Analysis of 112 Juveniles who Committed Homicide: Characteristics and a Closer Look at Family Abuse," *Journal of Family Violence* 13, no. 4 (1998): 365-375.

69. Patrick F. Fagan, "The Child Abuse Crisis: The Disintegration of Marriage, Family and the American Community," The Heritage Foundation, *Backgrounder Report*, no.1115 (May 15, 1997), http://www.heritage.org/Research/Family/BG1115.cfm (accessed February 21, 2009).

70. Jan E. Stets, "Cohabiting and Marital Aggression: The Role of Social Isolation," *Journal of Marriage and the Family* 53 (1991): 669-680.

71. Patrick Fagan and Kirk A. Johnson, "Marriage: The Safest Place for Women and Children," The Heritage Foundation, *Backgrounder Report*, no. 1535 (April 10, 2002): 3· http://www.heritage.org/Research/Family/BG1535.cfm (accessed February 21,2009)·

72. Linda J. Waite, "The Negative Effects of Cohabitation," *The Responsive Community Quarterly* 10, no. 1 (Winter1999/2000), http://www.gwu.edu/~ccps/rcq/rcq_negativeeffects_waite.html (accessed February 21, 2009).

73. U.S. Department of Health and Human Services, "Domestic Violence Fact Sheet," 1994.

74. United States Department of Justice, "National Domestic Violence Fact Sheet and Statistics," March 1998.

75. Jan E. Stets, "The Link between Past and Present Intimate Relationships," *Journal of Family Issues* 14, no. 2 (1993): 636-660.

76. The Crimes Against Children Research Center, The University of New Hampshire, http://www.unh.edu/ccrc/.

77. Patricia Tjaden and Nancy Thoennes, "Full Report of the Prevalence, Incidence, and Consequences of Violence Against Women: Findings from the National Violence

Against Women Survey," U.S. Department of Justice, National Institute of Justice, NCJ 183781 (November 2000): 17, http://www.ncjrs.gov/pdffiles1/nij/183781.pdf.

78. Jill King Greenwood, "Boyfriends of Moms May Put Tots at Risk," *Tribune-Review* (Pittsburgh, PA), November 23, 2007, http://www.unh.edu/ccrc/news/Phys-Abuse_TribReview_11_23_07.pdf.

79. Ibid.

80. Susan L. Brown and Alan Booth, "Cohabitation versus Marriage: A Comparison of Relationship Quality," *Journal of Marriage and the Family* 58, no. 3 (1996): 668-678.

81. Council on Families in America, *Marriage in America: A Report to the Nation*, The Institute for American Values (1995), http://www.americanvalues.org/html/r-marriage_in_america.html (accessed February 21, 2009)

82. David Popenoe and Barbara Dafoe Whitehead, *The State of our Unions: The Social Health of Marriage in America, 2002* (Rutgers University: The National Marriage Project, 2002), http://marriage.rutgers.edu/Publications/SOOU/TEXTSOOU2002.htm, (accessed February 21, 2009).

83. Rebecca O'Neill, "Experiments in Living: The Fatherless Family," Civitas: The Institute for the Study of Civil Society (September 2002): 14

Part II

Dangers Facing Children

In dealing with my child,
My Latin and my Greek,
My accomplishments and my money
Stead me nothing;
But as much soul as I have avails.
—Ralph Waldo Emerson

Every child comes with the message:
God is not yet discouraged of man.
—Rabindranath Tagore

4

Abortion

The worst threat to children's well-being is abortion, which ends a life before it has any chance to begin. This issue has new urgency because in November 2008, a fifty-five-page strategic plan was released by pro-abortion groups including Planned Parenthood, The Feminist Majority, the Guttmacher Institute, NARAL, and SIECUS. The document, "Advancing Reproductive Rights and Health in the New Administration,"[1] describes the groups' wish list—beginning with "Steps for the First 100 Days"—for an administration that they have ample reason to believe will follow their recommendations. Previously, the stated goal of abortion advocates was to "make abortion safe, legal, and rare." Now the goals include overturning the restrictions on abortion by enacting the Freedom of Choice Act and eliminating the conscience protection right for healthcare workers who are unwilling to perform abortions. President Obama has already reversed the Mexico City Policy that banned funding for abortions in foreign countries.[2]

The United States has the highest abortion rate among Western industrialized countries.[3] Over one million children are aborted in the United States every year. As abortion has moved from the desperate choice of a frightened teenager to the calculated decision of adult women who use abortion as birth control, some (between 8 and 10 percent) having as many as three or more abortions,[4] the abortion issue takes on a new poignancy, forcing us to examine the calloused way the nation views life—at one time the preeminent inalienable right to which all are endowed by the Creator, the cornerstone of the Declaration of Independence.

Following the lead of several states, the Supreme Court's 1973 decision in *Roe vs. Wade* made abortion legal throughout the United States; subsequently, over 46 million abortions have been performed with more than a million being added every year. In 1973, 45.6 million women were of childbearing age (ages fifteen to forty-four), and there were 745,000 abortions. By 2005, with sixty-two million women of childbearing age, there were 1,206,200 abortions.[5]

In the years after *Roe vs. Wade* became the law of the land, American culture became inured to the harsh realities of abortion. In fact, in a strange convoluted way, abortion became "good child policy." In April 2002, the *Chicago Tribune* published an opinion editorial[6] by Irving B. Harris arguing that New York City's lower crime rate today was due to the abortion of unwanted babies eighteen years ago. Had those babies come into the world, said the writer, they likely would have grown up to become criminals. "The only children we ought to produce," said Irving B. Harris, founder and chairman of The Harris Foundation in Chicago, "are wanted children." Harris, widely praised for his philanthropy for children, became a voice of moral relativism when he wanted Chicago to follow New York's lead in making the world safer tomorrow by slaughtering innocents today.

Harris' rhetoric flowers over a leaky cesspool of relativistic thinking and warped values. If you slaughter the innocents, you destroy the future. Without moral absolutes, children are at risk. When moral boundaries are blurred, children are no longer safe. Moral absolutes are necessary for children's well-being.

An important part of the abortion mantra is to "make abortion rare." Yet, more than 1.2 million abortions are performed in the U.S. every year. Even with a decline in abortion rates overall from 1990 to 2004—especially for teens and twenty to twenty-four-year-old women—this hoped-for change has not been universal: the rates for black women twenty-five and older have remained essentially unchanged with the exception of black women thirty to thirty-four, whose has increased by more than 6 percent.[7]

We have become so used to these cited figures that we are numb to the implications of the million plus figure. According to the CDC's abortion surveillance data, the abortion rate for unmarried women is 4.5 times greater than that of married women (7 per thousand for married women versus 31.7 per thousand of unmarried women).[8] Break the numbers down and the facts are that about 6.3 million American women become pregnant every year, and almost one-third of them are unmarried. Of those 2.1 million unmarried pregnant women, about one-quarter of them have abortions or miscarriages and 1.5 million have a child out of wedlock, swelling the ranks of unmarried mothers. Few of the unmarried pregnant women marry the father of their child or give the child up for adoption. These facts are a double-edged sword for children's well-being; too often, they either are aborted or are doomed to live in a household without a father.

Sadly, we are discovering that, though many unmarried women are living with the man who fathered their child, few consider marriage as an option or consider giving up the child for adoption to a couple on the long lists of infertile couples desperate to have a child. Young women today are told that marrying because you "have to" or giving up a child for adoption is "cruel." What a perverted twist of logic: it is not considered cruel to abort a child that is unwanted, but in some circles abortion is considered "brave" and "courageous" because, some argue, nothing could be worse for a child than being "unwanted." And, of course, some also argue that nothing could be worse for a woman than to be saddled with a child that is "unwanted."

Actually, something is much worse—discovering that a man wants to have sex with you but has no interest in marrying you, even when that sex results in a pregnancy. The truth behind the data is that abortion is overwhelmingly a choice of unmarried, rather than married, pregnant women.[9] Over and over, Crisis Pregnancy Center personnel hear unmarried women say that their "boyfriend," "live-in partner," or "significant other" is "making" them have an abortion. When a boyfriend is pressuring them to have an abortion, choosing to have the baby may not appear to be a manageable option among the "choices" that the women believe are available to them. Often the woman is told that if she does not "get rid of the baby," the man is "out of there."

Increasingly, as mentioned earlier, abortion is less a scared teen's impulsive "solution" than a twenty-something's "choice" between a man she loves and the baby he does not want. In short, abortion is no longer primarily an act of teenage desperation; instead, more and more it is the terrible choice of adults unwilling to accept responsibility for their behavior. Abortion is becoming more "rare" among the nation's teens, but a larger percentage of women in their mid to late twenties—women who should, by that age, be responsible, mature, and informed—are, to put it bluntly, using abortion as a form of birth control.[10] Over time, the percent of *repeat* abortions has been increasing. By the late 1990s, more than 46 percent of all abortions were being performed on women with previous abortions. More than a half million abortions each year are performed on women who have already had one or more previous abortions.[11]

Sensible people are glad to see that teen abortions are declining dramatically and that the total number of abortions also is declining. The abstinence message is getting through to teens; the pregnancy rate of ten to fourteen year olds has been cut in half since 1990.[12] Abstinence education would be worth the investment if it did no more than protect those ten to fourteen year olds.

A very meager amount of federal funds is appropriated for abstinence training. In fact, a HHS report at the end of 2008 revealed that only 22 percent of the total funding for adolescent programming went to abstinence education compared to 78 percent that went to pregnancy prevention and family planning services.[13] When the same report acknowledges, "about one-fifth of high school seniors reported having had sex with four or more partners in 2007,"[14] it seems imperative to provide teens with the information, skills, and programs in self-esteem that will enable them to remain abstinent during their vulnerable teenage years. Indeed, knowing the risks and understanding the consequences, what hard-hearted person could possibly recommend otherwise.

Sonogram technology is making possible increased awareness of the humanity of those babies in the womb. Currently, six states require verbal and written counseling about accessing ultrasound before an abortion can be performed; twelve states have requirements about ultrasound by abortion providers.[15] Obviously, those sonograms—especially the newer, high definition ones—are making a difference; they are 93 percent effective in preventing abortions. One study tracked seventy-five patients and all but five changed their minds about an abortion after seeing a sonogram of their baby in the womb.[16] In 1991, women ages twenty to twenty-four had over 535,000 abortions, about one-third of the total performed that year; by 2005, they had 26 percent fewer abortions. In 1991, teens nineteen and under had 327,000 abortions, but by 2005 they had 37 percent fewer abortions.[17]

The bad news is that over the past decade the share of abortions to women over twenty-five has grown from 46 percent of the total number of abortions to 50 percent in 2005. This contrasts with the teen share of abortions, which have declined during the same period; the share of abortions to women twenty to twenty-four stayed at about one-third of the total.[18]

The real shocker, as noted earlier, is that the percentage of women having repeat abortions (some three or more) has doubled since the mid-1980s and many are having an abortion after already having given birth to two or more children (the latter has risen from 22 percent in 1985 to more than 32 percent in 2005).[19] This is nothing less than a double tragedy: the potential wrapped up in the infant is destroyed and—though they may try to suppress the reality—part of the parents, mother and father alike, is destroyed as well. On the other hand, it seems a hopeful sign that women who had not previously had a live birth accounted for nearly three-quarters of the decline in the number of abortions from 1990 to 2005.[20]

These women who have previously given birth are, of course, experienced and informed. Yet, they engage in sexual behavior that has a high likelihood of producing pregnancy and all too often with men who are poor candidates for marriage and even worse candidates for fatherhood. Even so, a lifestyle of casual sex is commonplace; popular culture glamorizes it through contemporary shows like "Sex and the City."

Episode 59, "Coulda, Woulda, Shoulda,"[21] deals with the dimensions of abortion: Miranda is pregnant, decides to have an abortion but cannot go through with it for fear that she will be unable to have other children; Charlotte sees a fertility doctor because she cannot get pregnant and discovers that she has only a 15 percent chance of conceiving naturally. Carrie and Samantha both admit that they've had abortions (notice the plural) and have lied about it with subsequent boyfriends. Lest the reality be too much, the episode's denouement has Carrie searching out the restaurant where the waiter who got her pregnant years ago is stuck in a dead-end job—she walks away telling herself she made the right decision to abort that man's baby. The waiter's contrast with her wealth and sophistication is made obvious, and his "unworthiness" is portrayed as a valid reason for aborting the "unworthy" baby. Carrie admits her past to her current "yuppie" boyfriend who is non-judgmental and accepting of Carrie's past. So, the message is clear to twenty-plus single women: abortion is not a big deal, so have fun with casual sex.

After six years as an HBO series, "Sex and the City" was released on DVD and in 2008 as a movie that made $415 million in worldwide box office on a $65 million budget.[22] Now filming is beginning for a movie sequel to be released in the summer of 2010.[23] Sarah Jessica Parker, star of the show, called the original movie, "very serious and at many times very raw and emotional." The sequel, though, will be a "massive romp" because "we want our audience to have great fun."[24] Obviously, the millions in the audience have already bought into the idea that sex is nothing more than a very entertaining and meaningless "romp."

The data indicates that potential parenthood does not drive couples to marry—even when they are already living together. Though the median age for women's first marriage is now in the mid-twenties,[25] studies show that, contrary to the feminist myth, women do not have as many choices as they have been led to expect. Among cohabiting or sexually involved couples, the man can call the shots as to if and when the couple gets married; thus, unlike the "bad old days" when traditional values operated, regardless of sexual intimacy or even pregnancy, a couple does not get married until the man is ready regardless of how much the woman might desire marriage.

The abortion statistics indicate that even when confronted with a pregnancy, too many men are unwilling to make a commitment or take responsibility; plus, often the woman is unwilling to give up her independence for the sake of her child's well-being. In this respect, too, trends have changed dramatically. In 1960, most unmarried pregnant women married the father of their baby before the baby was born, but by 1994, most did not.[26]

Over the past three and a half decades, abortion has enabled women to ignore the possibility of pregnancy (though not without the risk of herpes, HIV/AIDS, and many other sexually transmitted diseases) and engage in sexual activity without marriage or any other commitment; this has made casual sex an easy possibility regardless of whether either person is able or willing to commit to a permanent relationship and regardless of whether either person is willing or able to take responsibility for the consequences. That is the driving force behind the so-called "pro-choice" movement. As a result, abortion, a so-called women's rights issue, is now deeply entrenched into American culture, and special interest groups are now calling for abortion to be enshrined as a "human" rights issue. But nagging facts just won't go away.

Abortion has made it easier for irresponsible men to turn their backs on women and the children they conceive. Women are left to deal with the consequences, and often they are not even aware of the worst complications. One study reported that only 25 percent of American women believed that they had received adequate counseling prior to their abortions.[27] Peer-reviewed research increasingly confirms the risks to women,[28] even though the prevailing view is that abortion is a minor procedure that resolves a major problem.

Pro-abortion rhetoric focuses on the danger of "back-alley" abortions, but legalized abortion are also not without risks. We do women a grave disservice to falsely reassure them that abortion is always safe. A study in Finland using official government data—STAKES, the statistical analysis unit of Finland's National Research and Development Center for Welfare and Health—showed that, while there is no way to pinpoint causal connections, there are associations between abortion and other dire outcomes: in that one-year study, abortion was 3.5 times deadlier than childbirth, suicide was 7 times higher among post-abortive women, and deaths from homicide were 4 times higher among post-abortive women.[29]

In December 2008, a peer-reviewed journal linked abortion with negative mental health results, underscoring the importance of full information for women considering an abortion. The *British Journal of Psychiatry* showed a connection between abortion and mental health problems, finding that the rates of mental disorder were about 30 percent higher among women who had had abortions.[30] Another earlier journal article reviewed over one hundred international studies and found a link between abortion and mental health problems.[31]

Also, evidence is mounting that there is a link between abortion and breast cancer—commonly called the ABC link. In 2006, eight medical organizations (including the Catholic Medical Association, the American Association of Pro-Life Obstetricians and Gynecologists, and the Breast Cancer Prevention Institute) concluded there is evidence that abortion raises a woman's risk of breast cancer.[32] While this evidence is denied by nearly a dozen studies, a peer-reviewed article in the *Journal of American Physicians and Surgeons* examines those studies, points out serious methodological weaknesses and flaws, and concludes that there is, indeed, an increased risk for breast cancer after an abortion.[33] Other consequences are less easy to quantify, but as noted above, abortion-related emotional and psychological problems are not uncommon after an abortion. In fact, such problems have earned a medical designation: "post-abortion syndrome."

Another disturbing fact that will not go away is the willingness to encourage abortion when doctors believe that the child will have a medical problem or disability. In fact, it is common today to claim a "right" for women to kill their unborn children only because the child likely will be born with a disability. Ninety-two percent of babies found in prenatal testing to have Down Syndrome are aborted.[34] At least 73 percent of unborn babies believed to have neural tube defects, such as spina bifida, share the same fate, with some researchers believing the rate to be between 80 and 100 percent.[35]

In fact, many times doctors encourage expecting parents to undergo prenatal testing (some involving risks of miscarriage and preterm labor) in order to diagnose disorders or "undesirable" disabilities early, so that the mother can "easily" undergo an abortion. In some cases, women who would happily give birth to a healthy child are encouraged to have an abortion if the tests show an elevated risk of the child being disabled. The implication is that no parent would want to deal with the financial and emotional burden of a child who has Down Syndrome or who will be blind.

This type of so-called "therapeutic" abortion, an outcome of both scientific advancement in prenatal testing and an unrestrained "right" to an abortion, is inherently discriminatory towards disabled and handicapped people. In effect, the doctors and abortion advocates are saying that human beings born with physical and mental disabilities are not fit to live. They justify this point of view by saying that they are just "relieving the suffering" that the disabled person will go through if born. This does not take into account the fulfilling lives that many disabled people enjoy, despite their handicap. It does not take into account the joy that others receive from their association with the disabled person as a *person*. Instead, they promote the destruction of human beings based solely on whether that child's potential "usefulness" is adequate for the parents and society.

Another troubling fact is the contradiction between the prevalent liberal view that abortion is a matter of "women's rights" and the reality that a frequent target of abortion is the "girl child" in the womb. It doesn't take a genius to recognize a dilemma here; that is, the two alternatives are mutually exclusive. Holding one point of view means that you cannot believe the other proposition. How can the pro-abortion advocates embrace the position that abortion is morally unobjectionable while condemning abortion for sex selection? Having the abortion option, they claim, is regrettable, but necessary. Sex selection abortion, however, is a morally reprehensible crime against the "girl child."[36] Such is the logical inconsistency of those pro-choice adherents who none-the-less condemn "pre-natal sex selection."

Amazingly, even the pro-choice activists at the United Nations admit the humanity of unborn girls and condemn aborting them. In their State of the World Population Report, the United Nations Population Fund

(UNFPA) reported, "At least 60 million girls who would otherwise be expected to be alive are 'missing' from various populations as a result of sex-selective abortions or neglect."[37] The United Kingdom (U.K.) has outlawed "sex selection for social reasons." The U.K. based bioethics group, Human Genetics Alert, argues, "If we allow sex selection it will be impossible to oppose 'choice' of any other characteristics, such as appearance, height, intelligence, etc. The door to 'designer babies' will not have been opened a crack—it will have been thrown wide open."[38]

These facts led William Saunders, Senior Counsel, Americans United for Life, the nation's oldest pro-life organization, to say, "The true 'plight of the girl child' is that she is being aborted out of existence. Recent demographic studies show a growing dearth of female births around the world. This trend is increasing, as couples (and governments) try to 'engineer families.'"[39]

The abortion dilemma of the radical feminists and other leftists will not be resolved anytime soon, and the ramifications continue to worsen. The bodies of the aborted babies may have been removed from sight, but the staggering long-term consequences of the "missing" lives will continue to accumulate dramatically.

Sow the wind, reap the whirlwind. The lie that produced the illogical abortion dilemma is the same lie that is snuffing out thousands of lives and wreaking havoc on human dignity. In due time, the bitter fruit of "choice" will be recorded in the pages of history.

Ironically, though, the landscape confronting the abortion movement has changed significantly. The abortion movement has a hidden self-destruct mechanism. Consider the data: abortion in America is on the decline. After *Roe vs. Wade*, abortions remained consistently high at over 1.55 million abortions annually throughout the eighties. But after hitting a high of 1.6 million in 1990, the trend declined throughout the nineties, reaching a new low of 1.2 million in 2005. What's going on? The answer starts with the cumulative power of the numbers. From 1972 to 2000, the number of abortions in the United States alone totaled over forty million, eliminating the equivalent of the entire population of Spain (40.2 million).[40]

The terrible tsunami that struck Southeast Asia[41] offers sobering perspective on the scale of abortion. If the killer wave had engulfed the entire island of Java in Indonesia (where the northern province of Banda Aceh was decimated), with its population of 19.9 million, the victims would still number *less than half* the total of the American death toll from abortion.

In the wake of the tsunami, authorities have noted that at least one-third of the over 200 thousand dead or missing are children. Stories of babies swept from their frantic mothers' arms broke our hearts. Early stories that speculated on the complete annihilation of some island tribes left us stunned and horrified. These images carry the tsunami impact one step further: once the waves claim their victims and recede, the survivors stand on the beach and grieve. And so it is with abortion.

While we may analyze "trends" and look at abortion in the aggregate, each and every abortion "statistic" is a tragedy for one, lone, individual woman and her child. The pro-abortion advocates offer a woman the opportunity to erase her "mistake" and get on with her life, as though nothing happened. But science and technology are capable of "showing" that something will have happened. With the widespread use of sonograms, more and more people are realizing that "abortion stops a beating heart."

Margaret Cho, the virulently pro-abortion stand-up comic, described pregnancy. She said, "pregnancy feels like there is somebody in there." She went on to say, with callous poignancy, about her own abortion, "The tenant was evacuated."[42] And that is something a woman does not soon forget. This is the engine of the self-destruct mechanism. Why are abortions declining? It may just be that a post-choice message is spreading. Two women, among the thousands regretting their abortions, wrote about their reactions. Marguerite wrote, "[M]y abortion has left me with a feeling of emptiness...I just keep picturing my baby." Lori wrote, "My abortion has left me empty, alone and in despair." Even cynical Cho revealed in her blog account that her abortion left her feeling "hollowed out and alone."[43]

You cannot sustain a movement on hollowed-out emptiness. This is the Catch-22 confronting the abortion movement; as women experience abortion personally, the truth cannot be contained. Witness the development and growth of the Silent No More campaign of post-abortive women, determined to help others avoid the choice they regret. Call this the "post-choice" movement. It's the wave of the twenty-first century.

In addition, aren't pro-choicers aborting their movement? Those choosing to abort their children have no one to whom to pass on their legacy.

There is good news on the horizon: between 1992 and 2005, the number of facilities providing abortions in the United States decreased by 25 percent in part because they could not get enough doctors to provide the abortions; more and more physicians are refusing to perform abortions.[44] By 2005, over 87 percent of U.S. counties had no abortion provider.[45] Some medical schools are seeking legal recourse to require abortion training because too many medical students are declining to become licensed for the procedure.[46]

Other good news is the increase in Crisis Pregnancy Centers (CPCs). At a time when some abortion clinics are closing because of the decline in business, CPCs are springing up everywhere. There were only five hundred CPCs across the United States in 1980. By 1990, there were an estimated two thousand and now it is estimated that there are at least four thousand, more than double the number of facilities providing abortions.[47]

Yet, abortion is still not rare, not even safe, and prominent voices continue to support it not only as a right but also as *good* for society. Nothing is heard more often these days than the claim that certain policies and programs must be enacted "for the children." Yet, America's culture is no longer child-friendly when the most that Americans, in general, hope for is that abortion will be safe, legal, and rare and when so many assert that children who are not wanted ought to be aborted.

If you slaughter the innocents, you destroy the future.

Notes

1. "Advancing Reproductive Rights and Health in a New Administration," Submitted to the Obama-Biden Transition Project by a coalition of pro-choice supporters, November 2008, http://otrans.3cdn.net/3b21d35e246c18a427_d7m6bw2o1.pdf.
2. Jake Tapper, Sunlen Miller, and Huma Khan, "Obama Overturns 'Mexico City Policy' Implemented by Reagan," ABC News, January 23, 2009, http://abcnews.go.com/print?id=6716958.
3. Stanley K. Henshaw, Susheela Singh, and Taylor Haas, "The Incidence of Abortion Worldwide," Family Planning Perspectives 25, Supplement (January 1999), http://www.alanguttmacher.org/pubs/journals/25s3099.html; Wm. Robert Johnston, "Abortion Statistics and Other Data," *Johnston Archive* (updated November 18, 2008): 1, http://www.johnstonsarchive.net/policy/abortion and Physicians for Reproductive Choice and Health (PRCH) and Guttmacher Institute, "An Overview of Abortion in the United States," slide and lecture presentation (January 2008): slide 45.
4. Sonya B. Gamble, Lilo T. Strauss, Wilda Y. Parker, Douglas A. Cook, Suzanne B. Zane, and Saeed Hamdan, "Abortion Surveillance—United States, 2005," *Morbidity and Mortality Weekly Report* (November 28, 2008): 57(SS13); 1-32, Table 13, and earlier reports, http://www.cdc.gov/mmwr/preview/mmwrhtml/ss5713a1.htm (accessed March 7, 2009).
5. The Guttmacher Institute, "Abortion in the United States: Incidence and Access to Services, 2005" *Perspectives on Sexual and Reproductive Health* 40, no. 1 (March 2008); U.S. Bureau of the Census, Population Division, "Annual Estimates of the Population by Selected Age Groups and Sex for the United States: April 1, 2000 to

July 1, 2006 (NC-EST2006-02)," National Population Estimates—Characteristics, www.census.gov/popest/national/asrh/NC-EST2006-sa.html.

6.   Irving Harris, "A Clue to Chicago's high murder rate you may not suspect," *Chicago Tribune*, April 16, 2002, http://pqasb.pqarchiver.com/chicagotribune/access/113906320.html?dids=113906320:113906320&FMT=ABS&FMTS=ABS: FT&type=current&date=Apr+16%2C+2002&author=&pub=Chicago+Tribune& edition=&startpage=19&desc=A+clue+to+Chicago%27s+high+murder+rate+yo u+may+not+suspect.

7.   Stephanie J. Ventura, Joyce C. Abma, and William D. Mosher, "Estimated Pregnancy Rates by Outcome for the United States, 1990–2004," *National Vital Statistics Report* 56, no. 15 (April 12, 2008): 14-17, Table 2, http://www.cdc. gov/nchs/data/nvsr/nvsr56/nvsr56_15.pdf (accessed March 8, 2009).

8.   Ibid., 22, Table 5.

9.   Gamble et al., "Abortion Surveillance," Table 1.

10. Janice Shaw Crouse, "Abortion: America's Staggering Hidden Loss," *Data Digest* VI, no. 1 (January-February 2005): 1-2, http://www.cwfa.org/images/content/ dd_jan-feb_05.pdf.

11. "Abortion More Prevalent for Birth Control," *World Net Daily*, January 24, 2005, http://www.wnd.com/news/article.asp?ARTICLE_ID=42526.

12. Ventura et al., "Estimated Pregnancy Rates," 22, Table 2.

13. U.S. Department of Health and Human Services, Assistant Secretary for Planning and Evaluation, "Health and Human Services Funding for Abstinence Education, Education for Teen Pregnancy and HIV/STD Prevention, and Other Programs that Address Adolescent Sexual Activity" (December 2008): 4, http://aspe.hhs. gov/hsp/08/AbstinenceEducation/report.shtml.

14. Ibid., 8.

15. The Guttmacher Institute, "Requirements for Ultrasound," *State Policies in Brief* (March 1, 2009): 1-2, http://www.guttmacher.org/statecenter/spibs/spib_RFU.pdf (accessed March 8, 2009).

16. Peter Bronson, "Angels in Lab Coats," *The Cincinnati Enquirer*, August 19, 2001, http://www.enquirer.com/editions/2001/08/19/loc_bronson_angels_in.html (accessed March 8, 2009).

17. Percentages of abortions by age are from Gamble, et al., "Abortion Surveillance," Table 1 and earlier reports; the total number of abortions are from Rachel K. Jones, Mia R. S. Zolna, Stanley K. Henshaw, and Lawrence B. Finer, "Abortion in the United States: Incidence and Access to Services, 2005," *Perspectives on Sexual and Reproductive Health, 2008* 40, no. 1 (March 2008): 9, Table 1 http://www. guttmacher.org/pubs/journals/4000608.pdf *(accessed March 8, 2009).*

18. Gamble, et al, "Abortion Surveillance," Table 1 and earlier reports.

19. Ibid., Tables 12 and 13 and earlier reports.

20. Percentages of abortions by number of live births are from Gamble et al, "Abortion Surveillance," Table 12 and earlier reports; the total number of abortions are from Jones, et al., "Abortion in the United States," 9, Table 1.

21. "Episode 59: Coulda, Woulda, Shoulda," HBO: "Sex and the City": Episode Guide: Summary: Season 4: Episode 59, http://www.hbo.com/city/episode/season4/episode59.shtml (accessed March 8, 2009).

22. "'Sex and the City' Sequel is Moving Along," WorstPreviews.com, February 5, 2009, http://www.worstpreviews.com/headline.php?id=11955 (accessed March 8, 2009).

23. Ibid.

24. "Sex and the City Sequel," posted under celebrity news on Popstar.com, February 18, 2009, http://news.popstar.com/Article/667.

25. In 1973, when abortion became legal in the United States, the median age of first marriage for women was 21 years of age; in 2005, it was 25.3 years of age. Source: U.S. Bureau of the Census, "Median Age at First Marriage for Women: 2005," Annual Social and Economic Supplement: 2005, Current Population Survey Reports, Series P20-553, and earlier reports, U.S. Bureau of the Census, "Estimated Median Age at First Marriage, by Sex: 1890 to the Present," Families and Living Arrangements, Historical Time Series, Marital Status, Table MS-2, http://www.census.gov/population/www/socdemo/hh-fam.html (accessed March 8, 2009).

26. In 1960, 60 percent of unmarried pregnant women married the father of their child before the baby was born. By 1994, only 23 percent of women in that situation married. U.S. Bureau of the Census report: Amara Bachu, "Trends in Premarital Childbearing: 1930-1994," Current Population Reports, Series P-23, no. 197(October 1999): 1-10, http://www.census.gov/prod/99pubs/p23-197.pdf (accessed March 8, 2009).

27. VM Rue, PK Coleman, JJ Rue, and DC Reardon, "Induced abortion and traumatic stress: a preliminary comparison of American and Russian women," *Medical Science Monitor* 10(10): SR5-16, 2004, http://www.ncbi.nlm.nih.gov/pubmed/15448616 (accessed March 8, 2009).

28. Martha Shuping and Chris Gacek, "Big Girls Do Cry: The Hidden Truth of Abortion," *Townhall Magazine*, (February 2009): 42. Note that this article also mentions that a 1993 Planned Parenthood fact sheet listed being pressured or coerced to have an abortion puts women at risk for negative psychological reactions.

29. As cited in David Reardon, "Abortion is Four Times Deadlier than Childbirth," *The Post-Abortion Review* 8(2) (April-June 2000), http://www.afterabortion.org/PAR/V8/n2/finland.html (accessed March 8, 2009).

30. David M. Fergusson, L. John Horwood, and Joseph M. Boden, "Abortion and Mental Health Disorders: Evidence from a 30-year Longitudinal Study," *The British Journal of Psychiatry* 193 (December 2008): 444-451, http://bjp.rcpsych.org/cgi/content/abstract/193/6/444, (accessed March 8, 2009).

31. John M. Thorp, Katherine E. Hartmann, and Elizabeth Shadigian, "Long-Term Physical and Psychological Health Consequences of Induced Abortion: Review of the Evidence," *Obstetrical and Gynecological Survey* 58 (1) (January 2003): 67-79, http://www.ncrtl.org/images/concept/evidencereview.pdf (accessed March 8, 2009).

32. The Coalition on Abortion/Breast Cancer, http://www.abortionbreastcancer.com/medicalgroups/index.htm (accessed March 8, 2009).

33. Joel Brind, "Induced Abortion as an Independent Risk Factor for Breast Cancer: A Critical Review of Recent Studies Based on Prospective Data," *Journal of American Physicians and Surgeons* 10, no. 4 (Winter 2005): 105-110, http://www.jpands.org/vol10no4/brind.pdf (accessed March 8, 2009).

34. Amy Harmon, "The DNA Age: Prenatal Test Puts Down Syndrome in Hard Focus," *New York Times*, May 9, 2007, http://www.nytimes.com/2007/05/09/us/09down.html?_r=1&sq=may%209,%202007&st= (accessed March 8, 2009).

35. U.S. Department of Health and Human Services, Agency for Healthcare Research and Quality, "42. Screening for Neural Tube Defects—Including Folic Acid/Folate Prophylaxis," 469. http://www.ahrq.gov/clinic/2ndcps/nrltube.pdf (accessed March 8, 2009).

36. Janice Shaw Crouse, "The United Nations Abortion Dilemma," *Townhall.com*, March 2, 2007, http://townhall.com/columnists/JaniceShawCrouse/2007/03/02/the_united_nations_abortion_dilemma (accessed March 8, 2009).

37.   "Infanticide, Abortion Responsible for 60 Million Girls Missing in Asia," *Fox News*, June 13, 2007. http://www.pop.org/2007061375/infanticide-abortion-responsible-for-60-million-girls-missing-in-asia-foxnewscom (accessed March 8, 2009).

38.   Human Genetics Alert, "The case against sex selection," Human Genetics Alert Campaign Briefing (December 2002): 2, http://www.hgalert.org/sexselection.PDF (accessed March 8, 2009).

39.   Personal interview conducted by Janice Shaw Crouse, March 1, 2007.

40.   Jones, et al., "Abortion in the United States," 9, Table 1.

41.   "Tsunami in Southeast Asia: Full Coverage," *National Geographic News*, January 18, 2005, http://news.nationalgeographic.com/news/pf/16914123.html (accessed March 8, 2009).

42.   Cho's remarks have been taken off her blog, but an account can be found at, "After Abortion," http://afterabortion.blogspot.com/2003_10_26_archive.html (accessed March 8, 2009).

43.   Janice Shaw Crouse, "Abortion Movement's New Antagonist: The Post-Abortive Woman," *Human Events*, November 27, 2006, http://www.humanevents.com/article.php?id=18198 (accessed March 8, 2009).

44.   Guttmacher, "An Overview of Abortion in the United States," slide and lecture presentation (January 2008): slide 33, http://www.guttmacher.org/presentations/ab_slides.html (accessed March 8, 2009).

45.   Ibid., slide 39.

46.   Ibid., slides 34 and 35.

47.   Vitoria Lin and Cynthia Dailard, *"Crisis Pregnancy Centers Seek to Increase Political Clout, Secure Government Subsidy,"* *Guttmacher Report on Public Policy* 5, no. 2 (May 2002), http://www.guttmacher.org/pubs/tgr/05/2/gr050204.html.

Though the mills of God grind slowly, yet they grind exceedingly small;
Though with patience He stands waiting, with exactness grinds He all.
—Friedrich von Logau

5

Childhood Sexual Exploitation

Child sexual exploitation has proliferated into a multi-billion dollar industry that is expanding to every corner of our modern-day world through electronic media. Yet, most parents don't think about obscenity, sex tourism, pornography, or sex trafficking as having anything to do with *their* children. Parents are naturally concerned about their children's well-being and safety, but the depravity of childhood sexual exploitation has been far removed from most American families. As the incidences of child sexual exploitation accumulate across the nation and as these scourges move relentlessly closer to our formerly safe neighborhoods and homes, parents are being forced to confront very unsettling threats to their children.

In February 2009, two separate cases of child sexual exploitation were in the national spotlight. In a three-night initiative called Operation Cross Country, the FBI rescued more than forty-five suspected prostituted teenagers, some as young as thirteen, in a nationwide effort to free young children from the illegal sex trade.[1] In another case, two teenage girls already accused of prostituting themselves were arrested for allegedly pimping other students for prostitution in Phoenix. The two girls are reported to have recruited at least five girls ages fourteen to seventeen.[2] One of the girls, it is alleged, had a pimp before she began pimping others—a typical situation where the cycle of abuse continues and spreads outward to affect others. Suddenly, parents have to come to grips with a very real and frightening new danger for the nation's children. In the Phoenix case, FBI Deputy Assistant Director Daniel Roberts said, "Unfortunately, the vast majority of these kids are what they term, 'throwaway kids.' They're kids that nobody wants, they're loners. Many are runaways."[3]

FBI Agent Roberts' comment supports the theme of this book—too many of our nation's children are without the family support that they need to be safe and to thrive into adulthood. Over and over again, one inescapable reality confronts us: kids need a mom and dad. The outside world is encroaching on individual families to the point that parents are having greater and greater difficulty protecting their children and shielding them from the corruption and coarseness of the culture that surrounds them.

A recent cell phone fad among kids as young as middle school is called "sexting"—sending nude or semi-nude pictures of themselves or other students and/or sexually explicit messages via cell phone. Authorities say that the practice is "shockingly common."[4] Recent estimates indicate that half of children ages eight to twelve, about 80 percent of teens and 93 percent of young adults ages eighteen to twenty-four have cell phones.[5] The National Campaign to Prevent Teen and Unplanned Pregnancy recently surveyed 653 teens (ages thirteen to nineteen), 20 percent said they had sent or posted nude or semi-nude pictures or video of themselves[6] and the most popular reason for doing so was to be "fun or flirtatious." Over 10 percent of the surveyed teens who admitted involvement were young teen girls ages thirteen to sixteen. Even more teens (about 40 percent) sent or posted sexually suggestive messages and nearly half received such messages.[7] In a Massachusetts middle school, six boys ages twelve to fourteen were caught with such images of a thirteen-year-old female classmate and these boys may face child pornography charges.[8] The same sort of thing happened in recent cases in Pennsylvania, Ohio, Indiana, Florida, New Jersey, Texas, and Utah.[9]

In writing about "sexting," Lori Borgman of the McClatchy-Tribune News Service stated the obvious and asked the pertinent question.

> There is a sense in which these kids have grown up "under the influence." Raunch has become a silent part of our cultural landscape, like a beige backdrop or small-print wallpaper. We hardly notice it. We rarely flinch....We have all grown numb. We recognize the symptoms—adolescent girls aspiring to be pole dancers, boys objectifying girls, girls objectifying themselves, absentee parents and kids with no boundaries. But do we ever get at what lies beneath? Do we ever flip over that big ugly rock to study the sow bugs beneath?[10]

Clearly, today's parents need to have open and frank conversations about video and text-messaging technology in the same way that they discuss the dangers of alcohol and drugs.[11] And those conversations need to be held at an earlier age than many would expect. Note that most of the "sexting" teens were trying to be popular with the classmates at school. This is a wake-up call for parents who need to think through and intentionally direct their interactions with their children in order to maximize the impact they have on building their children's self-image, self-confidence, and character. Nothing beats healthy relationships with both mom and dad to help teens to stay away from risky behavior.

Those who are genuinely concerned about the future of American children need to ask how young children have reached the point of thinking that it is no big deal to send sexually-explicit pictures and messages via a cell phone or text message. We have only to look at our cultural influences to see the numerous ways that children are sexualized. Look at the Halloween costumes available for young children; girls are offered skimpy outfits such as a French maid costume. Boys can dress up as a pimp. Clothing options for young girls include suggestive words and phrases imprinted everywhere from the back of their shorts and pants to the fronts of t-shirts or on thong underwear. (Yes, thongs are available for children all the way down to toddler sizes). Fortunately, thongs are not yet available in training pants. While little girls parade around in inappropriate clothing, little boys learn that it is okay to think of girls as merely sexual objects.

There is even a line of clothing for infants called "Pimpfants." This fashion collection has onesies with the phrase "My Mom is a M.I.L.F." MILF stands for Mother I'd like to f&#! Shall we blithely accept the deterioration of our society's culture and just passively accept the sexualization of children from the time they are helpless infants? Will we allow a morally cancerous development that only intensifies as our children get older? It is long past time for parents to emphatically say, "I think not!"

The average age of first exposure to Internet pornography is eleven years old;[12] often because of stumbling onto sites while doing homework. Kids searching "White House" can easily end up typing "com" instead of "gov" and end up at a porn site. Type into Google's image search engine words like "pretty," "beautiful," "cute," or virtually any girl's name and if the "safe search filter" is not properly activated many of the images that come up are sexually explicit in the extreme. Pornographers purchase domain names knowing that web surfers can unintentionally end up at their site. A child typing in a word like toys or a popular children's character like Pokemon or Beanie Babies can be misdirected to a porn site. The Kaiser Family Foundation estimates that 70 percent of teenagers have accidentally come across pornography on the web.[13]

Most parents would be shocked to learn the statistics about Internet porn. *GOOD* magazine[14] provides some staggering information about the pornography industry:[15]

- 12 percent of all Internet sites are pornography;
- 260 new porn sites go online daily;
- every second, nearly 30,000 Internet users are viewing porn;
- 35 percent of all Internet downloads are porn.

Statistics like these lend urgency to the recommendation that parents teach their children online safety in the same way that they approach other childhood danger areas. A British study indicates that teenagers spend an average of thirty-one hours a week online and nearly two hours a week looking at pornography. The implications for their intellectual and emotional well-being should not to be taken lightly. One in four teenagers said that they regularly communicated with strangers online but considered it harmless.[16] TopTenReviews.com reveals that nearly 90 percent of sexual solicitations of youth were made in chat rooms.[17] The implications of these facts are a cause for concern for any thinking person. Obviously, today's parents need to address healthy sexuality and healthy sexual attitudes sooner rather than later in an age-appropriate manner.

It's bad enough for children to stumble across pornography on the screen of their cell phone or computer. Even worse is that behind every pornographic image of a child on the more than 100,000 child pornography websites there is a real child who is being personally violated and commercially exploited, often in horrific and dehumanizing ways. These child victims are exploited over and over again as their images are forever cast out into cyberspace to be downloaded and traded by child pornographers every day through the thousands of child porn Internet sites.

These developments are not merely another increase in a continuum. By the mid-1980s child porn was almost completely eradicated; it was too difficult and expensive to deliver and very risky to produce or purchase.[18] Back then, peddlers and purchasers of child pornography had to know someone to make the connection to receive pornography, usually in a brown paper envelope. With the advent of the Internet, however, the porn problem re-emerged and exploded exponentially. With a click of the mouse, child pornography is available now from any computer. In addition, the continuing quest for something new and different drives those in the grip of pornography to demand images of younger and younger children and images that are more and more graphic and violent.[19] Some experts believe that there is a tipping point at which those who engage in what they call "online sexual deviancy" decide to act out what they have seen and thus become a danger to the children around them. We know that those who harm children are usually adults whom the child knows well—an uncle, cousin, neighbor, or teacher.[20] We also know that many who access child pornography are what the experts call "explorers"—meaning that they got started viewing child pornography because of the easy access. These "explorers" spend many hours and thousands of dollars surfing child porn websites.

Peer-to-peer contacts are another avenue for transmitting and receiving child pornography. An article in the *Buffalo News* last year revealed that at least half of the child pornography produced is traded for free. The traders download free images off the Internet and then barter them to obtain other images.[21] This development is very troubling to authorities and to parents because it increases the demand for and supply of pornographic images among the "explorers." Child molesters take pornographic photographs or video images of family members or neighborhood children and then trade those images. Amazingly, officials at the CyberTipline estimate that 60 to 70 percent of the child porn reports they receive involve this type of activity. Undercover police officers in eighteen countries scoured online sites for free child pornography in chat rooms, news groups, bulletin boards, and Internet networks. They found that the most activity was in the United States, which accounted for more than one-third of the proposed transactions.[22]

Sadly and inevitably, the increase in demand means an increase in victims. The demand for ever-younger victims is growing; there are records of infant victims. As long as there is demand, there will be more victims. If someone is willing to pay for or trade for the image, someone will produce and offer it for a profit. There is even a growing business in the production and consumption of composite images of children engaged in sexual acts, posed pornographically, and an increasing demand for images of naked body parts. Moreover, the children victimized by child pornography are not just victims at the time that the filming or photographing occurs. When those files are sent over the Internet and downloaded, there is no end to the distribution and no control over who, when, where, or for how long their recorded abuse will be available to anyone with a computer connection. With the content of child porn becoming more brutal and extreme, nameless and countless children are sexually abused and tortured—and their horror is replayed around the world over and over again.

In addition to those children who are commercially exploited for pornography, millions of children are sex slaves. Notice that I avoided the term "child prostitute" because it implies that the child who is being used as a commodity is a competent, decision-making agent. The victims of sexual exploitation should be called prostituted children or child sex slaves in order to convey clearly that the child is a victim of an adult criminal. The Department of Justice's Child Exploitation and Obscenity Section (CEOS) website says the average age of entry into prostitution for girls is between the ages of twelve and fourteen and for boys between the ages of eleven and thirteen.[23]

The Trafficking Victims Protection Act of 2000 (TVPA) defines severe forms of sex trafficking as a commercial sex act induced by force, fraud, or coercion, or in which the person induced to perform such an act has not attained eighteen years of age. A commercial sex act is defined as any sex act on account of which anything of value is given to or received by any person. This includes but is not limited to prostitution, stripping, pornography, and escort services. Sex trafficking is the recruitment, harboring, transportation, provision, or obtaining of a person for the purpose of a commercial sex act.[24]

Imagine the exploitation of children in any one of these evil enterprises and then face the strong likelihood that it is happening in your community or even your neighborhood. Look through the press release section of the local Federal Bureau of Investigation office, and you will find examples of exploited children from all fifty states. Sex trafficking is modern-day slavery, and many children worldwide are victims. To fathom the demand for the sexual exploitation of children is to plumb the depths of depravity, but it must be understood that it is the demand for prostitutes or pornography that drives sexual slavery.

It is important, also, to repeat the fact that children under the age of consent do not *choose,* with full knowledge, to enter a life of prostitution; there simply is no way that they can fully understand the ramifications of choosing that life. In addition, remember that sex with a minor is illegal in all fifty states; prostituting a child is a crime no matter when, where, how, or why it happens. Moreover, all adult prostitution is illegal in the United States except in a few counties in Nevada and if conducted indoors in Rhode Island.

So how does it happen that children in the United States are being prostituted? Many are runaway children who leave home because of neglect or physical and/or sexual abuse; others are "throwaway" children who are abandoned or neglected. These children engage in "survival" sex in order to obtain food, clothing, a place to live, and in some cases (and, for most, eventually) to feed drug addiction. Some children are lured or abducted and forced to prostitute for a pimp; others are seeking love and acceptance when they fall prey to a predator who at first acts like a kind, generous, and caring person. There are even occasional horrendous instances where parents force their own children to prostitute for money, for vicarious and perverted sexual pleasure, or to support their drug addiction. Yes, as abhorrent as it is to acknowledge the fact, these things *do* happen right here in the United States.

Traffickers and pimps often take the victims far from their homes so that they are isolated from family and friends and become dependent upon the abusers for their basic needs. A pimp's typical *modus operandi* is to find a vulnerable girl and play with her emotions, convincing her that he is her boyfriend and will provide the love and affection that is missing in her home. The pimp gives the girl treats, often including drugs. If she comes from a broken or abusive home life, the situation at first may seem like a step up for the young girl. Often the girl is tattooed with the pimp's name, which she considers to be a badge of honor. Then, as soon as the pimp has her under his control, he will turn her out on the streets to prostitute for him. He'll tell her that if she loves him, she will do this for him.

Runaways and street children are especially vulnerable and endangered. That is why the message of this book is so important; responsible citizens have to recognize how the breakdown of the family is affecting our children and acknowledge the importance of strengthening marriage and family in America.

According to the DOJ's Child Exploitation and Obscenity Section website:[25]

- approximately 55 percent of street girls engage in formal prostitution;
- of those, 75 percent are managed by a pimp;
- pimp-controlled CSEC (commercial sexual exploitation of children) is linked to escort and massage services, private dancing, drinking and photographic clubs, major sporting and recreational events, major cultural events, conventions, and tourist destinations;
- about one-fifth of these children end up in national organized crime networks and are trafficked nationally;
- they are taken throughout the United States in cars, buses, vans, trucks, or planes.

One story out of Phoenix, Arizona, details the exploitation of a twelve-year-old and a fifteen-year-old victim. The twelve-year-old told police she was molested by her father and was a repeat runaway. She met the wrong man at a mall (the criminal networks have made a science out of spotting vulnerable children and recognizing the situations that are advantageous to their purpose). Before long, that twelve-year-old was working sixteen hours a day being prostituted in Arizona, Las Vegas, and Los Angeles; earning between $300 and $1,300 a day, all going to the pimp. Both girls said the man was nice to them at first but then became threatening and sometimes violent.[26] Sadly, this same story could have happened and is happening in any city in the United States.

Regardless of how or why children come to the life of prostitution, it is a tragedy. Prostituted victims suffer beatings, rapes, serious bodily injuries, forced drug abuse, abortion, sexually transmitted diseases, and sometimes death. Their childhood is taken from them, and their lives are forever changed.

Some people may think that this issue doesn't warrant so much attention, however, the United States Department of State estimates that as many as one-half of the estimated 800,000 human trafficking victims are minor children and that up to 70 percent of the females are sexually exploited. The State Department's Office to Monitor and Combat Trafficking in Persons (*GITIP*) also estimates the number of victims trafficked annually into the United States at 14,500 to 17,000. This figure does not include the number of American children who are trafficked within the United States or trafficked abroad. The annual profits from human trafficking worldwide are thought to exceed $9.5 billion.[27] The United States Department of Health and Human Services reports that human trafficking is the fastest growing crime in the world; it is tied with illegal arms sales as the number two moneymaker for organized crime.[28]

Closely linked to sex trafficking is the ugly phenomenon of sex tourism—where apparently-respectable men fly off to an exotic locale to have sex with the local women and children, some as young as six years of age. Sadly, sex tourism is also big business with the United States. The city of Atlanta, Georgia is known as a sex tourism destination. Many of the men who fly into Atlanta to have sex with a child will make a return flight home in time for dinner. In the Internet age, the sex industry in Atlanta is advertised around the world through websites, blogs, and even Craigslist so you can place an order for a human being, fly in, sexually exploit that person, and leave in as little as a single day. Local government, law enforcement, and NGOs have launched a "Dear John" campaign to combat demand and to assist victims.

Traffickers and pimps understand the principle of supply and demand; they take their victims where there is a demand. As a consequence if a city has a reputation for sex tourism, pimps and traffickers will rotate girls and women into a city to keep their "supply" fresh and their customers coming back for new experiences. Major conventions and sporting events also attract a great influx of prostituted and trafficked women and girls. Wherever there is a demand, the exploited will be brought in to fill it. Cities like Las Vegas, Washington, DC, and Atlanta all have growing problems with sex tourism because they are tourist destinations, easily accessible by air and car, and are the sites of large conventions and sporting events. The end-users whose perversions drive the sex tourism business find it convenient to satisfy their desires without having to leave the country.

One reason predators may choose to stay in the United States to exploit children is the Prosecutorial Remedies and Other Tools to end the Exploitation of Children Today (PROTECT) Act of 2003. With the passage of this legislation, American citizens that go abroad to sexually abuse and exploit children will be prosecuted under U.S. law for those crimes. The punishment for those crimes committed abroad may be a sentence of up to thirty years here at home. In Fulton County, Georgia, by contrast, soliciting sex with a minor is punishable by only five to twenty years in jail.[29] The problem is NOT that the PROTECT Act is deficient, rather that the penalties and prosecution in the U.S. may be less severe than a PROTECT Act sentence related to activity in a foreign country.

The National Center for Missing and Exploited Children operates the CyberTipline for people to report incidents of child sexual exploitation in the United States. Their one-week summaries and project-to-date totals give a glimpse of the astounding extent of the problem. During 1 week alone, there were 1,282 reports of child pornography, 24 reports of child prostitution, and 5 reports of child sex tourism. Since the project began in 1998, there have been 556,542 reports of child pornography, 7,134 reports of child prostitution, and 2,969 reports of child sex tourism.[30]

Keep in mind that these are just the *reported* incidents. Imagine how many incidents go un-reported. It is important for parents to monitor their children when they are online; the dangers lurking beyond every mouse click are growing. Some parents use television as a "babysitter" and while that is not good parenting (partially because the children may watch inappropriate programs) at least television viewing does not involve personal contact and interaction with the child. By contrast, when parents use the computer as a "babysitter," inappropriate content is the least of parental concerns. Online predators will actively seek out children on the Internet, and if they can obtain home addresses and telephone numbers from the kids, they will try to make personal contact. Even if your child has no interest in viewing obscenity, it will come to them. Computer experts concerned with the protection of children highly recommend the use of a good Internet filter.

Sadly, some of the most popular networking sites for teens are teeming with predators. A February 2009 news article reported that MySpace removed ninety thousand registered sex offenders, an Facebook is coming under scrutiny too. Roy Cooper, the North Carolina attorney general, said, "These sites were created for young people to communicate with each other. Predators are going to troll in these areas where they know children are going to be."[31] Craigslist is also used to promote and recruit for prostitution, and, to illustrate the anything-goes approach it allows, there was even a posting of a seven-day-old baby for sale.[32] The use of Internet sites to buy, sell, recruit, and stalk children is becoming *more* prevalent, not less.

The commercial sex industry pervades daily life. The pimp lifestyle is glamorized and promoted on television shows and in movies. Pornography and predators are pervasive and readily accessible online. Prostitution and sex tourism are happening right under our noses. The nation's children are surrounded and too often caught by the tentacles of this predatory industry. Further, all aspects of the commercial sex industry continue to expand because they feed off one another. Stripping is a gateway into pornography and prostitution, the demand for prostitution leads to trafficking, pornography feeds aberrant desires and behaviors creating a demand for more, different and younger victims and when the prurient desires are no longer met with adult pornography, images of child pornography begin to fill the void. When pictures and videos no longer satisfy, live victims must be procured. It is a swirling vortex of evil.

Parents must be vigilant about what their children watch on television, what they access online, and who contacts them. Predators are very good at recognizing vulnerability and will exploit any weakness they find. Explaining the dangers of today's world to children is a delicate balance between causing fear and making clear the dangers that lurk not only just outside the front door, but also sometimes *inside* the home as well.

Notes

1. Devlin Barrett, "FBI rescues teen prostitutes in national sweep," Associated Press, *Houston Chronicle*, February 23, 2009, http://www.chron.com/disp/story. mpl/headline/nation/6276270.html.
2. "Two Arizona Teens Ran Prostitution Ring, Police Say," *Fox News.com*, February 24, 2009, http://www.foxnews.com/story/0,2933,499189,00.html.
3. Barrett, "Teen Prostitutes."
4. "'Sexting' Shockingly Common among Teens," *CBS News.com*, January 15, 2009, http://www.cbsnews.com/stories/2009/01/15/national/main4723161.shtml.
5. Brenda Rindge, "Teen 'sexting' risky behavior," *The Charleston Post and Courier*, January 6, 2009, http://www.charleston.net/news/2009/jan/06/teen_sexting_risky_ behavior67332/.
6. The National Campaign to Prevent Teen and Unplanned Pregnancy and *Cosmogirl. com*, "Sex and Tech: Results from a Survey of Teens and Young adults," (conducted online September 25–October 3, 2008): 1.
7. Ibid.
8. Melissa Sardelli and Erin Kennedy, "Sex young boys face child porn charges," *WPRI.com,* updated February 16, 2009, http://www.wpri.com/dpp/news/lo- cal_wpri_six_falmouth_boys_face_child_porn_charges_20090211.
9. Dalia Lithwick, "Teens, Nude Photos and the Law," *Newsweek*, February 23, 2009, http://www.newsweek.com/id/184814/output/print.
10. Lori Borgman, McClatchy-Tribune News Service, "Safe sexting? There's no such thing," *BradentonHerald.com*, February 24, 2009, http://www.bradenton.com/liv- ing/family/v-print/story/1249961.html.
11. Marcia Segelstein, "What parents need to know about porn and their kids," Per- spectives Column, *OneNewsNow*, February 24, 2009, http://www.onenewsnow. com/Perspectives/Default.aspx?id=426220.
12. Jerry Ropelato, "Internet Pornography Statistics," TopTenREVIEWS.com, http:// Internet-filter-review.toptenreviews.com/internet-pornography-statistics.html (ac- cessed February 9, 2009).
13. Donna Rice Hughes, "How Children Access Pornography on the Internet," Pro- tectKids.com, http://www.protectkids.com/dangers/childaccess.htm.
14. *GOOD*, http://www.good.is/sections/magazine/magazine.php.
15. Michael Arrington, "Internet Pornography Stats," TechCrunch.com, May 12, 2007, http://www.techcrunch.com/2007/05/12/internet-pornography-stats/.
16. "Teenagers 'spend an average of 31 hours online,'" *Telegraph.co.uk*, February 10, 2009, http://www.telegraph.co.uk/scienceandtechnology/technology/4574792/ Teenagers-spend-an-average-of-31-hours-online.html.
17. Ropelato, "Internet Pornography Statistics."
18. U.S. Department of Justice, Child Exploitation and Obscenity Division, "Child Pornography," updated November 2007, http://www.usdoj.gov/criminal/ceos/ childporn.html.
19. Sara Foss, "Child Porn Access, Crimes Grow," *Daily Gazette* (Schenectady, NY), October 26, 2008, http://www.dailygazette.com/news/2008/oct/26/1026_kid- porn/.
20. Ibid.
21. Susan Schulman and Lou Michel, "The United States is a major distributor of free child pornography," *Buffalo News*, updated February 5, 2009, http://www. buffalonews.com/339/story/182918.html?imw=Y.
22. Ibid.

23. U.S. Department of Justice, Child Exploitation and Obscenity Division, "Child Prostitution," updated November 2007, http://www.usdoj.gov/criminal/ceos/prostitution.html.

24. *Trafficking Victims Protection Act of 2000,* Public Law 106-386, codified at U.S. Code 22, §7102.

25. U.S. Dept. of Justice, "Child Prostitution."

26. Brian Webb/KTVK-TV, "Police report reveals more about Phoenix prostitution ring," *FOX11AZ.com*, March 14, 2007, http://www.fox11az.com/news/topstories/stories/kmsb-20070314-KTVKjc-phxprostitution.118db636.html.

27. U.S. Department of State, "Trafficking in Persons Report," Office of the Under Secretary for Global Affairs, Publication 11407 (Washington, DC, June 2008): 7.

28. U.S. Department of Health and Human Services, The Campaign to Rescue and Restore Victims of Human Trafficking, "Fact Sheet: Human Trafficking," updated Feb. 4, 2009, http://www.acf.hhs.gov/trafficking/about/fact_human.html.

29. Verna Gates and Mickey Goodman, "Sex Tourism Thriving in the U.S. Bible Belt," Reuters News Service, April 4, 2006, http://www.stopdemand.com/afaw-cs0112878/ID+175/newsdetails.html.

30. National Center for Missing and Exploited Children, "CyberTipline Fact Sheet," http://www.missingkids.com/en_US/documents/CyberTiplineFactSheet.pdf (accessed February 25, 2009).

31. Sam Jones and agencies, "MySpace removes 90,000 sex offenders," *guardian.co.uk*, February 4, 2009, http://www.guardian.co.uk/technology/2009/feb/04/myspace-social-networking-sex-offenders.

32. Associated Press, "Couple Arrested for Putting Days-Old Baby Up for Sale on Craigslist," *FoxNews.com*, May 28, 2008, http://www.foxnews.com/story/0,2933,358923,00.html.

Bitter are the tears of a child: Sweeten them.
Deep are the thoughts of a child: Quiet them.
Sharp is the grief of a child: Take it from him.
Soft is the heart of a child: Do not harden it.
—Pamela Glenconner

6

Child Abuse

At the present time in America on average there is a report of child abuse every ten seconds, and every day at least three children die as a result of abuse and neglect.[1] Such abuse is as shocking as it is common and reprehensible. The U.S. Department of Health and Human Services reports that every year in the United States there are over 3 million referrals of child abuse that involve "the alleged maltreatment of approximately 6 million children."[2] An estimated 80 percent of abused children carry physical, psychological, behavioral, and societal consequences that last a lifetime. The problems range from cognitive delays to high-risk behaviors, from anxiety to suicide attempts, from personality disorders to violent and destructive behavior.[3] Who does not recoil when innocence is stolen, whether in one awful trauma or through persistent, unrelenting acts of neglect, anger, sexual dominance, or vicious, sadistic physical abuse?

While the majority of American children move through the stages of childhood in a secure environment where they are both loved and protected, increasing numbers of children live in household arrangements where they are neglected and mistreated rather than cherished. Millions of children learn early that they rate a distant second or third in priority behind drugs and/or boyfriends.

The environment of abuse in which so many children experience pain and abandonment is not surprising when more than 6.6 million American children live in households where at least one parent is dependent on alcohol or drugs, whether prescription medications or illegal substances.[4] Little wonder many children live in fear of what might happen to them next. Their family instability, lack of supervision, and desperate conditions keep them from having the happy childhood that we would wish for all children; worse, their childhood mistreatment threatens their future, indeed, their health and life.

At the same time that our nation has improved so many living conditions for Americans across the board, we have produced a culture that is injurious to our children. We provide our children with billions of dollars of services, including safe drinking water, sewage treatment, and pasteurized milk. We have reduced the infant mortality rate by 90 percent and maternal mortality rates by 99 percent.[5] But it is virtually impossible for society to protect our nation's children from the conditions resulting from the sexual revolution and the breakdown of the family.

The sad reality is that we are spinning our wheels as a nation in trying to keep up with the problems of children who are denied the presence and protection of mature, concerned fathers. The latest figures show that federal spending on children is now 15.4 percent of the total federal domestic spending; yet UNICEF ranks the United States twentieth in children's well-being among the twenty-one rich democracies in the world.[6] How many more children will be abused before we acknowledge that the investment America needs to make for the nation's children is to encourage marriage. A married father-mother home is the safest and most nurturing place for the nation's children.

More than two thousand children in the U.S. die of child abuse and neglect every year. Children under four years of age account for nearly 80 percent of those fatalities, mostly infants and toddlers.[7] Sadly, the mother's boyfriends and fathers are most often the perpetrators of abuse deaths and mothers are more often responsible for the neglect fatalities.[8]

Whether the abusing adult is mean, controlling, selfish, mentally ill, drug addicted, or unable to cope, the abused child ends up emotionally scarred and psychologically damaged, often with feelings of self-loathing, fear, worthlessness, and guilt that can persist throughout the child's life.

The effects of child abuse depend on a variety of factors. One factor is related to the specific instance or instances, such as whether violence is involved and the child's relationship to the abuser. Other factors that impact the effect of child abuse are whether the child receives support and help afterward in handling the feelings of shame and humiliation and whether the child receives protection against future abuse or further trauma. Other events associated with the abuse or trauma can cause pain and inflict future harm, such as the death of a loved one, a handicapping injury, or physical disfigurement. Whether a specific child can cope with a horrible experience depends in part on the support, understanding, and sensitivity that he or she receives from adult caregivers as well as the individual child's resilience and inner strength.

Researchers are carefully investigating the factors that make a child "resilient" and able to cope, remain relatively unscathed, or even thrive despite living in an abusive environment. What they have discovered thus far is that certain individual characteristics (like optimism, self-esteem, intelligence, creativity, humor, and independence) peer acceptance and positive influences (like teachers, mentors, role models, and caring adults) as well as outside factors, including neighborhood stability and social supports, are extremely important in enabling a child to cope with and overcome abuse.[9]

Numerous other factors in an abused child's life also bear on how he or she responds when the abuse is exposed. Whether others know about the abuse impacts how children respond to their sense of powerlessness and how they handle the shame and guilt feelings. Often abused children distrust or fear anyone who is unfamiliar. At the time of the abuse, they have a tendency to act out their anger with peers; as they get older, they tend to perpetuate the abusive behavior patterns in their other relationships.[10]

These realities contradict false ideologies such as Judith Levine expressed in her book, *Harmful to Minors: The Perils of Protecting Children from Sex.* In Levine's misshapen view, "Sex is not harmful to children. It is a vehicle to self-knowledge, love, healing, creativity, adventure, and intense feelings of aliveness."[11] She argues that those on the religious right are denying children the opportunity to have sex with adults and with each other. Christian fundamentalists, she claims, "seem intent on pooping everybody else's party." She argues that there are "many ways" that "even the smallest child" can enjoy sex. After all Levine wrote, "Sexual expression is a healthy and happy part of growing up."[12] She expresses admiration for the Netherlands where the age of sexual consent is twelve years old.[13] She ridicules the idea that sex with children might be child abuse. No wonder SIECUS (Sex Information and Education Council of the United States) named the book one of the "40 Most Influential Books on Sexuality." The American Psychiatric Association and many members of the American Psychological Association as well as Congress soundly denounced her views and those of her followers. It should be noted, as well, that Judith Levine has a Master's Degree in journalism, hardly a qualification for evaluating psychological or psychiatric research.

Child Protective Services (CPS) agencies report dramatic increases in incidences of child abuse and neglect. The latest National Incidence of Child Abuse and Neglect (NIS-3) reveals a 67 percent increase in the incidence of child maltreatment since 1986 and a 149 percent increase since 1980.[14] The NIS-3 reports, not surprisingly, that children of single parents were "overrepresented" compared to their counterparts living with both parents. Children of single parents are at a 77 percent greater risk of physical abuse and an 80 percent greater risk of serious injury or harm. They are 3 times more likely to be educationally neglected and more than 2 times as likely to suffer some type of child abuse as children living with both parents.[15]

There are numerous repercussions to the child and derivative costs to the community when a child suffers abuse. Children who are abused and neglected fall prey to serious health and mental problems, including learning disabilities, mental retardation, delayed growth and developmental progress, cerebral palsy, and other neurological disorders, asthma, emotional and sexual problems, drug abuse, poor social skills, and vulnerability to gangs and violence.

Researchers report that the number of child abuse cases is increasing by more than 10 percent a year. The direct costs (child protection and foster care) to taxpayers exceed $20 billion and related costs add another $100 billion (crime, medical care, special education, etc).

The official figures are daunting—12.1 of every 1,000 American children (905,000 children) in 2006 were victims of confirmed abuse or neglect—and the experts who are responsible for federal child abuse studies report that the actual incidents may run 3 times higher.[16] The analyst found that:

- 64 percent were neglected (lacked food, clothing, shelter, hygiene, education, medical care or protection);
- 16 percent were physically abused;
- 8.8 percent were sexually abused;
- 6.6 percent were emotionally abused;
- 15 percent suffered mistreatment (abandonment, threats, congenital drug addiction).[17]

One of the difficulties with documenting abuse is that many of the children who are neglected or sexually abused do not show physical signs of harm. The abuse may not become apparent for years; and then when it does appear, it may not be understood to be associated with the childhood abuse. Many of those who work with abused and neglected children believe that the official data is "just the tip of the iceberg."

The increase in teen suicides has received media attention. The Centers for Disease Control (CDC) and the National Mental Health Association (NMHA) point out that suicide rates for teens have tripled since 1960—making it the third leading cause of adolescent death and the second cause among college students. But the reasons for the increase have not been adequately explored by the media.

Research from Columbia University Medical Center, published in the Journal of the American Medical Association, Archives of Pediatrics & Adolescent Medicine (APAM) cites different reasons for girls' and boys' suicides. The researchers collected data from over eight thousand students in New York City high schools in 2005. For females, recent dating violence is a primary cause of attempted suicide. In particular, Dr. Elyse Olshen, lead researcher for the study, reported that girls who have been physically abused by a boyfriend are 60 percent more likely to attempt suicide than those who have not. For boys, sexual abuse over an extended period of time is more likely to be the determining factor for male teen suicide.[18]

The National Institute on Alcohol Abuse and Alcoholism reported a clear link between childhood sexual abuse and alcoholism, depression, and tendencies to develop post-traumatic stress disorder. The study leader, Sharon Wilsnack, psychologist at the University of North Dakota-Grand Forks, cited abuse as the single strongest predictor of alcohol dependency, even stronger than a family history of drinking.[19] In addition, the study reported that their female respondents that were molested as children have more than double the depression rate of other women.

There is new evidence that sexual abuse is increasingly crossing gender lines with approximately one in six boys sexually abused (including a relative exposing genitals) before sixteen years of age.[20] The power differential between the adult and the child and deliberate, unwanted exploitation were facts taken into account in determining whether an act was "abuse." The Wilsnack study also cites other research that found even higher incidences of prior abuse when surveying older college students (average age of twenty-five years) who commuted to an urban university from a lower socioeconomic area.

A relatively new development is the worrisome increase in older women who are sexual predators of young boys, particularly female teachers who abuse their adolescent male students.[21] In 2002, the nation was shocked when a judge was lenient with a forty-three-year-old teacher, Pamela Diehl-Moore who pleaded guilty to second-degree sexual assault after admitting that she had had repeated sex with a thirteen-year-old boy over a six-month period. Pamela Rogers, a twenty-eight-year-old teacher in Tennessee, served only six months in jail for having sex with her thirteen-year-old student. Debra Lafave, another teacher, has been in and out of jail repeatedly for continuing the sexual relationship that she began with a former student when he was only fourteen years old. In her article, "When Beauty is the Beast," Jan LaRue describes many of the sixty female perpetrators of recent abuse against young boys.[22]

While sexual predators may target any child, the data as to which children are most vulnerable is overwhelming: the safest place for a child to live is with his or her married mother and father; all other household arrangements carry a higher risk of abuse and neglect.

- Abuse is 6 times higher in stepfamilies than in intact families.
- Abuse is 14 times higher in a single-mother family than in intact families.
- Abuse is 20 times higher with cohabiting parents than in an intact family.
- Abuse is 33 times higher with cohabiting partners than in an intact family.[23]

Unstable cohabiting households tend to be dangerous places for children, most especially those where the adult male is not the biological father. It is profoundly shameful that the United States leads the developed nations in the number of child maltreatment deaths. The child abuse death rate for American children is 3 times higher than Canada's, Japan's, Germany's, France's, and the United Kingdom's and 11 times higher thn Italy's.[24]

A dramatic headline in 2005 claimed that "a man" was "accused of impregnating" a ten year old.[25] It is not until the third paragraph that the accused man is identified as the girl's stepfather. The report informs us that DNA testing predicts with 99.99 percent probability that the stepfather is, indeed, the father of the child's baby. The final paragraph of the tragic account of the little girl reveals that she is now eleven years old and lives with her mother and her baby boy. This story reveals a common problem—rape of children by their stepfathers or by their mother's boyfriends. It bears repeating, though it is not surprising that child abuse is 33 times higher when the mother is living with a boyfriend rather than married to the father of her child. Nor is it a surprise that at least half of the child abuse and neglect cases are associated with alcohol or drug abuse.[26]

In a survey reported jointly by the National Institute of Justice and the Centers for Disease Control, 22 percent of the women disclosing a rape were children under twelve years old when it occurred. Another 32 percent of the victims were just slightly older, between twelve and seventeen years old. Thus, over half of the rape victims were mere children—young girls.[27]

Sadly, most of the perpetrators of these horrible acts were adult men and, too often, men that the young girl knew (and possibly trusted)—a stepfather, a mother's boyfriend, an uncle, a cousin, a neighbor, or a friend of her parent.

Households that are poor owing to patterns of dysfunctional behavior (particularly where alcohol and drugs are abused) are dangerous places for children. One study reported that children in families with an income of less than $15,000 per year were 22 times more likely to be abused than when the family income was over $30,000.[28] Doubtless, this finding is influenced by the fact that more than three out of five poor families with children are headed by single women, and when they cohabit, their children are at risk by the presence of a adult male with whom they have no biological relationship but with whom the child competes for the mother's time and affection. Abuse, however, can occur across the economic and social spectrum; it is not limited to the poorest families. Sadly, the abuse of one generation carries into adulthood and is often perpetuated against the next generation. Studies indicate that a parent who was abused as a child is more likely to abuse his or her own children.[29] As Herbert Ward so pithily said, "Child abuse casts a shadow the length of a lifetime."

Psychologists have identified several characteristics of adults who abuse children physically or emotionally.[30] Often they are under extreme stress (caring for a child with a disability or extreme behavioral problems or going through a personal problem like divorce, job loss, or financial crisis), are immature or lacking nurturing qualities, have difficulty controlling anger, have a history of being abused, are isolated from others, have physical or mental problems (depression or anxiety), or are addicted to alcohol or drugs. There are also personality traits that can contribute to abuse. For instance, people who view children as their property or those who are controlling are more likely to be abusive.

Priests are certainly the last group of people that one would expect to abuse children. Yet, in 2002 the biggest news story of the year was the hundreds of cases of sexual abuse of minors by priests in the U.S. Catholic Church.[31] The case had been building for two decades, and when the story broke, the church was accused of covering up the abuse for years. The *Washington Post* reported that out of the 178 dioceses in the United States 111 had covered up criminal sexual abuse by members of the priesthood.

The lesson of all this is that abusers can come from any strata of society—from teachers to priests, poor single-mother households, step-parents, and cohabiting partners—but no matter who they are or where they come from, a paramount priority in our society must be the protection of children from abuse.

There are excellent resources on the Internet for preventing and stopping child abuse. Anyone who suspects an abusive situation can find information at wee.helpguide.org. The following hot-line numbers should be readily available for access.

Here are some 24-hour toll-free hotlines:

- Childhelp USA's National Child Abuse Hotline, 1-800-422-4453 (1-800-4ACHILD);
- Rape Abuse and Incest National Network, 1-800-656-4673 (HOPE);
- National Domestic Violence/Abuse Hotline, 1-800-799-7233 (SAFE).

Conclusion

This year CBS News correspondent, John Blackstone, wrote an inspiring story about a brutally abused child who screamed and cried most of the night and growled like an animal for much of the day after being rescued from horrific circumstances. After years of treatment for both mental and physical wounds, that unbelievably damaged child made a remarkable transformation to become a smiling, confident young woman.[32] The credit for Mia's transformation goes to her adoptive mother who took her after child welfare workers rescued her from her father, who had killed her younger sister. Authorities said that Mia was "grievously sexually abused in ways that for the average individual…would be incomprehensible." Many of the psychologists believed that Mia was too damaged to ever recover, and her story highlights the difficulties of helping a child overcome horrible abuse. More importantly, though, her story illustrates the fact that with love, commitment, and appropriate help, even children who survive the worst abuse imaginable may be able to recover and go on to live productive and happy lives. Mia gives hope to those in society who care about those children who bear the brunt of ghastly abuse by some savage adult.

Notes

1. "The Relationship between Parental Alcohol, Drug Use and Child Maltreatment," Study Number: 14, Child Abuse.Com: Prevention Through Education and Awareness, http://www.childabuse.com/fs14.html.
2. U.S. Department of Health and Human Services, Administration for Children and Families, *Child Maltreatment, 2006*, Summary (Washington: GPO, 2008): xiv, http://www.acf.hhs.gov/ programs/cb/stats_research/index.htm#can.
3. Child Welfare Information Gateway, "Long-Term Consequences of Child Abuse and Neglect," U.S. Department of Health and Human Services, Administration for Children and Families (April 2008): 4, www.childwelfare.gov/pubs/factsheets/long_term_consequences.cfm.
4. "The Relationship between Parental Alcohol."
5. U.S. Centers for Disease Control and Prevention, National Center for Chronic Disease Prevention and Health Promotion, "Achievements in Public Health, 1900-1999: Healthier Mothers and Babies," *Morbidity and Mortality Weekly Report* (October 1, 1999): 48(38);849-858, http://www.cdc.gov/mmwr/preview/mmwrhtml/mm4838a2.htm.
6. Michael R. Petit, *Homeland Insecurity: Why new investments in children and youth must be a priority in the Obama Administration and the 111th Congress* (Washington: Every Child Matters Education Fund, January 2009): 2, http://www.everychildmatters.org/National/Resources/Homeland-Insecurity-Report.html (accessed March 17, 2009).
7. Ibid., 6.
8. National Center for Child Death Review Policy and Practice, "Fact Sheet: Child Abuse and Neglect," http://www.childdeathreview.org/causesCAN.htm.
9. "Long-Term Consequences," 3.
10. Ibid., 3-6.
11. Judith Levine, *Harmful to Minors: The Perils of Protecting Children from Sex* (Minneapolis: University of Minnesota Press, 2002): xx-xxx.
12. Ibid.
13. Ibid., 112.
14. Andrea J. Sedlak and Diane D. Broadhurst, U.S. Department of Health and Human Services, *The Third National Incidence Study of Child Abuse and Neglect* (Washington, DC: GPO, 1996): Executive Summary.
15. Ibid.
16. *Child Maltreatment 2006*, 25.
17. Childhelp, "2006 Child Maltreatment and Fatality Statistics," http://www.childhelp.org/uploads/h1/x6/h1x6ds5xBH2q_RPlWvyUzw/The-Department-of-Health-and-Human-Services--2006-Child-Abuse-STATS.pdf (accessed January 7, 2009).
18. Janice Shaw Crouse, "Teen Suicide: A Matter of 'Sexual Orientation' or Sex Abuse?" *Townhall.com*, June 13, 2007, http://townhall.com/columnists/Janice-ShawCrouse/2007/06/13/teen_suicide_a_matter_of_%E2%80%9Csexual_orientation%E2%80%9D_or_sex_abuse.
19. Marilyn Elias, "Study Links Sexual Abuse, Alcoholism among Women," *USA Today*, January 5, 1998.

20.   Shanta Dube, et al., "Long-term Consequences of Childhood Sexual Abuse by Gender of Victim," *American Journal of Preventive Medicine* 28.5 (2005): 430-438.

21.   These cases are described in more detail in Jan LaRue's article, "When Beauty is the Beast," Concerned Women for America, May 16, 2006, http://www.cwfa.org/articles/10763/LEGAL/pornography/index.htm.

22.   Ibid.

23.   Ibid.

24.   "Child Maltreatment Deaths per 100,000 population under 15 (1990s)," NationMaster, http://www.nationmaster.com/graph/hea_chi_mal_dea-health-child-maltreatment-deaths.

25.   "Man Accused of Impregnating a 10-Year-Old," KIROTV.com, June 29, 2005, http://www.kirotv.com/news/4664241/detail.html.

26.   Pat Fagan and Kirk A. Johnson, "Marriage: The Safest Place for Women and Children," The Heritage Foundation, *Backgrounder Report* No. 1535, April 10, 2002, www.heritage.org/research/family/BG1535.cfm.

27.   Patricia Tjaden and Nancy Thoennes, U.S. Department of Justice, National Institute of Justice, "Prevalence, Incidence, and Consequences of Violence against Women: Findings from the National Violence against Women Survey," Research in Brief, NCJ 172837 (Nov. 1998): 2, http://www.ncjrs.gov/pdffiles/172837.pdf.

28.   Jill Goldman, Marsha K. Salus, Deborah Wolcott and Kristie Y. Kennedy, "A Coordinated Response to Child Abuse and Neglect: The Foundation for Practice," U.S. Department of Health and Human Services, Child Abuse and Neglect User Manual Series (Washington, DC, 2003): 33, http://www.childwelfare.gov/pubs/usermanuals/foundation/foundatione.cfm.

29.   Cathy Spatz Widom and Susanne Hiller-Sturmhofel, "Alcohol Abuse as a Risk Factor for and Consequence of Child Abuse," *Alcohol Research & Health* 25, no. 1 (2001): 52-57, http://pubs.niaaa.nih.gov/publications/arh25-1/52-57.pdf.

30.   Joanna Saisan, Ellen Jaffe-Gill, and Jeanne Segal, "Child Abuse and Neglect: Warning Signs of Abuse and How to Report It," Helpguide, October 2008, http://www.helpguide.org/mental/child_abuse_physical_emotional_sexual_neglect.htm.

31.   For a summary of the controversy, read the excellent account by Michael Schwartz, "CWA Expert Says Catholic Bishops Avoided Responsibility," Concerned Women for America, June 19, 2002, http://www.cwfa.org/articles/658/CFI/cfreport/index.htm.

32.   John Blackstone, "The Remarkable Transformation of One Child," *CBS Evening News*, February 17, 2009, http://www.cbsnews.com/stories/2009/02/17/eveningnews/.

Part III

Outside Influences on Children

To understand your parents' love,
Bear your own children.
—Ancient Chinese Proverb

Having children no more makes you a parent
than having a piano makes you a pianist.
—Michael Levine

7

Foster Care

Any analysis of children's well-being in America must examine the nation's foster care system—those governmental programs tasked with providing for the needs of children who do not have parents or whose parents for one reason or another fail to care for them adequately.[1] The American Academy of Child and Adolescent Psychiatry identifies "parental problems" as the primary cause of children being placed in foster care.[2] Between 1,500 and 2,000 children are killed by their caretakers each year, and half of the murdered children are slain after they have come to the attention of child protective service agencies.[3] So, once again, this time in the foster care system, the breakdown of the healthy, traditional family is identified as a risk to the well-being of children.

Foster care is defined in federal statutes as "24-hour substitute care for children placed away from their parents or guardians and for whom the State agency has placement and care responsibility. This includes, but is not limited to, placements in foster family homes, foster homes of relatives, group homes, emergency shelters, residential facilities, child care institutions, and pre-adoptive homes."[4] Though often referred to by the amorphous non-judgmental term, "substitute care," foster care is, in reality, intended as a temporary safe haven for children who are at substantial risk of imminent harm. This care is intended to continue until the children can be either safely reunited with their parents/guardians or placed for adoption.

Children can be placed in foster care for a number of reasons. In the past, they were likely to enter because of family hardship or the death of a parent or guardian; today they are most likely to enter because of mistreatment. About 70 percent of children in foster care are put there by child protective services because the child has been abused or neglected. Most of the remaining 30 percent are teenagers placed in foster care by the juvenile justice system.[5]

Rates of maltreatment and types of maltreatment vary according to the age and sex of the victim. Girls are slightly more likely than boys (52 percent vs. 48 percent) to be victims of maltreatment.[6] Girls, however, are far more likely than boys to be the victims of sexual abuse. Children in the youngest age group, zero to three years, are much more likely to enter, remain, and re-enter the foster care system. One in five admissions is an infant, many of whom come into foster care directly from the hospital nursery; and they are more likely to be prenatally exposed to drugs (80 percent) and to be premature or of low birth weight (40 percent).[7] These infants also comprise the largest subgroup of confirmed cases of physical abuse and mental neglect.[8] Moreover, children entering the system as infants (age zero to one) stay in foster care 20 to 22 percent longer than older children (age one to eight).[9]

More than half of the children who are in foster care are at-risk for drug use, poor school performance, and incarceration.[10] Every year, approximately 800,000 children receive services from the foster care system and over 500,000 children end up placed in foster care[11]—including 40,000 infants; that's double the number from 25 years ago. Taxpayers fund foster care at $22 billion a year (over $40,000 per child). Even at that high cost, abused and neglected children often are not getting the care that they need—all too frequently we read in the newspaper of the brutal treatment or even death of some foster child whom the system failed to protect.

But the problem is bigger than just those tragic cases that make the headlines that turn our stomachs. On average, foster care children are yanked in and out of as many as three different foster care placements during the time that they need non-family care.[12] It doesn't take imagination to recognize that family instability, constantly changing living arrangements, and different household expectations have negative effects on children's school performance and general well-being.

Dr. Wade Horn, former head of the children and family division of the U.S. Department of Health and Human Services, called the foster care system a "giant mess."[13] One of the long-run consequences of that mess is additional costs for those formerly in foster care who end up incarcerated, homeless, or in need of residential or medical treatment.

Not surprisingly, 30 to 40 percent of foster care students need special education services.[14] Nearly all of the children face common educational problems—frequent school transfers, persistent low expectations, and lack of a basic social support system.[15]

State and local governments have primary responsibility for the children placed in foster care in their jurisdictions. For good or ill, these systems work most of the time without public scrutiny, although occasionally a foster care case grabs the headlines and causes some measure of public awareness. Such a case might involve the death or serious injury of a child or, at the other extreme, unwarranted intervention in the life of normal families by misinformed or misguided child welfare authorities. Otherwise, the worrisome faults of the foster care system are seldom brought into the glare of the public spotlight.

In some cases, the very system that is supposed to address a child's problematic situation is in such disarray itself that it fails to do its job—to protect those children for whom it has been given responsibility. Children in the custody of foster care authorities are sometimes neglected and abused by the people designated by those authorities to be their protectors. At the other extreme, child welfare authorities can become so overzealous in pursuit of accused child abusers that they trample on basic civil liberties. In fact, the wide range of problems in the foster care system is so documented that there are numerous references to the foster care "pendulum." [16]

Historically, several notable cases of overzealous intervention by child welfare authorities have made headlines, including a number involving bizarre allegations of rampant child abuse at childcare centers—in California, Florida, and North Carolina, for example.

Beginning in 1994 in Wenatchee, Washington, a ten-year-old foster child's allegations of abuse precipitated a string of similar allegations that eventually led to some thirty thousand cases against forty-three adults in that community. Most of the charged adults were eventually acquitted, and some, including a Pentecostal pastor, won financial judgments against child welfare authorities. But the episode tore the community apart and alarmed the whole nation.[17]

A series of reports, appearing in the *Washington Post* in September of 2001,[18] about the deaths of some 180 children in foster care in the District of Columbia revealed numerous examples of bureaucratic mistakes, bungling, and official negligence in the conduct of child maltreatment investigations and foster care placement during the 1990s. Council members called the child protection system's performance "horrific"; they described the system as "fragmented, under-funded, understaffed and under-observed." In this particular jurisdiction, child welfare authorities often failed to take basic preventive actions to protect children or they placed children in unsafe situations. Over 670 warnings to top officials were ignored, and mistakes were documented at each stage of the child protection process.[19]

Two other cases came to light after the *Washington Post* series. In December of 2001, a baby died of starvation; the caseworker assigned to the two-year-old boy's care had not seen the boy for over seven months. The follow-up investigation revealed that the caseworker was supposed to have been responsible for 135 children at the time.[20] The City Council announced that the system had "unquestionably failed" Katelynn Frazier, who died a horrific death in 2001 after being returned to her mother from the foster care system.[21]

Over the last several decades, the number of children whose circumstances require removing them from their home has increased dramatically and the number of foster parents available to care for children has decreased substantially.[22] Even so, the total number of children, 783,000, served in 2007 is the lowest number since data have been reported.[23] At the same time, an increase in the number of parents whose parental rights have been terminated means that the number of children who are waiting to be admitted to foster care is the highest since Adoption and Foster Care Analysis and Reporting System (AFCARS) data have been reported—nearly 85,000.

Intended as a temporary arrangement for children at imminent risk of harm until a more stable situation could be found, the foster care system has instead become more akin to a revolving door. The situation of these children is one of being in protracted limbo; they are invisible to the larger community; and they often lack both support systems and resources. A significant number of children spend years in the system, often shuttled from one foster home to another before either becoming eligible for adoption or, in some cases, aging out of the system without ever being adopted. Others end up going back and forth for years between a mother or father who neglects or abuses them and foster care situations that are sometimes only marginally better.

Approximately two-thirds of the children in foster care are black (non-Hispanic)—which is a significant overrepresentation of ethnic minorities[24]—and these children generally remain in foster care for longer periods of time than other children.[25] Even those children who do become eligible for adoption may wait several years before actually being adopted. The Adoption & Foster Care Analysis & Reporting System (AFCARS) stated that almost 30 percent of children waiting to be adopted had been in continuous foster care almost three years before being adopted.[26] To some degree, this may reflect the fact that about 30 percent of the children in foster care suffer from severe emotional, behavioral, or developmental problems. Physical problems are also commonplace.[27]

Growing public awareness of the problems of foster care in America has led to some much-needed reforms, yet serious problems persist. While most foster care situations do not result either in the death or serious injury of a child nor in the initiation of a "witch hunt" against innocent caregivers, few children or adults would describe their interaction with the foster care system as positive.

Although the foster care population remained fairly stable until 1980, from 1982 to 1992 the overall numbers increased a staggering 69 percent. Between 1982 and 1990, the population of children eligible for Temporary Assistance for Needy Families, TANF (formerly, Aid to Families with Dependent Children, AFDC), the government assistance program, increased by 73 percent.[28] Since at least the early 1980s, each year more children have entered the foster care system than have exited.[29]

Many observers have attributed the increase in foster care numbers in the late 1980s to the crack cocaine epidemic of that period. This led to a general increase in child abuse and neglect cases related to parental substance abuse and also to an especially marked increase in the number of infants placed in foster care as a result of pre- and post-natal drug use by their mothers. This conclusion is borne out by data from three states with the largest reported foster care populations. New York saw an increase of 89 percent in infant foster care admissions in 1985 to 1988. By 1988, nearly 3 percent of all infants born in New York City were placed in foster care, and most of those placements took place within a few days after birth. In Illinois, infant foster care placements increased by 58 percent during this period. In California, the total number of all children placed in foster care as a result of parental substance abuse doubled between FY 1984/85 and FY 1991/92.[30] Even though they acknowledged that alcohol and drug abuse are a factor in some 75 percent of foster care placements, the Pew Commission on Children in Foster Care focused its report on recommendations for improvements in the foster care system that it admitted was beyond repair.[31]

As we have seen, the typical "family" with children already in foster care or at risk of placement consists of a single, unmarried mother who is very likely to have a problem with substance abuse. Needless to say, some people in such situations do turn their lives around, but too often they do not; and it is the children who pay the price when they do not. Child welfare agencies devote large amounts of time and resources to family preservation that might be more wisely spent in placing eligible children for adoption, for example. The prevailing sentiment in the child welfare culture, however, seems to be that one form of "family" is just as valid as another. The safety of children ought to be the paramount goal of any child welfare program. Parents who have a record of serious neglect or abuse of their children—offenses which, if perpetrated against an adult, might be subject to criminal prosecution—should not repeatedly be given the benefit of the doubt.

In response to growing concern about the abuses endemic in, and to a degree inherent in, the foster care system, in 1997 Congress passed the Adoption & Safe Families Act (P.L. 105-89) based on the underlying principle that *safety* and *permanency* should outweigh all other considerations when it comes to child welfare. Effective implementation, management, and oversight are not possible without good information.

Before 1997, the most comprehensive database on numbers of children in foster care was the *Voluntary Cooperative Information System (VCIS)* begun in 1983 by the American Public Welfare Association (now the American Public Human Services Association). Although officially replaced in the late 1980s by the *Adoption & Foster Care Analysis & Reporting System (AFCARS)* at HHS, it remained the best comprehensive source of data until recent years. Even so, information from the states was voluntarily reported and legitimate numbers were difficult to attain; many states viewed data accumulation as a low priority. The data were no more than an approximation at best, prompting one federal official to recall privately that at times, when Congress requested numbers "we'd just make it up."[32] In the early 1990s, for example, the Iowa Citizen Foster Care Review Board did a hand tally and discovered six hundred children waiting for adoption in the state. This hard number came after they were told by child welfare officials that the total was about a 100, one-sixth of the actual number.[33] The VCIS data were always incomplete because states submitted incomplete data, and state systems were not uniform, making comparisons among states problematic at best. Thanks, in part, to a combination of adoption incentive payments and penalties for states that did not provide complete data, the AFCARS system has begun to provide the most reliable information ever available.

While reforms like the Adoption & Safe Families Act are having an effect, adopting children from foster care is filled with uncertainties. Although there are many couples that are willing to adopt, several factors make domestic adoption extremely difficult. Adoption can be expensive—estimates range from $15,000 to $50,000. Also, foreign adoptions have surged in popularity in recent decades in part due to the shortage of healthy American infants available for adoption. In addition, single motherhood is celebrated. These circumstances greatly restrict the options of infertile couples who wish to adopt an infant in the United States.

While recent reforms designed to ensure safety and permanency for foster children appear to be having an effect, nonetheless the ability of the foster care system to protect children is handicapped by the larger problems of society in general: out-of-wedlock pregnancy and the breakdown of marriage in general; substance abuse; and, arguably, by the devaluing of human life. Whether or not it is a coincidence, what we see is that the rise in levels of child abuse and neglect coincided with the growing societal acceptance of abortion. But observations (admittedly unscientific) based on human nature would strongly suggest more than mere coincidence. When the value of a child's life is based not upon his inherent worth, but rather upon whether or not he is *wanted* by his parents, an individual child's life becomes less valuable.

Families should be a refuge for children, a place where responsible parents, a married mother and father, consistently provide them with love and guidance. Yet more and more children are born into single-parent homes where the mother did not marry her child's father; and the drug abuse/poverty/foster care nexus reminds us that the plight of the average single mother is a far cry from the glamour and sophistication of the original television character made famous by single motherhood, Murphy Brown. In the real world, the typical child in foster care came from a home headed by a single mother with several children, who frequently has a history of substance abuse problems and who is cohabiting with a succession of boyfriends who may or may not be the father of one of her out-of-wedlock children.

The problems with foster care begin at the local level, and it is here that the most effective reforms must happen. Legislation can help, and new legislation passed by the 110th Congress makes it easier for the nearly 127,000 children in foster care who are waiting to be adopted.

Real improvement, however, will demand some fundamental changes in the child protection culture, including:

1.   Child welfare authorities cannot be all things to all people; they must set priorities and follow set processes. Thanks, in part, to mandatory reporting laws, these authorities are obliged to screen a multitude of reports, only a fraction of which are ever substantiated. One reason that so many children "slip through the cracks" of the child welfare bureaucracy is that caseworkers spend much of their time investigating false reports. In addition, caseworkers must divide their time between many competing tasks. They must screen and investigate reports, they must determine which children should be removed from their homes and placed in foster care, and they must do follow-up on those cases, including (for some families) labor-intensive "family preservation" services. It must be acknowledged that narrowing the scope of or eliminating mandatory reporting laws may mean that some cases of maltreatment may go undetected at the front end of the process. But under the current situation, even *substantiated* cases are often neglected, with sometimes-deadly consequences.

2.   Assault and criminal negligence should be treated as such—and by the proper authorities. Not only are caseworkers overwhelmed with the sheer volume of cases and tasks, they are also charged with functions that would be more properly handled by the police. Child abuse and severe neglect are, after all, forms of assault—with the parent as perpe-trator. Regarding maltreatment as pathology to be treated, rather than a crime to be prosecuted, endangers children. A pathological approach, rather than a criminal approach, also raises certain issues about the rights of the accused. Even good parents may find themselves accused of maltreating their children on the basis of an anonymous accusation and based on a supposed violation of a social service agency guideline rather than a public law. Law enforcement authorities, who are trained to do criminal investigation, should be the ones investigating these cases to determine whether or not a crime has been committed. If the evidence suggests that it has, then the case should be adjudicated in criminal court.

3.   Above all, real reform of the foster care system requires recognizing that some dysfunctional "families" are neither worth preserving nor are they realistic candidates for rehabilitation. Though this may sound like an odd statement for a family advocate to make, it is based on the plain fact that parents who abuse their children habitually are committing a crime. Returning children to abusive situations is irresponsible at best and criminal at worst. Real reform must also recognize that children in single-parent families, especially those headed by single, never-mar-ried mothers, are far more at risk for serious maltreatment than their counterparts in families headed by a married mother and father. Once children *are* removed from an abusive situation, they deserve to become

part of a family where they are loved and kept safe from neglect and abuse. Society must not tolerate a situation in which children spend their entire childhoods in foster care on the false presumption that one or the other of the parents is eventually going to mature sufficiently to get their act together. We must give children in long-term foster care opportunities to be adopted by loving families.

Notes

1. The author gives special thanks to Heide Seward who wrote an early version of this chapter when she was a research fellow at the Beverly LaHaye Institute.
2. American Academy of Child and Adolescent Psychiatry (AACAP), "Foster Care," *Facts for Families* 64 (updated May 2005), http://www.aacap.org/cs/root/facts_for_families/foster_care.
3. Richard J. Gelles, "Make the Child the Client," First Person: Essays, *The Pennsylvania Gazette*, (May/June, 2006), http://www.upenn.edu/gazette/0506/expert.html.
4. "Definitions," Title 45 Code of Federal Regulations, Part 1355, §1355.20 (a).
5. Moira Szilagyi, "Foster Care: Social Issues Affecting Children and Their Families," *The Merck Manual Home Edition* online, Children's Health Issues section, last revision/review July 2007, http://www.merck.com/mmhe/print/sec23/ch287/ch287f.html.
6. U.S. Department of Health and Human Services, Administration on Children, Youth and Families, *Child Maltreatment 1999,* (Washington, DC: GPO, 2001): 13.
7. Sheryl Dicker and Elysa Gordon, "Ensuring the Healthy Development of Infants in Foster Care: A Guide for Judges, Advocates and Child Welfare Professionals," Permanent Judicial Commission on Justice for Children and Zero to Three Policy Center (January 2004): 9.
8. Ibid., 4.
9. Ibid.
10. U.S. Department of Health and Human Services, "New Adoption Ad Campaign Launched," Administration for Children and Families, press release, July 13, 2006, http://www.acf.hhs.gov/news/press/2006/adoptuskids_teens.htm.
11. Child Welfare Information Gateway, "Foster Care Statistics," U.S. Department of Health and Human Services, Administration for Children and Families, June 2007, http://www.childwelfare.gov/pubs/factsheets/foster.cfm.
12. "Facts on Foster Care in America," *ABC News*, May 30, 2006, http://abcnews.go.com/print?id=2017991.
13. Ibid.
14. Scott Fromader, "Foster Care Youth: Serving and Preparing Youth Transitioning to Successful Adulthood," PowerPoint presentation, Wisconsin Department of Workforce Development (October 30, 2007): Slides 6 and 18, www.dwd.state.wi.us/dwdwia/powerpoint/103007fostercare_youth.ppt.
15. Dan Lips, "Foster Care Children Need Better Educational Opportunities," The Heritage Foundation. *Backgrounder No. 2039* (June 5, 2007): 3-4, http:/www.heritage.org/research/education/bg2039.cfm.
16. As early as 1996, the *New York Times* published an article lamenting the lack of expert consensus over the appropriate policies for children in foster care. [Alan Finder, "The Pendulum of Policies on Child Abuse." *The New York Times*, January 12, 1996.] The latest article was in the *Los Angeles Times* last year. [Miriam

Aroni Krinsky, "Finally, a foster care fix," *Los Angeles Times*, July 25, 2008.] The entire program, putting HIV/AIDS orphans in foster care, is called the Pendulum Project, http://www.pendulumproject.org/children_and_aids.html. *The Vanderbilt Law Review* published an article on the foster care "pendulum" [M. O'Laughlin, "A Theory of Relativity: Kinship Foster Care May be The Key To Stopping the Pendulum of Termination vs. Reunification," *Vanderbilt Law Review* 51(5) (October 1, 1998): 1427-1457.] and *The Law and Society Association* presented a paper on the subject, July 6, 2006. [Annette Appell, Sharon Sutherland and Justeen Hyde, "As the Pendulum Swings: Navigating Efforts to Act in the "Best Interests" of Children in Foster Care," paper presented at the annual meeting of *The Law and Society Association*, Jul 06, 2006.]

17.   Andrew Schneider and Andrew Barber, "Children sacrificed for the case," *Seattle Post-Intelligencer*, February 23, 1998.

18.   Sari Horwitz and Scott Higham, "Child Protection Deficiencies Aired: At Hearing, D.C. Council Members Say Government is at Fault in Deaths," Metro Section, *The Washington Post*, September 18, 2001, http://pqasb.pqarchiver.com/washingtonpost/access/8096875.html.

19.   Ibid.

20.   Scott Higham and Sari Horwitz, "Starvation Killed Baby under D.C. Protection; Caseworker Didn't See Family for 7 Months," Metro Section, *The Washington Post*, December 1, 2001, http://pqasb.pqarchiver.com/washingtonpost/access/93032466.html.

21.   Ann O'Hanlon, "Discipline Proposed in Katelynn's Death; 2 Alexandria Workers May be Suspended," *The Washington Post*, January 23, 2002, http://pqasb.pqarchiever.com/washingtonpost/access/101543096.html.

22.   AACAP, "Foster Care."

23.   U.S. Department of Health and Human Services, "Trends in Foster Care and Adoption—FY 2002-FY 2007," Administration for Children, Youth and Families, updated November 5, 2008, http://www.acf.hhs.gov/programs/cb/stats_research/afcars/trends.htm.

24.   Child Welfare Information Gateway, "Foster Care Statistics."

25.   National Foster Care Month, "Facts about Children in Foster Care," http://www.fostercaremonth.org/AboutFosterCare/StatisticsAndData/Documents/FCM07_Fact_Sheet_(national).pdf. Based on data from U.S. Department of Health and Human Services, "Child Welfare Outcomes 2002-2005: Report to Congress," (Child Welfare Outcomes Report), Administration for Children and Families, Executive Summary, http://www.acf.hhs.gov/programs/cb/pubs/cwo05/chapters/executive.html.

26.   U.S. Department of Health and Human Services, "Child Welfare Outcomes Report."

27.   AACAP, "Foster Care."

28.   U.S. House of Representatives, Committee on Ways and Means, *Overview of Entitlement Programs* (Washington, DC: GPO, May 15, 1992): 102-44; T. Tatara, *Characteristics of Children in Substitute and Adoptive Care: A Statistical Summary of the VCIS National Child Welfare Data Base* (Washington, DC: American Public Welfare Association, May 1993); Tatara, "U.S. child substitute care flow data for FY1992 and current trends in the state child substitute care populations," *VCIS Research Notes* No. 9 (August 1993) as cited in Eugene M. Lewit, "Children in Foster Care," *Home Visiting* 3 (Winter 1993): 197.

29.   Child Welfare Information Gateway, "Foster Care Statistics," 3.

30.   Lewit, "Children in Foster Care," 196-197.

31.   The Pew Commission on Children in Foster Care, "Fostering the Future: Safety, Permanence and Well Being for Children in Foster Care" (2004): 26, http://pew-fostercare.org/research/docs/FinalReport.pdf.

32.   Cheryl Wetzstein, "Lost in Foster Care?" *The Washington Times*, April 29, 2001.

33.   Ibid.

If our American way of life fails the child, it fails us all.
—Pearl S. Buck

8

Media

Today's children and youth live in an environment inundated by endlessly proliferating types of media. They have extraordinary media choices; what some authors call a "tsunami of media."[1] According to the Kaiser Family Foundation, children spend an average of six-and-a-half hours a day using the incredible variety of media available in their homes: television, video games, the Internet, or some other type of media.[2] Kaiser notes that children spend more time with media than in any other activity other than sleeping. Some experts aptly describe as "media clutter," the many options available to children in their own homes. Others are concerned that due to the increasing number of media choices available to children, it is difficult for parents alone to act as gatekeepers.

Certainly, the challenge of monitoring and guiding children's use of media, most especially television and the Internet, is daunting. The Brookings Institution devoted an entire issue of their journal *The Future of Children* to "Children and the Electronic Media."[3] One of their major points is that media technology is an integral part of children's lives now with television being replaced as the dominant media source by cell phones, iPods, texting, video games, instant messaging, social networks on the Internet (Twitter, MySpace, and Facebook) and email. They note the rise of multitasking that is common among children who use various media simultaneously.[4] Because government control of media is not desirable, the most effective pressure on the media industry must come from parents and other concerned members of the public.

Six prominent medical groups (American Academy of Pediatrics, American Academy of Child & Adolescent Psychiatry, American Psychological Association, American Medical Association, American Academy of Family Physicians and the American Psychiatric Association) are united in warning parents about the harms to children of too much media.[5] These warnings are increasingly important for parents to hear, and they dovetail with the message of this book: with greater numbers of single mother households and with more two-parent households where both parents work outside the home, increasing numbers of children have unrestricted and unsupervised use of media with all its good and bad dimensions. Parents have good reason to be concerned that their teens "are drowning in messages about sex, smoking, drinking, consumer goods, and a host of other behaviors and products that threaten their health and well being."[6]

The National Institutes of Health and Common Sense Media, a nonprofit advocacy group, is urging parents to "turn off the TV." They analyzed 173 studies and distilled 30 years of research about the effects of media consumption on children. In this analysis and summary, they demonstrate that a strong correlation exists between greater media exposure and adverse health outcomes for children.[7] The message of the studies was clear: more time with television, films, video games, magazines, music, and the Internet was linked to rises in childhood obesity, tobacco use, and sexual behavior. There was also a strong link, what the researchers called a "surprisingly lopsided finding," between heavy media use and drug/alcohol use and low academic achievement.[8]

There are over 116 million households in the U.S. in 2007 and the Consumer Electronic Association estimates that they owned 285 million television sets, more than 2 per household on average.[9] Just in the years between 1997 and 2000, the number of families that own a television, VCR, videogames, and a computer increased by 15 percent, with nearly half of the families (48 percent) owning all four media. In a dramatic change, those media have expanded beyond the living rooms and family rooms of the nation's homes into the children's bedrooms (57 percent).[10] Further, the media landscape continues to expand with CDs, DVDs, and MP3s. With choices available to children rapidly multiplying, they are the ones who are media savvy in today's families. Moreover, they are the ones who will determine how and which media future generations will use.

The technological evolution is rapidly playing out: families have switched from newspaper subscriptions (42 percent) to online access (52 percent).[11] Those children with computer access watch less television (fifteen minutes less time every day) than those without computer access; however, parents are more apt to supervise television viewing than to monitor what the kids are doing while they on the Internet or while they are playing video games.[12]

Parents often think that they do not have enough information about other media to influence effectively how their children use that media. One study found that mothers of sixth grade boys were concerned about video games, whereas mothers of teens were more concerned about rap music and the Internet.[13] Many parents are unaware that the V-Chip exists to help them control their children's television viewing; other parents dismiss such monitoring tools believing that their kids would just find a way around any blocking device.

Children in low-income families are as likely to own video game equipment as those in higher income families, but they are less likely to own computers or to have Internet access. Further, children in lower income families spend more time with media than do the children in higher income families. Fewer than half of all parents are aware of the rating systems that provide guidelines about the content of the various programs and games. Even parents who follow movie ratings to determine their children's movie viewing are unlikely to know about (84 percent do not) or use television rating systems. Parents that are knowledgeable report that they use the ratings system to determine the educational or informational value to their children (80 percent).[14]

The "three-hour rule" mandates that commercial television stations air at least three hours of educational programming for children; however, one study found that only two out of sixty-two mothers were aware of the rule.[15] A content analysis of the programming under the three hour rule in the Philadelphia area revealed that over half (57 percent) were considered moderately educational, while one-fifth were considered highly educational, and nearly one-fourth (23 percent) were judged minimally educational.[16] Further, children under the age of six spend about two hours a day with screen media—the same amount of time that they spend playing outside and three times as much time as they spend reading or being read to.[17]

Increasingly, programs are interactive, allowing children to adapt the media to their own learning style and adjust it to their individual learning pace. According to a survey by the Pew Internet and American Life Project, nearly 65 percent of teens who use the Internet are now actively creating content. They share artwork, photos, stories, or videos; they create Web pages or blogs; they write online journals; they maintain a personal Web page; and they remix content from online sources to create their own materials. These activities, along with the other technologies (85 percent of teens have at least a cell phone or BlackBerry and 45 percent have two or more), are an integral part of teen life today.[18]

The potential for using media effectively to empower children is expanding constantly, as is media's ability to expose children to negative experiences and harmful influences. Clearly, it is important, no, it is imperative for parents to educate themselves and know more about programming, rating systems, and current technology in order to help their children make reasoned, deliberate choices regarding their use of media.

Even two-year-olds today recognize "Big Bird" and immediately know that the "Golden Arches" means McDonald's. Such is the dramatic impact of advertising in the media even on toddlers. But the immaturity of their conceptual understanding makes it hard for them to differentiate between reality and acting, between people and puppets, or animals and animation. With their short attention spans, they may focus on some aspect or event of a program rather than understand the overall message; so parents must be aware that a child might see something entirely different from what the program intends him/her to see.

Although there are large bodies of research, there are few conclusions about the impact of media on young, pre-school children. A wise parent will watch programs with their very young child and talk with the child about what he or she is "seeing" and use the conversation to shape the child's understanding.[19]

One of the fastest growing demographic groups is pre-adolescent children aged nine to twelve, the "tweens," who are no longer little children, but are not yet teenagers. These are individuals who are "starting to develop their sense of identity and are anxious to cultivate a sophisticated self-image."[20] This stage of childhood is a very important, and lucrative, one for marketers who have been so successful that the Toy Manufacturers of America lowered their target age from fourteen to ten years of age. Astoundingly, Hollywood now utilizes children, barely teens and younger, to evaluate story concepts, commercials, movie trailers, and rough cuts for R-rated movies. By focusing on them as a separate advertising target, marketers have managed to subvert parents' role of gatekeeper because they have had virtually free rein in shaping tween attitudes about what is "cool."[21]

Some analysts call the tweens "the Internet generation" because they are so comfortable with the newest technology. Some of them are quite sophisticated users of new media; all of them are susceptible to the increasingly sexualized marketing schemes. Attitudes about body image (impossibly thin), physical beauty, popularity, happiness, and success are shaped by provocative advertising campaigns by Calvin Klein, Abercrombie & Fitch, Guess, and other brand-name clothing and apparel companies that are selling more than just their products; they are also selling inappropriate adult sensuality to children. This robs them of adolescent interest and has them focusing, instead, on things they aren't ready to handle in a mature responsible fashion. A 1998 study in Canada indicated that by tenth grade, over three-fourths of the girls and more than half of the boys were displeased with their looks.[22] The question, then, is whether parents and the public will continue to allow commercial interests to take precedence over the well-being of the nation's children.

Thoughtful young people see through and are critical of the media for portraying two extremes of teenagers. One frequent stereotype is the overachiever—the confident trendsetter, popular, smart, athletic perfect example. Another is the victim type—hates school, hates his or her parents, hates everything, is a troublemaker with a punk attitude and doesn't care about anything or anybody. Knowledgeable teens express a desire to see a typical young person who lives through the usual ups and downs of adolescence. They express appreciation for media content that is not patronizing. They prefer content that presents topics in a credible way with facts and information that are not pedantic, dull, or boring. They want materials that are meaningful in their lives.

Four gigantic media empires control the vast majority of children's media: News Corp., Viacom, Time Warner, and Disney. In addition, there are numerous smaller independent producers that provide programming to fill the three hours that are mandated for children's viewing. Some of the independent producers question whether the big media corporations, with their competitive mentality and bottom-line orientation, can put children's needs ahead of their responsibility to investors. Others argue, "What's good for kids is good business." These two points of view obviously clash and seem to be resolved by focusing on a specific "brand" of program. Phil Vischer, founder and CEO of Big Idea Productions, the creator of the "Veggie Tales" children's programs, said, "We can no longer trust the companies that are speaking to our kids." He argued that the big conglomerates are diversified and thus produce a variety of media, "some of which contradict the values that the public associates with the company."[23]

One of the most detrimental influences of media on children is marketing; and that marketing extends far beyond just television screens or computer monitors. Industry spending on advertising to children has dramatically increased over the past decade, with a price tag of over $2 billion now.[24] Brian L. Wilcox, chair of the American Psychological Association's Task Force on Advertising and Children said, "Probably the clearest evidence we have that television influences children's thinking and behavior is the fact that advertisers invest literally billions of dollars trying to influence perceptions, choices and behaviors of children through advertising. We know that advertisers wouldn't be investing the amount of money they do without clear evidence that those messages are influencing kids."[25] Studies indicate that on average we see three thousand advertisements per day.[26] The Russian space program even launched a rocket that had a thirty-foot Pizza Hut logo.

We have grown used to what the marketers call "ambient advertising"—ads on cars, buses, park benches, elevator walls, stadiums names, clothing, and on celebrities' sports equipment. Product placement has become a ubiquitous advertising tool targeting children. For instance, in the 1982 film, *ET*, having Reese's Pieces candy in a pivotal scene resulted in a 65 percent increase in sales of the product. Such product placement is now commonplace and a highly effective marketing tool.

The perceptions, choices, and behaviors of children are influenced through advertising. We know very well that advertisers wouldn't be investing the amount of money they do without clear evidence that those messages are influencing kids."[27]

Dan Acuff, a youth marketing consultant, calls attention to the efforts of advertisers to reach children in schools (free technology in exchange for access to the children) through promotions, contests, coupons, kids clubs, school relations, and event marketing.[28] Others, like Alison Alexander, a professor in the Telecommunications Department at the University of Georgia, is concerned about vulnerable, younger children adopting the commercial values of advertising because they cannot differentiate between the programming and the advertisements. She also is concerned about teens "being socialized into the consumer culture." Teens have a tendency to buy products that give identity and convey the non-verbal message that the owner of the clothes or item belongs to a certain group or social system. All of these teen practices are believed to help teens to gain peer approval; in the process, they make a lot of money for those who produce the products.[29]

It is quite instructive to see the deliberate intent behind the production and marketing of such "prestige" items. With the help of researchers and psychologists, advertisers carefully dissect and analyze what motivates children; they employ sophisticated, in-depth knowledge about kids' developmental, emotional, and social needs at the various stages of their development. Advertisements utilize that analysis to tap into children's behavior and dreams with very carefully calibrated marketing strategies.[30] The results of these unrelenting efforts can be seen in the fact that even very young children today can identify hundreds of specific logos and mascots.

The Federal Trade Commission found that 80 percent of the R-rated movies that they studied were marketed to children under seventeen. One studio's plan clearly stated a goal of making "sure that everyone between the ages of 12 and 18 was exposed to the film." The same is true of music and video games—marketing plans for 70 percent of mature-rated video games included ads placed in media reaching children under seventeen.[31]

Numerous studies have shown that the more an adolescent watches soaps, movies, and music videos, the more they become dissatisfied with their body and more determined to be thin. By age thirteen, over half of girls (53 percent) are "unhappy with their bodies" and (just as the Canadian study cited earlier found) that number grows to more than three-quarters (78 percent) by age seventeen.[32] By the time girls are only ten years of age, 40 percent have tried to lose weight by going on a diet.[33]

According to a Harvard study, 86 percent of teenage girls are on a diet or believe that they should be. This should surprise no one when fashion magazine models today are thinner than 98 percent of all the girls and women in America. This trend toward size 0-2 is relatively new and unrealistic because, for instance, Marilyn Monroe, the sex icon of a previous generation, wore a size 14.[34]

Many parents are distressed to learn that when girls watch between two and four hours of television per day their priorities change. They become overly concerned with "how they look" and give little thought to their studies or their future. "What they do" becomes irrelevant as they concentrate on their appearance and image.

More disturbing is *USA Weekend's* 11th Annual Special Teen Report (non-scientific, voluntary participation) survey of nearly 300,000 teens to discover what they feel about themselves. About half of the respondents feel good about themselves, but the other half has misgivings, especially about their appearance. Only four in ten consider themselves attractive—and increasingly, this is a problem for boys as well as girls. Almost nine in ten teens (85 percent) want to improve something about themselves (weight, grades, sports, relationships). A mere 15 percent like themselves as they are. Depression among teens is common. Nearly forty out of one hundred (37 percent) have a friend who has considered suicide. Teens generally don't think their family communicates often or well. The survey also revealed that minorities have fewer problems related to body image.[35]

As media options have proliferated, so too have concerns about the quality of media available to children and its impact on their lives and potential. Growing numbers of parents, educators, researchers, and policy makers note the absence of quality programming for children and young people. Most disturbing is the growing availability of questionable entertainment with gratuitous violence, sexual content, and negative role models. Numerous studies have documented the effects of media on children and the power of media in the lives of children and young people.

There are numerous non-positive ways that media shape the values and lifestyles of children and youth:[36]

- blurring the line between advertising and programming content;
- distorting children's perceptions of reality;
- building unrealistic expectations;
- creating a culture that glamorizes celebrity and fame rather than achievement;
- presenting harmful stereotypes, promoting intolerance and/or apathy;
- focusing on the banal and trivial;
- disparaging intellectual development, creativity, and culture;
- promoting group think and commercial agendas;
- establishing body-image ideals that are unrealistic and detrimental to self-esteem;
- blurring the distinction between right and wrong; good and evil;
- denigrating the influence of family, school, community, and religion;
- promoting negative trends in style and identity;
- isolating children and youth from more positive influences;
- over-riding and dulling critical thinking;
- limiting involvement in social and political life;
- encouraging sedentary lifestyles rather than activity and exercise.

If parents are involved with their children on a day-to-day basis, of course, they minimize these influences; but when parents are too busy to be closely involved in what their children are doing, the risk of negative outcomes multiplies. Further, youths can inadvertently stumble upon adult material on television or in electronic games and websites. Also, with the pervasive availability of media, parents cannot possibly keep track of where their children consume media. It is in their rooms, at school, at friends' homes, in hangouts, on phones, and at parties and events.

One psychologist explained, "Parents used to be the channel through which children learned about the outside world."[37] Family used to be isolated from the public as a safe haven, a place where the parents determined when and if and what the child experienced beyond the home. With the invasion of media, the family sphere now is permeable, and the outside world constantly pervades the living rooms, kitchens, and bedrooms of our homes. As one scholar aptly expressed it, "TV takes our kids across the globe before parents give them permission to cross the street."[38]

Few of us would deny the power and influence of television and other media on children's lives. As the *Future of Children* journal asked, "Do we then advocate simply leaving the nation's youth to the wiles of Madison Avenue, the purveyors of smut and violence, and Internet predators?[39]

Parents face the challenge of keeping media from becoming a wedge that drives the family apart; they also face the challenge of shaping their children's values, attitudes, and beliefs rather than allowing today's media to be the major influence on their children's future. Several celebrities have joined the effort to awaken the public to the cultural factors that pollute the environment that surrounds American children. The late comedian and former host of the popular "Tonight Show" television program, Steve Allen, said, "There is no doubt that our entire culture is experiencing a moral breakdown." Dean Jones, the movie actor and producer, said, "We need a national conscience telling those of us in Hollywood where the boundaries of decency are set." Michael Medved, film critic and author of *Hollywood vs. America,* described Hollywood's prevailing message as one of "hostility toward the traditional family."[40]

The good news, however, is that parents now have ready access to resources to help train their children to deal with the barrage of advertising they confront through media. The website, "Zillions," is a teen's version of *Consumer Reports*. There, parents and children can review the ratings for toys, crafts, and games and compare the ratings to the marketing claims about these products. There is an award-winning children's program called "Street Cents" that tests various consumer products for their "truth in advertising."

While there are laws on the books and V-Chip ratings, local stations have their hands full editing programming for children to eliminate inappropriate language, nudity, and gratuitous violence. There are obvious tensions between government regulation of the airwaves and broadcasters' responsibility for media content, between First Amendment rights and children's needs.

There are signs that the public is coming alongside the family in some areas to use the media for social marketing. The federal government is sponsoring a $10 million social marketing campaign to encourage parents to talk to the children about delaying sexual activity. The program, "Parents Speak Up,"[41] includes public service announcements, billboards, bus signs, posters, Web banners, and other motivational messages to encourage parents to talk with their children and to provide them with the appropriate information to be effective at covering the important topics. The Truth Campaign and the American Legacy Foundation[42] are getting information out to the public about dangers of smoking and to make it "cooler" for teens to reject tobacco. MySpace has launched a campaign, "How Do You Stay Teen?"[43] to encourage teens to enjoy age-appropriate activities in their teen years and postpone pregnancy and parenting. These are all important ways that the new media can be used in positive ways to enhance the well-being of American children.

The burgeoning growth of media will, without a doubt, affect America's homes and families. It remains to be seen whether we will succeed in harnessing the emerging new media technologies so that they will enhance children's well-being or detract from the influence of the parents. It is up to parents and other responsible adults to connect with today's youth where they are, "riding the airwaves," in order to teach them to understand when negative messages are being aimed at them and offer them "positive messages that compete with and offer attractive alternatives to the negative, unhealthful, or illegal messages that others offer."[44] This effort is not optional. It is an essential part of the task we face in rebuilding the family into the safe haven that it was meant to be for our children.

Notes

1   Elisabeth Hirschhorn Donahue, Ron Haskins, and Marisa Nightingale, "Policy Brief: Using the Media to Promote Adolescent Well-Being," *The Future of Children* 18, no. 1 (Spring 2008): 1, http://www.futureofchildren.org/usr_doc/ FOC_Brief_Spring08.pdf (accessed March 10, 2009).

2. National Institute on Media and the Family, "Fact Sheet: Children and Media Violence," (revised November 2006), http://www.mediafamily.org/facts/facts_vlent.shtml (accessed February 3, 2009).

3. "Children and the Electronic Media," *The Future of Children* 18, no. 1 (Spring 2008), http://www.futureofchildren.org/pubs-info2825/pubs-info_show.htm?doc_id=674322.

4. "Children and the Electronic Media: Executive Summary," *The Future of Children* 18, no. 1 (Spring 2008): 1, http://www.futureofchildren.org/usr_doc/media_summary.pdf.

5. National Institute on Media and the Family, "Fact Sheet."

6. Donahue, Haskins and Nightingale, "Policy Brief: Using the Media," 1.

7. Brian Stelter, "Report Ties Children's Use of Media to Their Health," *The New York Times*, (December 2, 2008), http://www.nytimes.com/2008/12/02/arts/02stud.html (March 10, 2009).

8. Ibid.

9. Number of households from U.S. Bureau of the Census, "Households by Type: 1940 to Present," Families and Living Arrangements, Historical Time Series: Households, Table HH-1(Internet release date January 2009), http://www.census.gov/population/www/socdemo/hh-fam.html (March 10, 2009).

10. J. Cory Allen and Kimberly Duyck Woolf, "The 5th Annual APPC Conference on Children and Media: A Summary," The Annenberg Public Policy Center, Report #39 (May 9, 2001): 7.

11. Ibid.

12. Ibid., 8.

13. Ibid., 11.

14. Ibid., 7.

15. Ibid., 11.

16. Allen and Woolf, "The 5th Annual APPC Conference: Summary," 9.

17. PBS Parents, "TV and Kids under Age 3," Issues and Advice: Children and Media, under "How prevalent is TV in the lives of very young children?" http://www.pbs.org/parents/childrenandmedia/article-faq.html (accessed March 10, 2009).

18. Donahue, Haskins, and Nightingale, "Policy Brief: Using the Media," 2.

19. Judith Myers-Walls, "Children: Media's Message Can Fool Kids," Center for Media Literacy, http://www.medialit.org/reading_room/article350.html (originally printed in *Media & Values* 35 [1986]).

20. Media Awareness Network, "Special Issues for Tweens and Teens," under For Parents: Marketing and Consumerism, http://www.media-awareness.ca/english/parents/marketing/issues_teens_marketing.cfm (accessed February 3, 2009).

21. Ibid.

22. Ibid.

23. Allen and Woolf, "The 5th Annual APPC Conference: Summary," 21.

24. Media Awareness Network, "How Marketers Target Kids," under For Parents: Marketing and Consumerism, http://www.media-awareness.ca/english/parents/marketing/marketers_target_kids.cfm (accessed February 3, 2009).

25. Rebecca A. Clay, "Unraveling New Media's Effects on Children," *Monitor on Psychology* 34, no. 2 (February 2003), http://www.apa.org/monitor/feb03/unraveling.html.

26. American Academy of Pediatrics Committee on Communications, "Children, Adolescents and Advertising," *Pediatrics* 118, no. 6 (December 2006): 2563, http://www.wsu.edu/~eaustin/pdf/AAP_statement.pdf.

27. Clay, "Unraveling New Media's Effects."

28.   Allen and Woolf, "The 5th Annual APPC Conference: Summary," 23.
29.   Ibid., 23-24.
30.   Clay, "Unraveling New Media's Effects."
31.   Media Awareness Network, "How Marketers Target Kids."
32.   National Institute on Media and the Family, "Fact Sheet: Media's Effect On Girls: Body Image and Gender Identity," (last revision September 6, 2002), http://www.mediafamily.org/facts/facts_mediaeffect.shtml (accessed February 3, 2009)
33.   Ibid.
34.   Kelly Nault, "Teenage Girls + Media = Low Self-Esteem." *EzineArticles.com*. http://ezinearticles.com/?Teenage-Girls-+-Media-=-Low-Self-Esteem&id=96389 (accessed February 3, 2009).
35.   "Special Teen Report on Teens & Self-Image," *USA Weekend Magazine*, May 1-3, 1998, http://www.usaweekend.com/98_issues/980503/980503teen_report_cover.html.
36.   Based on a similar list produced by the 4th World Summit on Media for Children and Adolescents, Rio de Janeiro, Brazil, April 2004.
37.   Joshua Meyrowitz interviewed by Barbara Osborn, "Altered States: How Television Changes Childhood," Center for Media Literacy, http://www.medialit.org/reading_room/article59.html.
38.   Ibid.
39.   Donahue, Haskins and Nightingale, "Policy Brief: Using the Media," 1.
40.   The Dove Foundation, "Quotes from a few friends," under About Dove, undated, http://www.dove.org/aboutdove.asp?ArticleID=6.
41.   Donahue, Haskins, and Nightingale, "Policy Brief: Using the Media," 3.
42.   Ibid., 4.
43.   Ibid., 5.
44.   Ibid., 2.

At work, you think of the children you have left at home.
At home, you think of the work you've left unfinished.
Such a struggle is unleashed within yourself. Your heart is rent.
  —*Golda Meir*

9

Child Care

In 1998, Sen. Chris Dodd (D-Connecticut) and other legislators introduced a child care bill that criticized stay-at-home mothers for choosing the "luxury" of motherhood over full-time employment. Senator Dodd showed how out of touch with reality he was when he said that mothers who choose to stay home with their children do so because they "want to go play golf or go to the club and play cards."[1] At almost the same time, others were claiming, "both parents now must work to pay the bills, and neither the workplace nor government has caught up with the crisis."[2]

Regardless how you view the issue of child care, there is no denying the impact of child-care concerns on American families and American culture. Two primary societal changes in recent years have increased the demand for child care. Over the past three decades, the number of children under five with employed mothers has more than doubled.[3] Obviously, these children must have child care while the mother works. The other factor that has had profound impact on the need for child care is the dramatic increase in the number of one-parent families, especially since that parent, usually the mother, is most often the sole financial provider for the children.[4]

One early warning that child care might contribute to the declining well-being of America's children came from the British psychologist Dr. Jay Belsky in 1986.[5] By 2001 the noted neuroscientist Stanley Greenspan, author of *Building Healthy Minds*, had convinced parenting guru, T. Berry Brazelton, to change his mind about day care. Together Brazelton and Greenspan published an influential monograph focusing on the "irreducible needs" of children.[6] The authors warned parents bluntly that they were "getting a lot of misinformation" about what is best for their children. Those two experts in child care explained the importance of a continuous, close relationship between a child and his or her parents, and they stressed the difficulty of building that relationship when both parents work outside the home.[7] By 2003, even the National Institute of Child Health and Development (NICHD) reported on research, which investigated whether too much time in child care (more than thirty hours a week) was producing socio-emotional problems and answered resoundingly. Excessive time in day care, they declared, "not only predicts problem behavior," but also predicts specific undesirable levels of "assertiveness, disobedience and aggression." Further, these problems remain "even when quality, type, and instability of child care are controlled," family background is taken into account, and quality-of-care effects are limited.[8]

In the past several years, however, research has taken a back seat to political correctness. Women's advocates have reacted to the research with outrage, blasting any scholar like Belsky[9] who presents evidence critical of child care, carelessly causing irreparable harm to the careers and reputations of several researchers. The reaction of state Senator Jackie Speier (D-San Francisco) is typical. When the NICHD study came out she said, "It's like just yank every woman out of the job and tell her to get back in her house and take care of her kids. We are living in the 21st Century. Everyone's got to get over that."[10]

On the other hand, those mothers who stay home with their children often feel "discriminated against fiscally and socially." Certainly, mothers at home don't get as much respect from American culture as do those in "paid work."[11] Women are no longer expected to marry before having children and then to make the sacrifices necessary to give their children hands-on parental nurturing. The prevailing cultural attitude that a woman's worth is determined by her market value has led to a concerted effort to force women into the marketplace, pressuring them to put career before marriage and to disrespect, if not actually disdain, motherhood. The idea that women must not be "tied down" by their responsibilities to their children fuels the push for federalized, universally-available child care and the campaign for subsidizing abortion on demand.

Often mothers feel as though they are on the front lines of the "mommy wars." Deborah Lewis and Charmaine Yoest wrote a "thoughtful policy agenda for reframing society's attitude toward mothers."[12] They called for a new vision of "radical motherhood" that allowed women to embrace the privilege of nurturing their children. We have still not reached the place where women feel that they have the option proposed by Lewis and Yoest.

Every fall, it seems, there is a child care "crisis" with polls demanding an increase in government funding for child care centers. In 2007, the claim was that about one in five (23 percent) women is delaying pregnancy or has decided against having another child because she cannot afford the child care costs. [13]

Not only is paid child care a severe strain on the budget of low-income mothers, even middle-class women, according to the National Association for Child Care Resource and Referral Agencies, are struggling to afford child care while the mother works during the day. Such initiatives always advocate greater federal and state "involvement" in child care and cite exorbitant figures for private child care. The cliché is that "if working families can't afford child care, law enforcement will end up taking care of the kids."[14]

When the reports cite "agonizing decisions" that parents have to make and the "stark reality" that parents face, they fail to mention some of the choices the families make, or the warped spending priorities established in some families. They do not mention the families who choose a boat, second car or truck, larger house, big-screen television, expensive vacation, or other luxury item instead of paying for quality child care or having the mother take a break from her career to nurture the family's children. Instead, the activists assume that the public ought to pay for an individual family's child care costs so that the family, regardless of its income or spending priorities, can use its disposable income on some luxury item. The underlying premise, assumed though not stated, is that no one should ever have to sacrifice in order to do whatever they want to do. Thus, the lobbying and political pressure for states to provide government-subsidized all-day pre-kindergarten has increased dramatically as both the number of single-parent families and two-wage-earner couples has increased.

Not surprisingly, even middle-class families complain about the cost of child care. Before they have children, young couples sometimes get on a merry-go-round of spending when they buy an expensive home, high-priced vehicles, and other luxury items; then they find that they cannot hop off the ride when the children come. The wife cannot afford to cut back on her working hours or quit work because the wife's income is needed to make the mortgage and car payments as well as the other extra payments—for surround-sound big screen television entertainment centers, second car, cleaning service, etc. Typically, child care costs equal a major share of the wife's income; but even then, the family seldom wants to forgo that extra paycheck.

There are a wide variety of options for child care being employed today for the approximately twelve million children younger than five whose mothers are employed: 30 percent are cared for on a regular basis by a grandparent during the mother's working hours. Slightly more than 30 percent are in an organized care facility (day care center, nursery, or preschool). About 25 percent receive care from their fathers, 3 percent from siblings, and 8 percent from other relatives when mothers are at work.[15] In addition, there are school- or work-based child care centers, church and corporate child care centers, and numerous "early learning center" franchises that purport to formally educate children even before they are potty trained.

Those who beat the drum about a child care "crisis" talk about the cost of the numerous commercial options available to those who are able to pay for someone else to raise their children. Mostly though, they talk about a lack of government-funded child care that would enable mothers to return to work while their children are infants, with tax dollars under-writing the expense. Federal and state spending for child care went up from $3.2 billion in 1996 to $10.5 billion 2002.[16] Now in addition to the *$10 billion* on child care provisions, we spend more than $15 billion on other child well-being programs, like child support enforcement, adoption assistance, and children and family services programs.[17] Those who are determined to institute full male-female equality in the workplace realize that to achieve that goal, women must be freed from the duties and responsibilities of motherhood. Thus, they push both for taxpayer-funded abortion and child care.

These efforts, often the work of ideologues, to "help" mothers stay in the workplace are not consistent with the desires of mothers themselves. A National Study of Women's Awareness, Attitudes, and Opinions found that eight out of ten American women agree with the statement, "If I could afford it, I would like to stay home and be a full-time mother."[18] Similarly, a poll by Wirthlin Worldwide revealed that when parents ranked nine options for caring for pre-school children, government-run child care centers came in dead last![19]

These parents, no doubt, know that by the time a child turns six years of age, about 85 percent of his or her personality is already formed and that the child's experiences in the family are vitally important for his or her personality development.[20] But parents also need to fully understand the new research about brain development. The first years of life are crucial for intellectual, social, and general development 80 percent of the brain develops by age three.[21] The care that a baby receives has dramatic and long-term effects on how that child develops and learns, how they cope with stress, and how they react and interact with the world around them. Studies at Baylor University indicate that loving care can actually help a baby's brain to grow; there is a strong relationship between brain activity and brain growth. There are neural pathways that develop in a child's first three years that "act like roadmaps for later learning."[22]

Too often, when it comes down to a choice between a mother's goals and her children's well-being, the kids lose out. They lose out at the personal level and at the policy level when "women's rights" take precedence over children's needs. The politicians, ideologues, and activists who promote policies "for our children," are often the ones most politically correct in their questionable ideas about what is best for children. The research findings are overwhelming: one of the children's greatest needs is their mothers' presence and attention. In her book, *Home-Alone America: The Hidden Toll of Day Care, Behavioral Drugs and Other Parent Substitutes*, Mary Eberstadt[23] lays out in a very readable form the research about the detrimental effects on the nation's children when they spend too much time in day care. She explores the "immediate emotional experience" that day care, divorce and an overuse of Ritalin and similar drugs cause for children. In the plainest of terms, she says: "It would be better for both children and adults if more American parents were with their kids more of the time."[24] Yet, in the United States, many children of working mothers are placed in child care before they are four months old, and they spend an average of 33 hours a week in child care.[25]

With the range of child care options springing up in every community, town, and city of America, we are marching bravely toward the feminist goal of "freeing women from motherhood."[26] Millions upon millions of families use day care or other methods of child supervision each week, primarily because of the rising number of working mothers, in spite of the fact that we've known for years that the outcomes are undesirable when children spend too much time in day care. Regrettably, though, the negative findings of the comprehensive studies are buried in the small print while the headlines trumpet muddled messages that designed to obfuscate the facts and make parents feel fine about putting their children in full-time day care.

So what does happen when mom and/or dad drive away leaving the child at a child care center? A University of Minnesota study measured the presence of a stress hormone, cortisol, in toddlers. Those who attended child care showed a significant increase in the hormone (7 out of 10) on their days in child care compared with no increase in the hormone on their days at home.[27]

How safe is day care? In one year, 1997, at least 31,000 children, 4 years old and younger, were treated in emergency rooms for injuries that occurred in child care or school.[28] Is the high injury rate merely a neutral convenience or are there unsuspected hazards for children? What the research is finding is that children in day care centers have a greater likelihood of becoming: sick,[29] stressed,[30] passively withdrawn,[31] aggressive, defiant, and disobedient.[32]

Psychologist Dr. Ken Madig notes that an increasing number of children suffer a "character disturbance" called Antisocial Personality Disorder (APD). "The symptoms of APD include emotional detachment and uncontrollable inner rage, and its origins can be traced to disruptions in parent-infant bonding."[33]

Contrary to how they advertise, day care centers are not educational institutions that also teach social skills. Too often, the child is "stuck on the middle;" as Lewis and Yoest put it, "Even in good day care situations, children are often competing for the attention and affection of the adults there."[34] Turnover in employment due to burnout (not to mention low pay) is often high as many day care situations are "overcrowded or otherwise emotionally sterile environments in which the child has been forced as an infant to fight for attention and adopt behavior based on the contradictory messages about acceptable behavior that they have received from parents and daytime caregivers."[35]

The landmark study from the National Institute of Child Health and Human Development (NICHD)[36] mentioned earlier was a decade-long survey of the relationship between child care and child development. It is the largest and most authoritative long-term study of child care in the United States. That study—the NICHD Study of Early Child Care and Youth Development (SECCYD)—found that a child does best when nurtured at home by his or her own mother and that children who spend many hours (thirty hours or more) in child care show more behavioral problems (disobedience, defiance, destructiveness, and aggression) and more episodes of minor illness (stomach flu, ear infections, upper respiratory infections) than those in fewer hours of child care. The amount of time a child spends in child care is also associated with the degree of attachment in the mother-child relationship; the more time in child care the weaker the child's attachment to the mother tends to be and the less the mother's sensitivity to the child's needs. In his research, Dr. Belsky found that, in contrast with infants who are at home with their mothers, infants in "early and extensive non-maternal care" have a greater likelihood of failing to develop secure infant-parent bonding. [37]

What the NICHD study found to be the strongest predictor of a child's positive behavior is the degree of the mother's sensitivity and awareness of her child's wants and needs.[38] In other words, a sensitive mother produces socially adjusted children who are less likely to engage in disruptive behavior and less likely to be involved in conflicts with their peers or caregivers. The key is for a mother to spend enough quality time with her child to be attuned to his or her deepest needs. Further, those mothers with positive personalities tended to have children with better outcomes and well-being; and those families with well-organized routines and positive family environments produced children with more advanced social and cognitive development.[39]

The evidence is quite clear that a higher number of working hours for mothers is associated with lower academic achievement scores and lower cognitive development.[40] "As a mother's work hours increased, children's grades were lower, work habits were poorer and the children displayed less resilience, resourcefulness, and adaptability in the classroom."[41]

A recently completed British study provides the longest and most detailed study of child care ever conducted in the United Kingdom. Lead by Penelope Leach, Kathy Sylva, and Alan Stein, the study began in 1998 and continued to 10 years following the development of 1200 children and their families. In brief, they concluded, "children looked after by their mothers do significantly better in developmental tests than those cared for in nurseries, by child minders or relatives."[42]

In Britain, as in America, the headlines often inaccurately reflect the study being reported. While the headline, "Official: Babies do Best with Mother" was accurate, the rest of the article focused on what they called a "controversy" over how best to bring up children. Despite the finding of the study, the article editorialized about the benefits of commercial child care. They warned, "Love doesn't necessarily produce the best child care" and that "mummy care is not necessarily the gold standard" for children. They reported, "78 percent of working mothers say a nursery is the ideal child care." They ended with an appeal for federally funded child care.[43]

Some of the findings of the research related to the benefits of family-based child care have appeared in unlikely places. Amazingly, UNICEF just published a report, "Child Care is Bad for Your Baby, Working Parents are Warned."[44] The BBC laid the facts on the line with a provocative headline, "Selfish Adults 'Damage Childhood.'" They declared, "Childrearing is one of the most challenging tasks in life and ideally it requires two people."[45]

The National Child Care survey estimated that in centers caring for one-year-olds, the average group size was 10 children, the average ratio of children to staff was seven to one, and older children (ages two through five) were frequently crowded into groups of fifteen. Some studies have estimated an average of seven different people in a single day and as many fifteen a week provide care for each day care child.[46] Author Brian Robertson agrees in his book, *There is No Place Like Work*, "Day care workers' tasks are more akin to crowd control than to the formation of young minds."[47]

With first-hand knowledge of conditions, some day care workers confess that they wouldn't put their own children in day care.[48] At its worst, the hazardous environment of day care has even contributed to some tragic and preventable deaths. Some of the older children found twenty-two-month-old Demar Joseph-Amir Hicks apparently strangled by the straps of his car seat at "Mama D's" home day care center; he died two days later. The two caregivers, with twenty-three children in a home facility that was licensed for fourteen children, were each charged with child neglect, child endangerment, and culpable negligence.[49] Another child care death was attributed to the caregiver "violently throwing the crying infant into a playpen" because she couldn't stop him from crying.[50] Then every summer we face the horror of more deaths from children left in vehicles. Over half of the 361 deaths over a ten-year period were due to the child being "forgotten" by a caregiver.[51]

But what happens to school-aged kids? When children are too old for day care and are in public schools, they often end up as latchkey kids. Approximately fourteen million children (about 25 percent) stay home alone after school or with siblings and without supervision on a regular basis.[52] Studies by the American Academy of Pediatrics have found, not surprisingly, that latchkey kids "are more susceptible to misbehavior, risk-taking, and anxiety."[53] These latchkey kids are "more likely to use alcohol and other illegal drugs. One study of five thousand eighth-graders (twelve- and thirteen-year-olds from a range of economic and ethnic backgrounds) concluded that children who care for themselves for eleven or more hours per week were twice as likely to consume alcohol, smoke cigarettes, and use marijuana as children who were supervised."[54] The AAP study stated unequivocally, "Until about the age of eleven or twelve, most children are not able to handle stressful or emergency situation that require mature decision-making on their own."[55] The editor of the AAP book, Edward L Schor, said in an interview, "Even children approaching adolescence...should not come home to an empty house in the afternoon."[56] In spite of the expert advice, the latest Census Bureau figures reveal that about one-third of all middle-school-aged children (twelve to fourteen years of age) provide "self-care" while added to this total are 6 percent of children ages five to eleven who also take care of themselves after school.[57]

Another problem with "self-care" is that television is a common "babysitter" when children remain unsupervised. Half of the nation's youth spend more than two hours a day watching TV, yet 76 percent said they would choose more time with their parents if they had the option.[58] One of the benefits of new technology is that kids are spending a lot of time in cell phone or online conversations with their parents. "Instant messaging, long a part of teenagers' lives, is working its way into the broader fabric of the American family," said Michael Gartenberg, of Jupiter Research.

Some family therapists see this development as very positive for those people who have a hard time talking face-to-face, and it can be a good way to smooth things over after a fight or to deal with touchy family issues in a less confrontational manner. Since the new technologies are more a teen's turf, some teenagers are more comfortable communicating via those media about the issues that bother them.[59] College students, in particular, find security in phoning home frequently.[60] Parents are reminded, however, that children's exposure to electronic media is increasing and is associated with a number of negative outcomes. Since time with parents and parental involvement in their children's lives is crucial to their well-being, parents need to monitor kids' time with electronic media. Researchers report that students today typically spend more than half of their time either playing video games or talking on a cell phone.[61]

Conventional wisdom would presume that parents would be spending less time with their children today than ever before. Ironically, that is not the case. On the plus side, several studies indicate that married couples are spending more time with their children now than they did forty years ago. In 2000, married mothers spent almost 13 hours a week more than in 1965 and married fathers spent 6.5 hours a week, compared to 2.6 hours in 1965. Single mothers, too, spend more time now with their children than in 1965.[62] Experts say, in part, the difference is that now there are fewer children in a family and each child gets more of his/her parents' time; in addition, parents are more concerned today about dangers their children face, so they try to keep a closer eye on them. Plus, working mothers have far less time for other activities—they sleep less, watch less television, and spend less time with their husbands.[63]

Mounting research evidence links "language-rich home environments"[64] with a child's reading success and school achievement. Those parents that talk at length with their children are helping them with their reading comprehension and increasing their children's lifelong academic success; no wonder those who specialize in literary research are encouraging parents to "increase the quantity and quality of their conversations with their children, beginning at birth."[65] More parents need to be educated as to the importance of talking with their infants, children, adolescents, and teens; only 26 percent of parents report being "very aware" of the importance of talking with their children.[66]

A University of Michigan study on families' use of time found that on average parents spend seventeen hours per week with their children.[67] The study also reported that children whose mothers work outside the home are spending more time in school and/or day care and less time in free play, reflecting "the widespread demographic changes in U.S. families." Further, Sandra L. Hofferth, the author of the study, said, "These data show how children's lives are being affected by the family time crunch."[68] A recent study published in the *Journal of Marriage and Family* also reported that single mothers spend less time (83 to 90 percent as much) with their children than married mothers.[69] And, there is a racial component as well. The majority of white mothers are married (83 percent) while less than half of the nonwhite mothers are married.[70]

Our culture has come a long way—the wrong way—from when Herbert Hoover remarked, as he did numerous times, that America's children are her greatest natural resource. Too often now children are viewed, not as one of the most treasured elements of the family whose nurture is central to its purpose, but as a problem that the parents must "solve." Far too often, the "solution" is to foist the children off onto a paid caretaker who will assume the shaping of that child's character and future. Too often, that caretaker's view of the child is the view that the child absorbs as his self-image.

Instead of only asking the typical question of what is best or more convenient for the adults, we must ask the serious question: "What is best for our children?" The best environment to foster a child's intellectual development is one in which his or her mother is actively involved literally hands-on on a day-to-day basis; the likeliest environment for this to take place is the home.[71] Many families are hearing the message: an estimated 5.6 million mothers stayed home to care for their children in 2005, about 1.2 million more than a decade ago.[72] In addition, more women are learning that they can keep one foot in the workplace while raising their children. About 36 percent of moms of infants work full time, while another 17.3 percent work part time. (A quarter of never-married mothers work full time while their children are infants).[73] Among married-couple families with related children under eighteen years old only about 40.5 percent had a mother who worked full-time, year-round. That leaves nearly 60 percent with a mother who did not work, worked part-time, or worked only part of the year.[74]

But, the children are not the only ones stressed when day care is a daily routine. Over 85 percent of working mothers also work out the primary child-care responsibilities in the family.[75] The mother is the one who has to arrange for child care; and one in ten face significant problems in arranging for child care.[76] For working parents, "coordinating summer child care can be a logistical nightmare" and most working parents are "on their own when it comes to arranging summer child care."[77] While younger children spend most of their year in a child-care center,[78] summer care is a problem for school-aged children of working parents. For working middle-class parents, child care expenses can increase fully 34 percent during the summer. Some parents spend as much as $7,000 for summer child care.[79] Nearly one-quarter of school-age children (six through twelve years old) attend local summer programs, like day camps and summer recreation programs, nearly one-third are in the care of relatives, and less than 10 percent have in-home child care.[80] Almost 30 percent of ten to twelve-year-olds are in self-care during the summer months, and these children spend significantly more time alone (more than ten hours a day) during the summer than during the school year.[81]

About 38 percent of children in child care are in multiple child care arrangements—in formal center-based care part of the day and with family, neighbor, or other informal caretaker arrangements during other parts of the day.[82] Working mothers are more likely to drop off and pick up children from child care, increasing a mother's total commute time by 28 percent.[83]

All of these factors weigh into the generally held opinion that it is harder to raise children today than it was when today's mothers were children (72 percent), and mothers today (52 percent of mothers of one child and 63 percent of mothers of more than one child) worry about being a good mother. [84]

When we stay too busy to spend time with our children, we miss out on the invaluable lessons that we can learn from being with them and seeing the world through our children's eyes. John Greenleaf Whittier captured it when he wrote, "We need love's tender lessons taught as only weakness can; God hath His small interpreters, the child must teach the man." Many of us need to get back to that special place where we learn the lessons that only our children can teach us.

Parents who ignore the research findings put their children at greater risk. Obviously, some children are resilient enough to overcome the disadvantages, and some mothers have no other options; but many parents, learning of the risks involved, will want to make lifestyle changes that will enable the mother to be at home with her children most of the time and away from them no more than ten hours a week. Loving parents are unwilling to expose *their* children to unnecessary risks. It is said often that quality, not quantity, of time spent together is what matters most; however, as it relates to the well-being of children and families, *quantity* of time and *quality* of time seem to be of equal importance and to go hand in hand.

Notes

1.   Rich Lowry, "Dodd's bogey," *National Review*, (March 23, 1998), http://www.articlearchives.com/government-public-administration/government-bodies/644973-1.html (accessed March 14, 2009).
2.   Lee Grant, "Confronting the Crisis: Child Care in America," *Parade,* April 11, 1999.
3.   U.S. Department of Labor, Bureau of Labor Statistics, unpublished tabulations from the Current Population Survey, Annual Social and Economic Supplement, 1976-2007.
4.   The White House (Clinton), Council of Economic Advisors, "The Economics of Child Care" (December 1997) and "Child Care," The U.S. House Ways and Means Committee Green Book (2000): 571-632, both found through The Almanac of Policy Issues website, http://www.policyalmanac.org/social_welfare/archive/child_care_economics.shtml.
5.   Jay Belsky, "Infant Daycare: A Case for Concern?" *Zero to Three: Bulletin of the National Center for Clinical Infant Programs* 7, nos. 1-5 (September, 1986-June 1987): 1-7.
6.   T. Berry Brazelton and Stanley Greenspan, *The Irreducible Needs of Children: What Every Child Must Have to Grow, Learn and Flourish* (New York: Da Capo Press, 2001).

7. Ibid., 26.
8. NICHD Early Child Care Research Network, "Does amount of time spent in child care predict socioemotional adjustment during the transition to kindergarten?" abstract of article found in *Child Development* 74 (2003): 976-1005, https://secc. rti.org/abstracts.cfm?abstract=33.
9. Jessica Garrison, "Toddlers' Time in Child Care Linked to Behavior Problems," *Los Angeles Times*, April 19, 2001, http://articles.latimes.com/2001/apr/19/news/mn-52933.
10. Ibid.
11. Rebecca Camber, "Strain of work is pushing families to breaking point," *The Daily Mail*, November 1, 2008, http://www.dailymail.co.uk/news/article-1082267/Strain-work-pushing-families-breaking-point.html.
12. Deborah Lewis and Charmaine Yoest, *Mother in the Middle* (Grand Rapids, Michigan: Zondervan Publishing House, 1996), Back cover.
13. Janice Shaw Crouse, "The Perennial Child Care Crisis," Concerned Women for America, August 29, 2007, http://www.cwfa.org/articles/13761/BLI/commentary/index.htm; and Fight Crime: Invest in Kids, "One in Five Women are Deciding against or Delaying Having a Child Because of the High Cost of Child Care and Preschool, Poll Shows," press release, August 14, 2007, http://www.fightcrime.org/releases.php?id=347.
14. Ibid.
15. U.S. Bureau of the Census, "Nearly Half of Preschoolers Receive Child Care from Relatives," press release, February 28, 2008, http://www.census.gov/Press-Release/www/releases/archives/children/011574.html.
16. Brian M. Riedl, "The Myth of the Child Care Crisis," The Heritage Foundation, *Backgrounder Report* No. 1649 (May 2, 2003): Executive Summary, http://www.heritage.org/research/welfare/bg1649.cfm.
17. Adam Carasso, Gillian Reynolds, and C Eugene Steuerle, "How Much Does the Federal Government Spend to Promote Economic Mobility and for Whom?" The Economic Mobility Project: An Initiative of the Pew Charitable Trusts (February 4, 2008): 17. http://www.urban.org/UploadedPDF/411610_economic_mobility.pdf.
18. Family and Home Network, "Recent Surveys and Opinion Polls Regarding Work/Family Balance," 2002, http://www.familyandhome.org/media/Media_pr_surveys.htm.
19. Ibid.
20. Monique Laberge, "Children's Health Encyclopedia: Personality Development," Answers.Com, 2009, http:/www.answers.com/topic/personality-development.
21. National Association of Child Care Resource and Referral Agencies, "Child Care in America" (2009 Fact Sheet): 1, http://www.naccrra.org/randd/.
22. National Association of Child Care Resource and Referral Agencies, "New Research on Brain Development is Important for Parents," *The Daily Parent* 1 (NACCRRA copyright 2009), http://www.childcareaware.org/en/subscriptions/dailyparent/volume.php?id=1.
23. Mary Eberstadt, *Home Alone America: The Hidden Toll of Day Care, Behavioral Drugs and Other Parent Substitutes*, (New York: Sentinel, 2004).
24. Ibid., 1 and Back Matter.
25. Ibid.
26. Historians claimed that the modern feminist movement alienated black women because of its emphasis on "freeing women from motherhood." The following reference is only one page of over forty pages. Laura Hussey, "Are Social

Welfare Programs Pro-Life? A Study of Low-Income Mothers," http://www.allacademic.com//meta/p_mla_apa_research_citation/1/3/8/8/3/pages138835/p138835-6.php.

27.   Marilyn Elias, "Day care raises shy toddlers' levels of stress hormone," *USA Today,* July 15, 2003.

28.   *Child Care Safety Checklist for Parents and Child Care Providers*, (Washington, DC: U.S. Consumer Product Safety Commission), http://*www.cpsc.gov/cpscpub/ pubs/childcare.pdf (accessed March 15, 2009).*

29.   David M. Bell, Dennis W. Gleiber, Alice Atkins Mercer, Robi Phifer, Robert H. Guinter, A. Jay Cohen, Eugene U. Epstein, Manoj Narayanan, "Illness Associated with Child Day Care: A Study of Incidence and Cost," *American Journal of Public Health* 79, no. 4 (April 1989): 479-84.

30.   Rome Neal, "The Negative Effects of Childcare?" *cbsnews.com*, July 17, 2003. http://www.cbsnews.com/stories/2003/07/16/earlyshow/living/parenting/printable563639.shtml.

31.   Brian Robertson, *There is No Place Like Work,* (Dallas, TX: Spence Publishing Company, 2000), 26.

32.   Kathryn Hooks, "'Hands-On' Love," Concerned Women for America, July 8, 2003.

33.   Dana Mack, *The Assault on Parenthood,* (New York: Simon and Schuster, 1997), 182.

34.   Lewis and Yoest, *Mother in the Middle*, 142.

35.   Ibid., 183.

36.   U.S. Department of Health and Human Services, "The NICHD Study of Early Child Care and Youth Development: Findings for Children Up to Age Four-and-a-Half Years," National Institute of Child Health and Human Development, NIH Pub. No. 05-4318 (January 2006): 17-25, http://www.nichd.nih.gov/publications/pubs/upload/seccyd_051206.pdf.

37.   Jay Belsky and Michael J. Rovine, "Nonmaternal Care in the First Year of Life and the Security of Infant-Parent Attachment," *Child Development* 59, no. 1 (February 1988): 157-167, http://www.jstor.org/pss/1130397.

38.   American Psychological Association, "Study Finds that Child Care Does Impact Mother-Child Interaction," press release, November 7, 1999.

39.   U.S. Department of Health and Human Services, "The NICHD Study," 25.

40.   Erin Parker, "The Effects of Maternal Employment on a Child's Language and Cognitive Development, and Academic Achievement," (doctoral dissertation, Lamar University, n.d.): 1-4. http://dept.lamar.edu/lustudentjnl/Archived%20Editions_files/The%20Effects%20of%20Maternal%20Employment%20on%20a%20Chil ds%20Language%20an%C3%A0.pdf.

41.   Ibid.

42.   Yvonne Roberts, "Official: babies do best with mother," *The Observer*, October 2, 2005. http://observer.guardian.co.uk/uk_news/story/0,6903,1583072,00.html.

43.   Ibid.

44.   Alexandrea Frean, "Child Care is Bad for your Baby, Working Parents are Warned," TimesonLine (U.K.), December 11, 2008, http://www.timesonline.co.uk/tol/life_and_style/health/child_health/article5321524.ece.

45.   Mark Easton, "Selfish Adults Damage Childhood," *BBC News*, February 2, 2009, http://news.bbc.co.uk/go/pr/fr/-/2/hi/uk_news/education/7861762.stm.

46.   Robertson, *There is No Place Like Work*, 26.

47.   Ibid., 27.

48.   Ibid., 25.

49. Abby Simons, "Bloomington mom, daughter indicted in day-care death," *Star Tribune* (Minneapolis-St. Paul,) February 30, 2009, http://www.startribune.com/templates/print_this_story?sid+39991927.

50. Jay F. Marks, "Case will move ahead in Custer County baby's day care death," *NewsOK* (online version of *The Oklahoman*), March 5, 2009, http://newsok.com/case-will-move-ahead-in-custer-county-babys-day-care-death/article/3350568.

51. Jan Null, "Fact Sheet: Hyperthermia Deaths of Children in Vehicles," San Francisco State University, Department of Geosciences, February 27, 2009, http://ggweather.com/heat/.

52. Ann Pleshette Murphy and Jennifer Allen, "Summer Child Care for Working Moms," *ABC News*, June 14, 2006, http://abcnews.go.com/print?id=2073583.

53. Edward L. Schor, editor-in-chief, American Academy of Pediatrics, *A Complete and Authoritative Guide: Caring for Your School Age Child Ages 5-12,* (New York: Bantam Books): 328.

54. Ibid., 411-412.

55. Ibid., 42.

56. DisneyFamily.com, "Latch-Key Kids," ParentPedia: What the Experts Say, http://family.go.com/parentpedia/school-age/milestones-development/children-latch-key-kids/ (accessed March 8, 2009).

57. Census Bureau, "Nearly Half of Preschoolers."

58. Robertson, *There is No Place Like Work*, 12.

59. John Schwartz, "That Parent-Child Conversation is Becoming Instant, and Online," *The New York Times*, January 3, 2004, http://query.nytimes.com/gst/fullpage.html?res=9C03E7DC1731F930A35752C0A9629C8B63.

60. Jennifer Burk, "Phone Home: More College Students Talking to Parents Regularly," Young Money.com, December 18, 2006, http://secure.youngmoney.com/show?print_article.175.

61. KidsData, "Parent Reports of How Children Spend Their Time: 2006," Lucile Packard Foundation for Children's Health, August 2006, http://www.kidsdata.org/parentpoll/.

62. Robert Pear, "Married and Single Parents Spending More time with Children, Study Finds," *The New York Times*, October 17, 2006, http://www.nytimes.com/2006/10/17/us/17kids.html?ex=1318737600&en=b&4912d675c16e7&ei=5088&partner=rssnyt.

63. Ibid.

64. Laura Pappano, "The Power of Family Conversation," *Harvard Education Letter* 24, no. 3 (May/June 2008), http:/www.edletter.org/insights/familyconversation.shtml.

65. Ibid.

66. Ibid.

67. Sandra L. Hofferth, "Major Changes in How American Children Spend Their Time," University of Michigan Institute for Social Research, Panel Study of Income Dynamics, Child Development Supplement, (1997), http://www.scienceblog.com/community/older/1998/D/199803338.html.

68. Ibid.

69. Amy Molnar, "Married Mothers Spend More Time with Their Children than Single Mothers," *Medical News Today*, November 25, 2008, http://www.medicalnewstoday.com/articles/130735.php. (Journal article: Sarah Kendig and Suzanne Bianchi, "Single, Cohabiting, and Married Mothers' Time with Children," *The Journal of Marriage and Family* 70, Issue 5 [December 2008]: 1228-1240.)

70.   Gary Langer, "Poll: Work, Worry and Accomplishment Define Mothering," analysis of the ABC News/Good Housekeeping Poll, *ABC News*, April 7, 2006, http://abcnews.go.com/print?id=1813264.
71.   Rachel Mahaffey and Eva Arlia, "Career or Family?" Concerned Women for America, October 18, 2004.
72.   Leslie Bennetts, "Will you Regret Staying Home with Your Baby?" *Glamour Magazine*, March 1, 2007, http://www.glamour.com/sex-love-life/2007/03/stay-at-home-mom.
73.   U.S. Bureau of the Census, Current Population Survey, Detailed Family Income Tabulations for 1999, Tables FINC-03 and FINC-=04 (March 2000).
74.   Ibid.
75.   Langer, "Poll: Work and Worry."
76.   Lynda Laughlin, "Child Care Constraints among America's Families," U.S. Bureau of the Census, Housing and Household Economics Statistics Division, unofficial report, 2008. http://www.census.gov/population/www/socdemo/child/child-care-constraints.pdf.
77.   Melinda Ligos, "Personal Business: Child Care Woes can make for a Sticky Summer," *The New York Times*, April 27, 2003. http://query.nyties.com/gst/fullpage.html?res=9907EED8163DF934A15757COA9659C8B63.
78.   Murphy and Allen, "Summer Child Care for Working Moms."
79.   Ligos, "Personal Business."
80.   "Fact Sheet: Summer Child Care Arrangements," based on, Jeffrey Capizzano, Sarah Adelman, Matthew Stagner, "What Happens When the School Year is Over? The Use and Costs of Child Care for School-Age Children during the Summer Months," Occasional Paper 58, The Urban Institute, June 2002.
81.   Ibid.
82.   Jeffrey Capizzano and Gina Adams, "The Number of Child Care Arrangements Used by Children under Five: Variation Across States," New Federalism: National Survey of America's Families, Series B, Number B-12, March 2000, http://www.urban.org/publications/310268.html.
83.   Lynda Laughlin, "Sex and the City: Why Women and Families Matter," Greater Greater Washington Blog, posted February 20, 2009, http://greatergreaterwahsington.org/author.cgi?username-lynda.
84.   Ibid.

Nothing you do for children is ever wasted. They seem not to notice us, hovering, averting our eyes, and they seldom offer thanks, but what we do for them is never wasted.
—Garrison Keillor

10

Childhood Obesity

It is in the news...everybody is talking about it; facts are accumulating and concern is mounting. Three of five Americans are overweight; one in five is obese.[1] There is broad general agreement that childhood obesity has reached epidemic proportions in America; Dr. David Ludwig of Children's Hospital Boston calls it a "tsunami" of childhood obesity.[2] The *Journal of the American Medical Association (JAMA)* reports that the rates for childhood obesity have tripled during the past three decades.[3] Because of obesity-related health issues—such as high blood pressure, heart disease, stroke, and diabetes—researchers conclude that life expectancy over the coming decades could decline by two to five years.[4]

Among health professionals, there is genuine concern that the social, economic, and human behaviors that have contributed to the childhood obesity epidemic threaten long-term "medical, psychosocial and financial consequences" beyond America's capacity to respond.[5] And it is not just an American problem. Some experts see childhood obesity as a global challenge.[6] The World Health Organization (WHO) estimates are that nearly one in six of the world's population is overweight—that is more than a billion people—outnumbering those who are under-nourished.[7]

Overweight kids have become an all-too-common reality. Numerous sources estimate that approximately 40 percent of American children are either overweight or obese;[8] since the mid-1970s the obesity rate for young children (ages two to five) and youth (ages twelve to nineteen) tripled and for older children (ages six to eleven), the obesity rate quadrupled.[9] That's about 110 million children now classified as overweight or obese.[10]

With at least 300,000 deaths per year and nearly $100 billion in economic costs per year attributable to obesity, Americans must come to grips with the problem and find a solution.[11] Indeed, four of the top ten causes of American deaths—coronary heart disease, diabetes, stroke, and cancer—have "well-established links" to what Dr. Michael Pollan calls our "national eating disorder."[12]

In fact, a June 2006 online survey of over two thousand adults indicated that fully 84 percent of the population sees childhood obesity as a "major problem."[13] And the problem is not static, but continues growing.

> Weight-related illnesses once limited mostly to adults, such as Type 2 diabetes, high blood pressure, liver problems, and premature heart disease, now are being diagnosed in teens. If this trend continues, today's children could be the first in generations to enjoy shorter life expectancies than their parents do. As such, it is no surprise that the United States Surgeon General has identified obesity as "the fastest growing cause of disease and death in America."[14]

Certainly, the American Heart Association (AHA) realizes the problem. In 2002 the AHA released a statement about arteriosclerosis beginning in childhood and warned the public about the dangers of poor diet and little exercise.[15] The *New England Journal of Medicine (NEJM)* also declared that the worldwide epidemic of childhood obesity was "progressing at an alarming rate," that risk factors for coronary heart disease are already identifiable in overweight children, and that higher BMIs in childhood are associated with coronary heart disease in adulthood.[16] Such warnings are very timely.

Parents cannot simply assume that their children will naturally outgrow "baby fat" as they mature. This is bad news for the 22 million overweight children under age five. Duane Alexander, director of the Institute of Child Health and Human Development at the National Institutes of Health, reports that children typically will not lose their extra weight as they get older.[17] Alexander is not alone; numerous studies have found that obese children tend to become overweight adults; they also tend to have the medical conditions that go along with obesity: heart disease, high blood pressure, stroke, and diabetes.[18] Neville Rigby, policy director for the International Obesity Taskforce, noted that the "childhood obesity time bomb has already exploded" with increasing numbers of children falling victim to type-two diabetes, a condition usually associated with overweight adults.[19]

A recent study published in the medical journal, *Pediatrics*, provides the "strongest evidence to date" that adult obesity is connected to being overweight as a child. Philip R. Nader, the lead researcher, explained that this study focused on one thousand children from ethnically diverse and economically disadvantaged households and followed them at regular intervals from ages two through twelve. The basic finding was that if toddlers or young children are overweight at least once, they are 5 times more likely to be overweight at age twelve; and the more times they are overweight, the greater the likelihood that they will be overweight at twelve. A child's weight in elementary school is an even stronger predictor for being overweight in junior high: being overweight once as a child means being 25 times more likely to be overweight at twelve, overweight 3 times in elementary school means more than three hundred times more likely to be overweight at twelve years old. [20]

There is agreement around the world that the easy availability of junk food increases obesity. Gerald Hastings, Stirling University, Scotland, a spokesperson for the 10th International Congress on Obesity (a conference held every four years for more than two thousand academic and health professionals) said, "No one can deny there is a link between food marketing and children getting fatter." Hastings added that the extensive commercial advertising of "energy-dense foods such as confectionery and soft drinks" pushes children toward unhealthy diets.[21] Over half of Americans believe that the government should play a more active role in regulating the food industry's marketing focused toward children and that the government should take companies to court if they misrepresent and mislead children about the nutritional value of foods.[22]

At the top of parents' concerns is the type of food available to children at school. The majority of adults (83 percent) believe that unhealthy foods (snack foods, sugary soft drinks, and fast foods) should be limited.[23] One-third of parents also think that zoning regulations should put fast-food restaurants off-limits near schools.[24] Already, ten states have banned the sale of junk food at schools—some just until after lunch, others all day.

Science supports parental concerns about junk food. And with good reason since Americans reportedly eat one in five meals in cars and one in three children eats fast food *every day*![25] Some endocrinologists argue that junk food by its very composition—high-calorie, low fiber—encourages children to overeat. A study in an endocrinology journal reported that bad diets create a "toxic environment" that "dooms children to being overweight."[26] According to Dr. Robert Lustig, the lead researcher of the endocrinology study, highly processed foods are "essentially addictive" and create hormonal imbalances that stimulate children to overeat.[27]

Until we make changes in their diet, our children will continue to be "overfed and undernourished."[28] Researchers cite other problems with a junk food diet, claiming that high levels of triglycerides in teenage girls can lead to what they call "metabolic syndrome" with a greater risk for heart disease and diabetes.[29]

The campaign against junk food is going worldwide; a group of international obesity experts is calling for a global ban on advertising junk food. The International Obesity Taskforce is asking the World Health Organization (WHO) to take the lead against the "exploitative marketing techniques" aimed at children by the fast food, junk food, and sugary children's cereal industries.[30]

In early 2007, The Federal Communications Commission chairman, Kevin J. Martin, and commissioners Deborah Taylor Tate and Michael J. Coops, together with Senators Sam Brownback (R-KS) and Tom Harkin (D-IA), worked together to form a Task Force on Media and Childhood Obesity with a broad range of representatives from the public and private sectors. They assembled a panel of media moguls, food industry giants, celebrities, advertising and marketing geniuses, beverage company executives, consumer advocacy leaders, health experts, and leaders of nonprofit organizations devoted to children's well-being. I was privileged to serve on the "Media and Childhood Obesity" task force of distinguished individuals, and our responsibility was to work together to address the many dimensions of the issue and to recommend action on the epidemic of childhood obesity. We were tasked with recommending serious and concrete efforts to mitigate the impact of marketing in the media on children's health and well-being.

We reviewed the data and analyzed the situation; we heard reports from those most aware of the realities and challenges facing those who want to work effectively at finding solutions. The Kaiser Family Foundation issued a report reviewing more than forty studies of the role of media in the nation's dramatically increasing rates of childhood obesity. One of their major conclusions is that "children's exposure to billions of dollars worth of food advertising and marketing in the media may be a key mechanism through which media contributes to childhood obesity." Estimates indicate that $10 to $15 billion is spent annually on food advertising targeting children—over $3 billion a year on fast food advertising alone.[31] Marketing executives know where the money is: studies estimate that children under twelve years of age spent $35 billion of their own money and influenced over $200 billion of their household spending in

2004.[32] Children determine their preferences and make their demands based on viewing over 200,000 commercials in around 15,000 hours of television viewing during their childhood and adolescence.[33]

Dr. David Ludwig of Children's Hospital, Boston has compiled a twenty-five-point obesity index that is appalling. Since 1950, there has been a 500 percent increase in the consumption of soft drinks. Over 50 percent of school districts today have contracts with beverage companies to sell soft drinks on school property, yet a single soft drink per day over time increases a child's risk for obesity by 60 percent. In 1970, only 2 percent of a child's daily calories came from fast food; today it is more than 10 percent. Food advertising targeting children totals in excess of $10 billion, yet the entire federal budget for nutrition education is only one-fifth the costs for advertising one popular-with-kids product—Altoids mints! Yet, as noted earlier, estimates of the direct costs of obesity to the American economy exceed $100 billion.[34]

At the same time that children are consuming more "empty" calories, they are also getting less exercise. Many factors have combined to foster a more sedentary lifestyle, even for children. In many communities, children are not allowed to walk or ride bicycles to school. Numerous schools have eliminated recess and physical education from the school day. At home, the children are watching more television and playing video games for longer and longer amounts of time during the day. Twenty-six percent of American youth watch four or more hours of television a day. More than half (57 percent) of American children have a television in their bedroom, nearly 40 percent (39) have video game equipment, 30 percent have a VCR, 20 percent have a computer, and 11 percent have Internet access in their rooms.[35] A large number of studies in childhood obesity cite having a television in a child's bedroom as linked closely to children being overweight or obese.[36] And with television, of course, comes a virtual barrage of advertising.

Numerous experts in the fields of pediatrics and public health have identified advertising, especially television advertising, as one of the "most pernicious" factors driving the alarming increases in childhood obesity. In fact, the Institute of Medicine found that there is strong evidence that television advertising of foods and beverages has a direct effect on what children choose to eat.[37] Children aged eight to twelve years old see the most television commercials (twenty-one per day, fifty-one hours a year). Kids thirteen to seventeen years old see seventeen ads a day in forty-one hours a year of viewing, and even youngsters ages two to seven see twelve food ads a day, or thirty annual hours worth. Most of these ads (34 percent for candy, 28 percent for cereal, and 10 percent for fast food) are for junk food, only 4 percent are for dairy products, and 1 percent for fruit juices.[38]

One of the most controversial aspects of advertising in children's programming is having program characters and hosts featured in commercials that run during the program in which they appear. Another is the practice of having well-known cartoon characters featured in commercials during a children's program. It is important to note that experts agree that children under age six cannot distinguish between programming content and advertising.[39] The message is clear: since young children cannot separate the cartoon character from the product being advertised, psychologists criticize the practice of mixing the program content with the advertising.

A further challenge for the Media and Childhood Obesity Task Force was determining the extent of our recommendations regarding regulation because cable television is often a worse offender than the networks. The three major advertisement-supported cable networks (ABC Family, Cartoon Network, and Nickelodeon) have the highest food ad time—32 percent of their total advertising (compared to 13 percent of the advertising time on the major networks). Anyone who has observed even a limited amount of children's programming will not be surprised by the fact that half (50 percent) of all advertising time on children's shows is food advertising.[40] There is no question that the nation's children are significantly influenced by the extent and type of advertising and that it represents a significant public health threat to children.

The task force was reminded that the Federal Communications Commission has been involved in children's television issues for more than forty-five years. As early as 1960, television broadcasters were admonished to recognize the "particular needs of children." Specifically, the FCC is responsible for both providing excellent educational and informational programming for children as well as to protect children from "excessive and inappropriate commercial messages." And, in the Children's Television Act of 1990, Congress declared that children are uniquely susceptible to the persuasive messages contained in television advertising.[41] The Kaiser Family Foundation estimates that children view between 4,400 and 6,000 ads per year, and a large number of these messages are for foods lacking in nutritional value—mostly candy, sugary cereals, junk food, and fast food.[42]

A few broadcasters (Disney, for example) are to be commended for incorporating healthier messages into their children's programming. And at least some advertisers are voluntarily taking steps to counter the flood of television advertising for unhealthy foods. In November 2006, ten of the largest food and beverage companies, including McDonald's, General Mills, and Kellogg's, promised that half of their advertising directed to children would promote healthier food and encourage more active lifestyles. Earlier, Kraft foods promised to conform their advertising to good nutritional standards. The Kellogg Company announced in June 2007 that it would phase out advertising its products to children under twelve unless the foods meet specific nutrition guidelines for calories, sugar, fat, and sodium. They also promised to stop using licensed characters and branded toys to promote foods that do not meet the nutritional guidelines. Their decision will affect about half of their products, including Froot Loops, Rice Krispies, Apple Jacks, and Pop-Tarts. Their action stalls out two lawsuits threatened against them by the Center for Science in the Public Interest and the Campaign for a Commercial-Free Childhood.[43]

Such cooperation by food manufacturers is necessary to turn around the onslaught of advertising for products that provide poor nutrition to children. To date, however, positive efforts are falling short. Advertising continues to overpower the educational and informational broadcasting that benefits children, and the positive efforts have not limited the overwhelming amount of advertising that can have a negative influence on children's food choices.

Currently, the Children's Television Act (CTA) contains restrictions on the amount of allowable advertising to children—only 10.5 minutes per hour on weekends and no more than 12 minutes per hour on weekdays. The law provides for modification (with due process) "in accordance with the public interest."[44] In fact, the American Academy of Pediatrics recommends limiting advertisements during children's programming to no more than five to six minutes per hour (which, amazingly, would cut the advertising *by half*.) [45]

In addition, the CTA already provides potential control over programming through its license renewal process to encourage more wholesome, kid-friendly fare in children's programming. Further, the CTA's provisions are meant to encourage three hours of "safe spaces" for children's television viewing. If a broadcaster airs at least three hours a week of core educational programming (having as a "significant purpose" to provide regular programming that meets the educational and informational needs of children), its license renewal can receive Media Bureau staff approval rather than have to go through full commission approval.[46] An alert reader will notice that these provisions do not affect advertising; there exists a conflict between the programming (which can have positive impact) and the program's advertisements that can undercut its educational and informational value for the child. The Federal Communications Commission has no authority to revoke the licensing of those programs where such contradictions exist.

In another symbolic action, Nickelodeon has joined with the Boys and Girls Clubs of America and the Alliance for a Healthier Generation over the past four years to sponsor a "Let's Just Play" campaign. In addition to public service announcements (PSAs) and more than three thousand local events, Nickelodeon went dark from noon to 3 p.m. to encourage kids to go outside and play. Nickelodeon also committed more than $30 million and 10 percent of their airtime to promoting health and wellness messaging. Nickelodeon also awarded approximately $2 million in grants for after-school programs. An estimated fifty thousand kids participated in an educational program to promote healthier lifestyles.[47]

Lest we heap too much praise on these laudatory actions and the compliance with the restrictions on television advertising, we should note that the timing coincides with the increased popularity of the Internet with children and adolescents. With more kids and teens moving from television to the Internet, advertising is also moving in that direction where the marketing of junk food is unregulated; even video games are used to sell products. The International Association for the Study of Obesity (IASO) is calling for an all-inclusive ban on advertising of junk food to children because of the intense marketing currently prevalent in both television and the internet.[48] The Kaiser Family Foundation's research indicates that 85 percent of businesses advertising to children on television also had interactive websites for children promoting their branded products. In one three-month monitoring project, over twelve million children visited websites promoting food and beverage products. Almost two-thirds (64 percent) of the sites use viral marketing—the children are encouraged to send emails to their friends about the product.[49]

For further information on the nation's progress in preventing childhood obesity, the Institute of Medicine of the National Academies reports on ways that families, schools, industries, the media, communities, and government can work together to address the rising rates of obesity in children and youth. They also examine the progress made by obesity-prevention initiatives over the past two years and outline steps for future efforts.[50] They recommend focusing on prevention, evaluating current policies and programs for effectiveness, monitoring progress, and disseminating promising practices through cooperative efforts among government, industry, communities, schools, and families.

Certainly, any solution to childhood obesity must include reforming the nation's sedentary lifestyle. Evidence is accumulating that monitoring "screen time" is just as important as monitoring television. With the increased use of video games and surfing the internet, parents must broaden their concern. The *Journal of Pediatrics* describes "screen time activities" (including television, DVDs, computers, and video games) as encouraging inactivity and consumption of junk food. They cite the recommendations from The American Academy of Pediatrics that children should watch no more than two hours of television or computer screens per day, boys should take at least thirteen thousand steps a day and girls should take at least eleven thousand steps per day.[51]

Research studies reveal that a child's taste for protein-rich foods (meat and fish) is inherited. On the other hand, a child's taste for vegetables and desserts is an acquired taste that can be influenced. Parents then should offer a variety of vegetables and healthy foods, like fruit, for dessert. Dr. Leonard H. Epstein, who has researched childhood obesity issues for over thirty years and is at the Department of Pediatrics at the State University of New York at Buffalo (SUNY-AB), developed a "Traffic Light Diet" for children.[52] The diet links food to the three colors of a traffic light. Red indicates high-calorie foods that should be eaten rarely. Yellow denotes moderate-calorie foods that can be eaten occasionally. Green is for low-calorie foods that can be consumed freely. This kind of practical approach can be easily used and, thus, is very effective in teaching children good nutritional habits.

Finally, we must recognize the connection between the breakdown of the family and childhood obesity. While obesity organizations have stopped referring to "the national retreat from family life" as an influence in the trends toward obesity or to the "rarity" of the homemaking mother as a reason for the "frequency of fast-food eating" among American families, they do encourage the family to work together toward good nutrition. They try to persuade families to sit down together over dinner rather than grab fast food to eat in the car coming home from work after picking up the kids at school or day care. The American Obesity Association (AOA) recommends that parents and children re-establish the practice of "preparing food together" so that "children can learn about healthy cooking and food preparation." They encourage eating at regular times, without other activities such as television occupying the family's attention and without rushing through the meal. They recommend limiting fast-food eating to no more than once a week.[53]

There is a demonstrable link between poor children and unhealthy children. Writing in *Pediatrics*, Dr. David Wood chronicles the connection between the phenomenal increase in the number of single-parent, female-headed households and the rising number of poor children and children who are unhealthy and have poor nutrition[54]—which could influence the dramatic increase in the number of children who are overweight or obese.

USA Today reports that the America on the Move Foundation found that 71 percent of children get information about how to be healthy from their mothers, while only 43 percent get that information from their fathers.[55] An even more noteworthy finding relates to an unexpected ramification of the breakdown of the family and comes from the researchers at the national Centers for Disease Control and Prevention (CDC). Their Pediatric Nutrition Surveillance System tracked over 177,000 children and learned that "the rate of overweight at 4 years of age was highest among children who were never breastfed" or were breastfed for less than a month. The protective effect of prolonged breastfeeding was especially strong for non-Hispanic white children. Thus, the CDC recommends breastfeeding infants for at least a full year in order to counter the childhood obesity "epidemic."[56]

The flip side of the childhood obesity epidemic is the increase in bulimia, anorexia, and body image disorders among children, teens, and young women. It is ironic that while we worry legitimately about childhood obesity we must also be concerned that so many normal weight teenagers, especially girls, falsely perceive themselves as overweight. Teenagers' desire to be thin produced an annual "Eating Disorders Awareness Week" that tries to bring some reality to perceptions about the ideal woman's figure. They point out that Marilyn Monroe, considered one of the most beautiful women in history, was a size 14[57] and that the average American woman is 5'4" and weighs 140 pounds. That makes the fashion models, typically around 5'11" and weighing only 117, thinner than 98 percent of American women.[58] This disparity is made all the greater by the practice of distorting perceptions of what is natural and beautiful by "photo shopping" the pictures of models to make them appear to have Barbie-like dimensions and flawless features.

The conventional wisdom is that negative comments about a child's weight can have long-lasting impact, especially comments by a mother or father.[59] Parents and siblings are cautioned to not make derogatory comments about a child's body shape or weight.[60] Parents are advised to focus on healthy eating and an active lifestyle rather than on a child's weight control. Miles Goldstein, a therapist at an eating disorders clinic, told a *Washington Post* reporter that he always advises parents not to address weight issues.[61] Joanna Chakerian added, "Often a parent's comment can be very destructive. Our comments don't save our daughters from distress; more often than not, they contribute to their struggles with their body images."[62]

Instead of talking about body image or weight, parents should promote healthy meals so that children will have the energy necessary for physical activity, sports, and learning.[63] A study in *Pediatrics* revealed that both boys and girls are especially attuned to their fathers' attitudes about thinness/lack of fat; if thinness is very important to the father, the children are apt to become constant dieters.[64]

While parental attitudes and cooperation are tremendously important, parents alone cannot change the bigger picture of childhood obesity. To reverse the swelling tide of childhood obesity we will have to have political leadership at every level of government in combination with leadership coming from the private sector and the advocacy community. It has to be clear that children's health *must* take precedence over private or corporate profit. In addition, cultural changes must be a priority. We must all work together—parents, school nutritionists, primary care physicians, advertising and food industry leaders, and celebrities—for a fundamental shift in the social environment so that healthy eating and an active lifestyle are the norm.

Dr. David Ludwig, Children's Hospital Boston, says, "If we were to reverse environmental factors back to those of the 1960s, most of the obesity epidemic would disappear."[65] He notes:

> In the past 40 years, fast food, junk food and soft drinks have become a prominent part of the landscape. Further, food advertising directed at children has exploded, and portion sizes have ballooned. Schools have become purveyors of fast food and soft drinks through contracts with the food and beverage industry that help fund school programs—even as they cut physical education classes from their curricula to save money. At the same time, children are becoming more sedentary, spending more time watching TV and using computers.[66]

We can't return to the 1960s, and few of us would want to do so; but if we are to turn back the epidemic of obesity, we must reform our lifestyle and return to some of those attitudes and values. We have to learn to live with this era's stresses for our sake as well as for our children's sake. During tough times and stressful situations people are more likely to sacrifice nutrition by eating fast food—"it's inexpensive, tasty and immediately gratifying, things we all like when we're stressed about other issues."[67] One school authority recalled a situation in which a preschooler accompanied his mother when she came to the school for a consultation with a teacher: "The little boy was carrying his breakfast: a bag of Cheez Doodles and a sugary soda. The mother explained that she was running late and they didn't have time for a meal."[68] Parents are the grocery gatekeepers; they are the ones who stock the pantry and determine the snacks that are available to the children in the house.

Despite the challenges, there is a lot of optimism among pediatric health personnel. Dr. Mark Jacobson, a member of the American Academy of Pediatrics' task force on obesity, believes that the problem of childhood obesity can be reversed because it is now finally on "everybody's radar screen" and because there has been a "huge outpouring of commitment from schools, government, public health agencies, private industry, medical groups and parents."[69]

My experience with the media and obesity task force led me to a different view. There was an abundance of symbolic action, but few people or organizations are taking substantive or effective actions. The plain fact is that a lot of money, jobs, and company bottom lines are involved in the products and lifestyles that are associated with kids gaining weight. Sadly, we are a long way from agreement about the best way to address the issue of childhood obesity. In the meantime, parents have to be reminded that, when it comes to their kids, "the buck stops" with parents.

Notes

1. George Will, "Where the Obesity Grows," *The Washington Post*, (March 8, 2009), http://www.washingtonpost.com/wp-dyn/content/article/2009/03/06/AR2009030602070.html (accessed March 19, 2009).
2. Children's Hospital Boston, "Explosion of child obesity predicted to shorten U.S. life expectancy," press release, March 16, 2005, http://www.eurekalert.org/pub_releases/2005-03/chb-eoc031605.php.
3. Jeffrey P. Koplan, Catharyn T. Liverman, and Vivica I. Kraak, "Preventing Childhood Obesity: Health in the Balance," *The Journal of the American Medical Association,* 295, No. 8 (February 22, 2006): 941, http://jama.ama-assn.org/cgi/content/extract/295/8/maxtoshow=&HITS=10&hits=10&RESULTFORMAT=&fulltext=childhood+obesity&searchid=1&FIRSTINDEX=0&resourcetype=HWCIT (March 19, 2009).
4. Children's Hospital Boston, "Explosion of child obesity."

5.   Risa Lavizzo-Mourey, "Childhood Obesity: What it means for Physicians," *Journal of the American Medical Association* 298, no. 8 (August 22-29, 2007): 920-922, http://jama.ama-assn.org/cgi/content/extract/298/8/920.

6.   Anna M.G. Cali and Sonia Caprio, "Obesity in Children and Adolescents," *The Journal of Clinical Endocrinology and Metabolism* 93, no. 11, Supplement 1s31s36 (November 2008), http://jcem.endojournals.org/cgi/content/abstract/93/11_Supplement_1/s31 (accessed March 19, 2009).

7.   Malcolm Burgess, "Banning Junk Food Ads May Help in Fat Fight," *Daily News and Independent Online* (South Africa), September 5, 2006, http://www.dailynews.co.za/index.php?fSectionId=3532&fArticleId=qw1157443201701B223 (accessed March 19, 2009).

8.   Steven M. Schwarz and Michael Freemark, "Obesity," eMedicine: Pediatrics, updated November 1, 2007, http://emedicine.medscape.com/article/985333-overveiw.

9.   Institute of Medicine of the National Academies, "Progress in Preventing Childhood Obesity: How Do We Measure Up," Report Brief (September 2006): 1, http://www.iom.edu/?id=36999.

10.   Cali and Caprio, "Obesity in Children."

11.   Christine L. Williams Laura L. Hayman, Stephen R. Daniels, Thomas N. Robinson, Julia Steinberger, Stephen Paridon, and Terry Bazzarre, "AHA Scientific Statement: Cardiovascular Health in Childhood," *Circulation 106*, no. 1 (July 2, 2002): 143-160, http://circ.ahajournals.org/cgi/content/full/106/1/143.

12.   Will, "Where the Obesity Grows."

13.   Beckey Bright, "More Americans See Childhood Obesity as Major Problem in U.S., Poll Finds," *Wall Street Journal,* July 5, 2006, http://online.wsj.com/article/SB115190208989196887.html?mod=health_home_inside_today_left_column&csid (accessed March 19, 2009).

14.   Edward J. Markey, Chairman, House Subcommittee on Telecommunications and the Internet, letter to the Federal Communications Commission, April 16, 2007, 1, http://markey.house.gov/docs/telecomm/Letter%20to%20FCC%20on%20Childhood%20Obesity.pdf (accessed March 19, 2009).

15.   Williams, et al., "AHA Scientific Statement."

16.   Jennifer L. Baker, Lina W. Olsen, and Thorkild I. A. Sorensen, "Childhood Body-Mass Index and Risk of Coronary Heart Disease in Adulthood," *The New England Journal of Medicine* 357, no. 23 (December 6, 2007): 2329-2337, http://content.nejm.org/cgi/content/full/357/23/2329 (accessed March 19, 2009).

17.   Lorraine Heller, "More Evidence Links Obesity in Early Childhood and Later Life," foodnavigator-usa.com, September 7, 2006, http://www.foodnavigator-usa.com/Science-Nutrition/More-evidence-links-obesity-in-early-childhood-and-later-life (accessed March 19, 2009).

18.   Ibid.

19.   Fiona Macrae, "Children Falling Victim to Adult Diabetes," *Daily Mail* (U.K.), February 27, 2006, http://www.dailymail.co.uk/health/article-378393/Children-falling-victim-adult-diabetes.html# (accessed March 19, 2009).

20.   Philip R. Nader, Marion O'Brien, Renate Houts, Robert Bradley, Jay Belsky, Robert Crosnoe, Sarah Friedman, Zuguo Mei, and Elizabeth J. Susman, "Identifying Risk for Obesity in Early Childhood," *Pediatrics* 118, no. 3 (September 2006): e594-e601. http://pediatrics.aappublications.org/cgi/content/abstract/118/3/e594?maxtoshow=&HITS=10&hits=10&RESULTFORMAT=&fulltext=september+2006+obesity+health+harm&searchid=1&FIRSTINDEX=0&sortspec=relevance&resourcetype=HWCIT (accessed March 19, 2009).

21. Burgess, "Banning Junk Food Ads."
22. Bright, "Childhood obesity is major problem."
23. Ibid.
24. Ibid.
25. Will, "Where the Obesity Grows."
26. University of California, San Francisco, "Childhood obesity caused by 'toxic environment' of western diets, study says," press release, August 11, 2006, http://pub.ucsf.edu/newsservices/releases/200608105/ (accessed March 19, 2009).
27. University of California, "Toxic Environment."
28. Will, "Where the Obesity Grows," quoting Dr. Michael Pollan.
29. Reuters Health News, "Heavy Teen Girls Risk Metabolic Syndrome," redOrbit.com, November 25, 2005, http://www.redorbit.com/news/health/314170/heavy_teen_girls_risk_metabolic_syndrome/# (accessed March 19, 2009).
30. Burgess, "Banning Junk Food Ads."
31. Kaiser Family Foundation, "Kaiser Family Foundation Releases New Report On Role Of Media In Childhood Obesity" press release, February 24, 2004, http://www.kff.org/entmedia/entmedia022404nr.cfm and Kaiser Family Foundation, "The Role of Media in Childhood Obesity," Issue Brief (February 2004): 5, http://www.kff.org/entmedia/upload/The-Role-Of-Media-in-Childhood-Obesity.pdf (accessed March 19, 2009).
32. Ibid.
33. *Children's Television Act of 1990,* Public Law 101-437, codified at U.S. Code 47 (1990), §303a.
34. Dr. David Ludwig, "An Obesity Index," reproduced in Children's Hospital Boston press release, "Explosion of child obesity."
35. Emory H. Woodard, IV, "Media in the Home 2000: The Fifth Annual Survey of Parents and Children," The Annenberg Public Policy Center of the University of Pennsylvania (2000), 3, http://www.annenbergpublicpolicycenter.org/Downloads/Media_and_Developing_Child/mediasurvey/survey7.pdf (accessed March 19, 2009).
36. U.S. Centers for Disease Control and Prevention, "Going Behind the Screens," Youth Media Campaign, press release, August 1, 2007, http://www.cdc.gov/Youth-Campaign/pressroom/PDF/6.2.09-ScreensBG.pdf (accessed March 19, 2009).
37. Institute of Medicine, Committee on Food Marketing and the Diets of Children and Youth, *Food Marketing to Children and Youth: Threat or Opportunity?* (Washington, DC: The National Academies Press, 2005), http://iom.edu/CMS/3788/21939/31330.aspx (accessed March 19, 2009).
38. Walter Gantz, Nancy Schwartz, James R. Angelini, and Victoria Rideout, "Food for Thought: Television Food Advertising to Children in the United States, "Kaiser Family Foundation (March 2007): 3, http://www.kff.org/entmedia/7618.cfm (March 19, 2009).
39. Kaiser Family Foundation, "The Role of Media," 8.
40. Ibid.
41. *Children's Television Act of 1990.*
42. Gantz et al., "Food for Thought," 18.
43. Andrew Martin, "Kellogg to Phase Out Some Food Ads to Children, *The New York Times,* June 14, 2007, http://www.nytimes.com/2007/06/14/business/14kellogg.html (accessed March 19, 2009).
44. *Children's Television Act of 1990.*
45. American Academy of Pediatrics Committee on Communications, "Policy Statement: Children, Adolescents, and Advertising," *Pediatrics* 118, no. 6,

(December 2006), 2563-2569, http://pediatrics.aappublications.org/cgi/content/full/118/6/2563 (accessed March 19, 2009).

46. "Educational and informational programming for children," Title 47 Code of Federal Regulations, Part 73, §73.671(c), http://cfr.vlex.com/vid/73-671-educational-informational-programming-19852061 (accessed March 19, 2009).

47. PRNewswire, "Nickelodeon Expands Partnership with Boys and Girls Clubs of America for Let's Just Play Campaign," redOrbit.com, September 12, 2006, http://www.redorbit.com/news/health/653640/nickelodeon_expands_partnership_with_boys__girls_clubs_of_america/index.html (accessed February 13, 2009).

48. International Association for the Study of Obesity (IASO), "Obesity Experts Back Junk Food Marketing Ban," press release, March 15, 2008, http://www.iotf.org/IASOmarketingreleaseMarch1508.htm (accessed March 19, 2009).

49. Kaiser Family Foundation, "First Analysis of Online Food Advertising Targeting Children," press release, July 19, 2006, http://www.kaiserfamilyfoundation.org/entmedia/entmedia071906nr.cfm (accessed March 19, 2009).

50. Institute of Medicine, Committee on Progress in Preventing Childhood Obesity, *Progress in Preventing Childhood Obesity: How Do We Measure Up?* (Washington, DC: The National Academies Press, 2007), http://www.iom.edu/?id=36999 (accessed March 19, 2009).

51. *The Journal of Pediatrics*, "Study Suggests Too Much Screen Time and Not Enough Physical Activity May Lead to Childhood Obesity," press release, April 16, 2008, http://www.jpeds.com/webfiles/images/journals/ympd/JPEDS_Laurson3.pdf (accessed March 19, 2009).

52. Susan M. LoTempio, "When Bigger Isn't Necessarily Better," *UB Today: A Publication of the University of Buffalo Alumni Association,* (Winter 2009): 13-16, http://www.buffalo.edu/UBT/features/probingObesity.php (accessed March 19, 2009).

53. American Obesity Association, "Childhood Obesity" (last updated May 2, 2005), http://obesity1.tempdomainname.com/subs/childhood/prevention.shtml (accessed March 19, 2009).

54. David Wood, "Effect of Child and Family Poverty on Child Health in the United States," *Pediatrics* 112, no. 3 (September 2003): 707-712, http://pediatrics.aappublications.org/cgi/reprint/112/3/S1/707 (accessed March 19, 2009).

55. Nancy Hellmich, "Danger signs of child obesity," *USA Today*, September 13, 2006, http://www.usatoday.com/news/health/2006-09-12-childhood-obesity_x.htm (accessed March 19, 2009).

56. The Howard Center for Family, Religion and Society, "Fat Chance," *New Research* 18, Issue 04 (April 2004). http://www.profam.org/pub/nr/nr_1804.htm (accessed March 19, 2009).

57. Kelly Nault, "Teenage Girls + Media = Low Self-Esteem," *EzineArticles.com.* http://ezinearticles.com/?Teenage-Girls-+-Media-=-Low-Self-Esteem&id=96389 (accessed February 3, 2009).

58. National Eating Disorders Organization, "Fact Sheet: National Eating Disorders," May 2008, http://www.nationaleatingdisorders.org/uploads/file/in-the-news/NEDA-In-the-News-Fact-Sheet(2).pdf (accessed March 19, 2009).

59. Abigail Natenshon, "Parental Influence Takes Precedence over Barbie and the Media," Empowered Parents website, undated, http://www.empoweredparents.com/1prevention/prevention_09.htm (accessed March 19, 2009).

60. Jennifer Huget, "Watch What You Eat, Yes. But Also Watch What You Say and Do around Your Daughter," *The Washington Post,* March 3, 2009, http://www.

washingtonpost.com/wp-dyn/content/article/2009/03/02/AR2009030201756.html (accessed March 19, 2009).

61.   Joanna Chakerian, "An Innocent Word Can Be a Heavy Burden," *The Washington Post*, February 24, 2009, http://www.washingtonpost.com/wp-dyn/content/article/2009/02/23/AR2009022302368_pf.html (accessed March 19, 2009).

62.   Huget, "Watch What You Eat."

63.   Rosie Schwartz, "The Flip Side of Childhood Obesity," *The National Post (Canada)*, April 21, 2008, http://www.canada.com/topics/bodyandhealth/story.html?id=57c2bfec-a1c4-4e34-b6a6-1d9a73525cc5 (accessed March 19, 2009).

64.   Alison E. Field, Carlos A. Camargo, Jr., C. Barr Taylor, Catherine S. Berkey, Susan B. Roberts, and Graham A. Colditz, "Peer, Parent, and Media Influences on the Development of Weight Concerns and Frequent Dieting Among Preadolescent and Adolescent Girls and Boys," *Pediatrics* 107, no. 1 (January 2001): 54-60, http://pediatrics.aappublications.org/cgi/content/abstract/107/1/54 (accessed March 19, 2009).

65.   Children's Hospital Boston, "Explosion of child obesity."

66.   Ibid.

67.   Tedd Mitchell, "Beware of Recession Obesity: Don't Risk Your Children's Health to Save a Few Bucks," Health Smart, *USA Weekend,* March 8, 2009, http://www.usaweekend.com/09_issues/090308/090308healthsmart-recession-health.html (accessed March 19, 2009).

68.   Hellmich, "Danger signs of child obesity."

69.   Ibid.

Children have never been good at listening to their elders,
but they have never failed to imitate them.
—James Baldwin

11

Health, Safety, and Behavior

Exuberant, high energy health is generally the norm in early childhood; the absence of good health in children is especially distressing. Indeed, few things melt the hearts of people like a sick or injured child. This was brought home to me recently when a beloved child in our extended family, Lily, was diagnosed with leukemia. We are learning things that nobody wants to know. More than ten thousand cases of cancer occur annually among children under fifteen years of age. Each year there are about 1,500 cancer deaths among children, and one-third of them are from leukemia.[1] The most shocking thing I've learned is that research on childhood cancer is atrociously underfunded. According to Kristin Conner, Executive Director of CURE Childhood Cancer, "Pediatric cancer receives only 2 percent of all federal research dollars targeted for cancer research."[2] We see ribbons for all sorts of diseases, like AIDS and breast cancer. But there is far too little awareness of the paucity of funds for childhood cancer, which is second only to car accidents as the number one killer of children.[3]

In Lily's case, a mother and a father are sacrificing their careers for the three years that she will need treatment, so that they can provide the intensive and often around-the-clock care that she needs to survive. Grandparents and other relatives are providing a supportive network and encouragement. Her family is doing everything that they can do to ensure that she gets the very best care possible.

Not all children get that kind of care, and there is nothing that can replace a family's devotion and commitment: nobody loves a child with the same fierce intensity as his or her parents. The government can only do so much. Taxpayer funding can only do so much. The case of young Deamonte Driver illustrates that point.

In a rare but tragic case in Maryland, Deamonte Driver, a twelve-year-old boy died on February 25, 2007 from a severe brain infection caused by the bacteria from an infected tooth.[4] Deamonte's story illustrates the problems facing many children who lack a married mother-father family. Even though his family was eligible for Medicaid coverage, the Driver family's coverage had lapsed. The never-married mother explained that three of her five sons had gone to stay with their grandparents in a two-bedroom mobile home while the paperwork to confirm their eligibility was mailed to the shelter where they used to live. Deamonte's bill for two weeks at Children's Hospital was expected to be between $200,000 and $250,000;[5] he also had more than six weeks of additional medical treatment as well as physical and occupational therapy at another hospital. So, although an $80 tooth extraction[6] would probably have taken care of the original problem and saved his life, neither he nor his brothers had received routine dental attention. The problem? No one had taken care of the paperwork necessary for treatment.

Less than one-third of Maryland children who were eligible under Medicaid saw a dentist in 2005. Deamonte's death was a "shocking wake-up call" that prompted a "flurry of legislation" to correct what everyone is calling "the failures of our health care system."[7] Health official, Harry Goodman, told a newspaper reporter, "We got everything we asked for." Indeed, the Maryland legislature appropriated another $7 million in state funds, to be matched by federal funds.[8]

Tragic cases like Deamonte's cause heartbreak, but pouring more money into federal bureaucratic programs doesn't solve situations like this. Federal systems can only do so much. It makes us feel better to spend more, but does it work? Why do we continue to think that increasing the federal bureaucracy will take care of problems?

This failure of publicly funded health care occurred despite recent increases in federal Medicaid spending—an increase of $146 billion from 2000 to 2007[9]—proving that merely spending more dollars will not solve the problem. The whole approach to services must be reformed in order to achieve better coordination and responsive service for the nation's poor. Nor will monetary increases, even in the billions of dollars, help if fraudulent spending at both the state and federal levels is not addressed. Those who vote for increased Medicaid funding are, as Senator Mike Pence said, "...well-intentioned. But their plans would expand a failed government culture that has neglected the poor Americans it is supposed to serve. Throwing more taxpayer money at a structurally flawed program is not an audacious hope. It is a false one."[10]

We are already spending a fortune, and still children like Deamonte continue to fall victim to the overwhelming problems facing never-married mothers. Often these mothers, like Deamonte's mother, have multiple children and no father (or fathers) around. In the dozens of stories about Deamonte, there is no mention of a father. Most unmarried mothers who try to make it on their own do so typically with inadequate education and resources; in too many cases they lack a support system to provide backup help in times of crisis. These moms need all the support and encouragement that our welfare system was designed to provide, and, though many try valiantly to make the cumbersome system work, it too often fails. At the same time, we need to increase awareness among young girls and women of the overwhelming difficulties and almost insurmountable problems inherent in single motherhood.

Further, we need to restore the cultural expectation that marriage precedes having children and that fathering a child obligates a man to marry the mother of his child so that he is there to provide the help that both the mother and the child need—not just for health and survival, but also to thrive in all dimensions of the good life promised by democratic society.

All citizens have a vested interest in seeing that the nation's children have every advantage to stay healthy—nutritious food, good hygiene, protection from harm or injury, immunizations, and plenty of exercise. And, when they are ill, all of us want the very best of care along with the most cutting-edge research into prevention and cures for those illnesses that strike children. Good health starts with good preventive care.

Immunizations

Health experts recommend an immunization series that protects against diphtheria, tetanus, whooping cough, measles, hepatitis B, and polio. These diseases are among the dreaded diseases that used to be common in childhood. Now the public schools require proof of vaccination before children can enroll; this ensures that parents take care of children's immunization to protect each of them, but also to protect the other children in their community as well. It is important that all children get the appropriate vaccines because in some countries where the immunization rate has declined, the diseases have come back to cause ravaging epidemics.[11]

Before vaccinations began in the 1930s, over 150,000 people a year contracted diphtheria, and the disease killed over 15,000 people a year in the U.S.[12] Before the measles vaccine was introduced in 1962, almost 500,000 cases of measles were reported in the U.S.; gradually those numbers dropped until, by 2005, there had only been 405 cases in this century.[13] But measles is still a problem in other countries. About 23 million people around the world get the disease, and about 480,000 die from measles every year.[14] With international travel quite common, the disease continues to threaten people the world over. During the 1950s polio was rampant, paralyzing children by the thousands. By the end of the 1970s, after the Salk and Sabin vaccines were widely used, polio was eradicated in the U.S.[15]

Hepatitis A and Hepatitis B are liver diseases that formerly were very common. The "A" version does not cause long-term illness or damage, but about one hundred people a year die from the disease. The "B" version can become chronic, about one million American citizens are chronically infected with Hepatitis B, and about four to five thousand die each year from it.[16]

The World Health Organization began a worldwide program of vaccinations against smallpox in 1967, and twelve years later the disease had been wiped out; now smallpox is the only disease to be "eradicated from the Earth."[17]

A respected international medical journal, *Lancet*,[18] evaluated the impact of global vaccination initiatives and discovered that foreign governments have overstated their compliance with immunization agreements. Some of the poorer countries with the greatest risk "overstated their gains by four-and-fivefold."[19] The Global Alliance for Vaccines and Immunizations (GAVI) gave out almost double the amount earned for performance awards to nations (compared to what they were entitled to receive based on their actual compliance with expectations). Instead of paying out $290 million, they should have paid only $150 million.[20] An official with GAVI, also funded by the Gates Foundation, said, "All we can say is that there is over-reporting, and the over-reporting occurs in the presence of financial incentives."[21]

The Centers for Disease Control announced in September 2007 that childhood immunization rates in the U.S. remained at or near record highs.[22] With a record 81 percent of children getting the full set of vaccinations[23] (ranging from a high of 91 percent in Maryland to a low of 63 percent in Nevada) an estimated thirty-three thousand lives per year are saved in the U.S. [24] Despite those gains, more than 20 percent of America's children are not "fully immunized against the infectious diseases to which they are especially vulnerable."[25]

Environmental Pollutants

Children are more vulnerable to environmental pollutants than are adults; in addition, their exposure to air pollution during childhood can lead to respiratory problems when they are adults. Because the population is concentrated in urban areas with high levels of vehicular traffic and industrial zones, 55 percent of the nation's children live in a county where air pollution is an issue (that is, however, down from 65 percent in 1999).[26] Further, one in three U.S. public schools is in a "danger zone" for air pollution—within a quarter mile of highways serving as major trucking routes, where diesel exhaust particles produce environmental pollutants.[27] In some metropolitan areas, almost half of the student population attends school where there is a potentially increased risk for asthma and other chronic respiratory problems.[28] Over the past twenty years, there's been a significant rise in the prevalence of asthma in children—by 2006, 9 percent of children had asthma[29] and most of them will have allergic triggers. The annual cost of pediatric asthma attributable to the environment is about $2 billion.[30] The 2006 Surgeon General's report noted that 60 percent of America's children (nearly twenty-two million) are exposed to secondhand smoke. In a special report in 2007, the Surgeon General joined with the American Academy of Pediatrics, the Environmental Protection Agency, and the Administration for Children and Families to alert the public to the fact that secondhand smoke causes premature death and disease in children.[31] Many children's health problems—like bronchitis, pneumonia, earache, sudden infant death syndrome, and respiratory problems—can be traced to living where they breathe secondhand smoke.[32]

Many warnings have been given regarding children's exposure to lead; it can have a harmful impact on a child's central nervous system and sufficient contact with it can result in learning and behavior problems.[33] Even though lead is outlawed in products now, some lead-based products still exist (particularly in imported products from countries where the prohibition against the use of lead based paints is not rigorously enforced) and can cause problems.[34] But the latest report from the Centers for Disease Control and Prevention shows very substantial improvement in the number of children with high lead levels compared to twenty years ago, "even in historically high-risk groups for lead poisoning."[35] Federal researchers found that just 1.4 percent of children had high lead levels in 2004, while 9 percent did as recently as 1988. They are crediting the drop to the removal of lead from gasoline, a trend that began in the 1970s, along with reducing children's exposure to lead in house paint, soil, and water.[36]

Water and Housing

The U.S. Environmental Protection Agency monitors public water systems and requires them to meet federal health-based standards. However, about 15 percent of the population receives drinking water from private water systems that are not regulated.[37] That reminds me of a time when I was a child and we lived briefly in a small middle-American town. The water supply for our house was from a rainwater cistern and we didn't like the taste, so for months we hauled drinking water from a well across the street where the water tasted wonderful. After six months or so, my parents had the water tested: our cistern water was pure, but the well water was polluted. Obviously the taste of water is not always a sufficient indicator of its potability.

The annual "National Ground Water Awareness Week" is usually the second week of March; during that time, the EPA reminds the public that underground formations and aquifers supply water to more than 90 percent of all public drinking water systems. It serves as a timely reminder of the need to protect the nation's underground sources of water.[38]

Today, less than 5 percent of American children live in physically inadequate or crowded housing (compared to 9 percent in 1978). Having passed that milestone does not mean, however, that there are no problems with children's housing. Today, the problem is likely to be the cost burden of the housing; severe cost burdens—exceeding 50 percent of the family's income—affect 45 percent of very-low-income renters with children.[39]

In recent years, there has been the increase in run-away children and homeless children. The National Center on Family Homelessness (NCFH) released a 220-page report in March, 2009, indicating that one in 50 American children is homeless—that is about 1.5 million children, a little over half of whom are black (55.2 percent).[40] With the economic crisis of 2009, knowledgeable researchers are projecting that child homelessness will be the worst since the Dust Bowl Era or the Great Depression. It is noteworthy that 75 percent of homeless children are accounted for by only eleven states.[41] NCFH aptly summarized the conditions experienced by homeless children saying they "endure a lack of safety, comfort, privacy, reassuring routines, adequate health care, uninterrupted schooling, sustaining relationships, and a sense of community." These influences, reported NCFH, combine to "create a life-altering experience that inflicts profound and lasting scars."[42] Given the billions spent on the financial bailout, the report asks, "What does it say about our country that we are willing to bail out banks, but not our smallest, most vulnerable citizens?"[43]

Dental Care

In recent years, we have learned much about the importance of good dental care for children's overall health and well-being. Data from the Centers for Disease Control cites tooth decay as one of the most common chronic infectious diseases among U.S. Children.[44] (Recall the story of Deamonte Driver in the introduction of this chapter.) Fortunately, most children (76 percent) begin regular dental care by going to the dentist once a year after age three, but the percentage drops to 68 percent among children in poor families.[45] Nevertheless, more than one-fourth of U.S. children ages two through five and half of those twelve through fifteen have cavities. Among low-income families and ethnic and racial minorities, the numbers go up dramatically.[46] In total, Americans spent over $102 billion on dental services in 2008.[47] Parents today have better information about the importance of caring for children's teeth, even baby teeth; most know that drinking sweet drinks is harmful to tooth enamel—the sugar and the acid are equally destructive. Many parents, however, are not taking advantage of the new developments in dental care for children. Only one in three U.S. schoolchildren has received dental sealants that protect them from cavities.[48]

Health Care

There has been a constant barrage of news items about the number of children not having health insurance and, of course, no one wants to see children denied the health care that they need. But the data shows that 88 percent of the children in America were covered by health insurance at least some time during 2006, down one point from 2005.[49] Private health insurance provided coverage for 65 percent, and public health insurance covered 30 percent.[50] Public health insurance is primarily Medicaid, but it also includes other programs (Medicare, SCHIP—the State Children's

Health Insurance Programs, CHAMPUS/Tricare—the program for members of the armed forces and their dependents). Nine percent of children in poor and 8 percent of those in near-poor families had "no usual source of health care" with older children more likely to lack care than younger ones.[51] While most of those children could have access to Medicaid, their parents did not avail themselves of those services.

As is obvious from the tragic death of Deamonte Driver and the numerous others like him who have died untimely deaths, having access to health services—preventive care, health education, appropriate and timely screenings and immunizations, as well as sick care—is important for children to remain healthy.

Crimes against and by Children

The rate of serious violent crimes against children has declined by more than two-thirds since the peak (forty-four per thousand in 1993 and fourteen per thousand in 2005).[52] Males are more likely than females to be victims of serious crimes; black youth are more likely to be victims than white youth, and older teens are more likely than younger ones to be victims of violent crimes.[53]

The rate of youths committing serious violent crimes (aggravated assault, rape, robbery) in 2005 was seventeen crimes per thousand juveniles ages twelve through seventeen. That rate has dropped by two-thirds since the peak in 1993 (fifty-two crimes per thousand juveniles).[54] Youths in this age bracket are more than twice as likely as adults to be victims of serious violent crimes; but, like the rate of commission of crimes by youths, the rate of victimization has fallen sharply (fourteen crimes per thousand juveniles aged twelve through seventeen in 2005) since 1993.[55]

Accidental Injury and Death

Fatal injuries to children have declined over the past two decades, but they are still the leading cause of death for children up to age fourteen. Non-fatal injuries remain the major cause of disability for children. For every fatal injury, there are 33 hospitalizations and 1350 emergency room visits. Falling, striking something after tripping or falling, or being struck by an object are the leading causes of children's injuries. Other common injuries include poisoning, being cut or pierced, and traffic accidents.[56]

Injury is the cause of 80 percent of adolescent deaths, including those from automobile accidents and firearms. Non-fatal injuries to adolescents are more likely to be related to violence (24 percent assaults), sports-related activities (39 percent), or traffic accidents instead of falls as is typical of younger children. For each fatal injury to an adolescent, there are eleven hospitalizations and nearly three hundred emergency room visits.[57] While one-third of adolescent poisonings (a small number, only six visits per thousand) are unintentional, more than half are self-inflicted and about one-third of those require hospitalization.[58]

Death rates for children from all causes—injuries, cancer, birth defects, homicide, heart disease, pneumonia—have dropped by half since 1980. Of these adolescent deaths, more than half are from motor vehicle accidents and firearm injuries; others are from poisoning and drowning. The homicide rates for adolescents remained at 9 deaths per 100,000. Firearms accounted for four of five homicides and nearly half of all suicides.

Tragically, parents need to be aware of the fact that suicide is now the third leading cause of death for children ages 10-14 (1.3 deaths per 100,000) followed by homicide (1 death per 100,000)[59] and that among teenagers 15-19 the rate climbs to 8 deaths per 100,000. Suffocation, mainly from hanging, accounted for 40 percent of suicides,[60] and boys are more likely to be successful in their attempts than are girls. Parents also need to be aware of the wide variety of causes for suicide attempts as well as the symptoms indicating that a teen might be a risk.

While there are numerous references in popular literature in recent years attributing teen suicide to adolescent struggles with homosexuality, the data does not bear out those claims. The National Alliance on Mental Illness,[61] suicide prevention organizations,[62] and numerous psychologists and health workers cite substance abuse, divorce of parents, parental unemployment, household financial problems, isolation from family or friends, rejection by a boyfriend or girlfriend, domestic violence or abuse, lack of success at school, and depression as the most common causes for a teen suicide. More than 90 percent of teens will give clear warning signs that they are contemplating taking his or her own life; these warnings should be taken seriously.[63]

Behavior

The well-being of children and adolescents is often affected by their own immature or dysfunctional behavior, including illegal and high-risk activities, substance abuse behaviors (smoking, alcohol, and drug use) and sexual activity.

- Smoking among adolescents has dropped dramatically (about half) since the late 1990s. It is the lowest today that it has been since the inception of the survey that measures the rate of teen smoking.[64] Among 8th graders, smoking has decreased from 10 percent in 1996 to only 3 percent in 2007. Among 10th graders, smoking has dropped from 18 percent in 1996 to 7 percent in 2007. With 12th graders, the drop was from 25 percent in 1997 to 12 percent in 2007.[65] A March 2009 study reported that twelve-year-old students whose parents allow them to watch R-rated movies are more likely to say that it is easy for them to get cigarettes. The researchers question whether those children were influenced because of their parents' permissive parenting style, allowing activities that are not age appropriate, or because they viewed smoking scenes in the movies.[66]

- Alcohol use is associated with some of the worst outcomes for adolescents (car accidents, injuries, death, problems in school, fighting, crime, and other serious consequences). Heavy drinking at a single occasion (five or more alcoholic beverages in a row) or in a brief period (two weeks) is especially problematic. Again, white and Hispanic teens are more likely to abuse alcohol than are black teens.[67] The good news is that heavy drinking has declined among teenagers. Among 8th graders, drinking declined from 15 percent in 1995 to 10 percent in 2007. Among 10th graders, it declined from 24 to 22 percent and among 12th graders, from 30 to 26 percent.[68]

- Drug use is especially dangerous for teens; it can have disastrous short-term and long-term consequences. Use dropped in the early 1990s and then surged upward in the late 1990s; it is just now approaching the lower levels of the early 1990s. This is good news because all these levels dropped a percentage point from 2006 to 2007. Now, illicit drug use "during the past 30 days" has declined from 15 to 7 percent of 8th graders, 23 to 17 percent of 10th graders, and 26 to 22 percent of 12th graders.[69]

The comprehensive report of official government data, *America's Children 2007*, has begun using the term "sexually transmitted infections" (STIs) instead of the term, "sexually transmitted diseases" (STDs) that was previous used. For over two years, I was a participant in former Surgeon General, Dr. David Satcher's, bipartisan and broadly left-right task force dedicated to creating a "Call to Action for Responsible Sexual Behavior."[70] At a task force retreat, I asked why there was a language change from STDs to STIs. The head of Planned Parenthood responded, saying that anybody can get an infection so the term STI was adopted in order to make sexually transmitted diseases sound less serious. Using the term "disease" scares people, especially teenagers, she replied and it makes them think they have a serious problem. Ironically, the task force voted to use the term "STD" because that term is preferred by the

CDC (participants noted that the World Health Organization promoted the term "STI").

The *America's Children 2007* report describes the consequences of adolescent sexual activity and emphasizes the desirability of teenage abstinence:[71]

> Early sexual activity is associated with emotional and physical health risks. Youth who choose abstinence avoid risks associated with sexual activity, such as contracting sexually transmitted infections (STIs) and becoming pregnant. STIs, including HIV, can infect a person for a lifetime and have consequences including disability and early death; meanwhile, delaying sexual initiation is associated with a decrease in the number of lifetime sexual partners, and decreasing the number of lifetime partners is associated with a decrease in the rate of STIs. Additionally, teen pregnancy is associated with a number of negative risk factors, not only for the mother but also for her child.

Parents will want to note that during the years when abstinence education was supported by federal funds, the rates of teen sexual activity, teen abortions, and teen pregnancies declined.[72] Since 1991, the CDC's Youth Risk Behavior Survey has monitored risk behaviors among students in grades 9 through 12, including sexual behaviors that the CDC characterizes as contributing to "unintended pregnancy and sexually transmitted diseases."[73] The same year the *2007 Child Stats* report waters down the language and refers to abstinence as means of avoiding "sexually transmitted infections"—not diseases but what it considers to be the less threatening term infection, which it at least admitted could "infect a person for a lifetime and have consequences including disability and early death."[74] But in the 2008 report, there is no mention of abstinence, only the use of contraceptive pills and condoms, and there is no mention of the fact that STIs can have lifetime consequences, merely the possibility that teens engaging in early sexual activity could contract sexually transmitted infections and become pregnant—gone is any hint of encouragement for teens to remain abstinent.[75] The diluting of the wording is all the more unfortunate in light of the fact that the 2006 birth data indicate that we are seeing an uptick in teen birthrates.[76]

While the number of students who report having had sexual intercourse declined from 1991 (54 percent), the rate leveled off to 47 percent in 2003 and hovered there until 2005.[77] The differences between grade levels are significant for 9th graders the rate is 34 percent, while for 12th graders it is 63 percent. Racial and ethnic differences also exist: the decline for whites was 50 to 43 percent, among blacks it was an 82 to 68 percent decline.[78]

Johns Hopkins University released a sociological study in 2007[79] confirming what pro-family groups have been saying for decades: that family instability correlates with bad behavior in children. They reported, "Children who go through frequent transitions are more likely to have behavioral problems than children raised in stable two-parent families and maybe even more than those in stable single-parent families."[80] The study—based on the National Longitudinal Survey of Youth (NLSY), a 21-year project focusing on women and their children—utilized a cognitive achievement test for children ages five to fourteen that catalogued their behavioral problems and related them to the children's home situation (marital and cohabitation changes). The authors report that a child undergoing three changes in family structure would have a behavioral problem score six points higher than a child would from a stable family structure. Multiple family transitions were linked with juvenile delinquency (vandalism, theft, and truancy). It is noteworthy that the study found that family transitions were also associated with lower scores in mathematics and reading. They found that white children were affected more deeply by family transitions than black children were.[81]

The bottom-line message for all Americans from research studies and the many trends we have examined, however, is quite clear: we must do all we can to strengthen the natural family and promote it among young people as the best household arrangement for raising healthy, well-developed children. It is only fair that young people, particularly those who are approaching parenthood, know the facts and understand that the data is clear in all the areas of children's well-being: children need a married mother and father to avoid many of the negative outcomes that have plagued the nation's children over the last four decades. There is nothing more important that we can do "for our children" than to teach these facts to the next generation's mothers and fathers.

Notes

1.   American Cancer Society, *Cancer Facts & Figures 2007*, http://www.cancer.org/downloads/STT/CAFF2007PWSecured.pdf (accessed March 12, 2009).
2.   Mary Welch, "Woman of Impact: Pediatric Cancer Fundraising Champion," *Atlanta Woman Magazine*, September 5, 2008, http://www.atlantawomanmag.com/Articles/2008/Web_October/Woman_Of_Impactx_Pediatric_Cancer_Fundraising_Champion.html (accessed March 12, 2009).
3.   Helen Jonsen, "Childhood Cancer: Where's the Money?" Commentary, *Forbes Magazine*, September 12, 2008, http://www.forbes.com/2008/09/11/pediatric-cancer-philanthropy-oped-cx_hj_0912jonsen_print.html For more see: http://townhall.com/columnists/JaniceShawCrouse/2009/01/12/learning_about_leukemia (accessed March 12, 2009).

4.   Mary Otto, "For Want of a Dentist," *The Washington Post,* February 28, 2007, http://www.washingtonpost.com/wp-dyn/content/article/2007/02/27/AR2007022702116.html.

5.   "Laura Owings, "Toothache Leads to Boy's Death," *ABC News*, March 5, 2007. http://abcnews.go.com/print?id=2925584.

6.   Ibid.

7.   Matthew Hay Brown, "Deamonte Driver, One Year Later," *Baltimore Sun.Com*, blog posting, February 25, 2008, http://weblogs.baltimoresun.com/news/politics/assembly/2008/02/deamonte_driver_one_year_later.html.

8.   "Deamonte Driver Didn't Die in Vain," Fact-esque, blog posting, April 28, 2008, http://casadelogo.typepad.com/factesque/2008/04/deamonte-driver.html.

9.   U.S. Department of Health and Human Services, Centers for Medicare & Medicaid Services, National Health Expenditure Data, "National Health Expenditures by type of service and source of funds, CY 1960-2007," http://www.cms.hhs.gov/NationalHealthExpendData/02_NationalHealthAccountsHistorical.asp#TopOfPage (accessed March 12, 2009).

10.   Rep. Mike Pence, "More Money Won't Assure Quality Care," *Investor's Business Daily,* editorial, March 6, 2009, http://www.ibdeditorials.com/IBDArticles.aspx?id=321238557281943.

11.   U.S. Centers for Disease Control and Prevention, "A Parent's Guide to Childhood Immunizations 2008," National Center for Immunization and Respiratory Disease, Department of Health and Human Services, (Washington, DC: GPO, 2007): 9, http://www.cdc.gov/vaccines/pubs/parents-guide/default.htm.

12.   Ibid., 16.

13.   Ibid., 9.

14.   Ibid., 15.

15.   Ibid., 10.

16.   Ibid., 16-17.

17.   Ibid., 10.

18.   Stephen S. Lim, David B. Stein, Alexandra Charrow, and Christopher J. L. Murray, "Tracking progress towards universal childhood immunisation and the impact of global initiatives: a systematic analysis of three-dose diphtheria, tetanus, and pertussis immunisation coverage," *The Lancet* 372, Issue 9655 (December 13, 2008): 2031-2046, http://www.thelancet.com/journals/lancet/article/PIIS0140-6736(08)61869-3/abstract?version=printerFriendly.

19.   David Brown, "Number of Children Immunized Has Been Inflated for Years," *The Washington Post*, December 12, 2008, http://www.washingtonpost.com/wp-dyn/content/article/2008/12/11/AR2008121103318_pf.html.

20.   Lim et al, "Tracking progress," Summary.

21.   Brown, "Number of Children."

22.   U.S. Centers for Disease Control and Prevention, "National Infant Immunization Week (NIIW) Background," Vaccines and Immunizations, 2009, www.cdc.gov/vaccines/events/niiw/2009/downloads/pr_docs/web-bckgrd-508.doc.

23.   U.S. Federal Interagency Forum on Child and Family Statistics, *America's Children in Brief: Key National Indicators of Well-Being, 2008* (Washington, DC: GPO, July 2008): 9, http://www.childstats.gov/pdf/ac2008/ac_08.pdf.

24.   Reuters News Service, "Record Number of U.S. Kids Vaccinated," September 5, 2008, found at http://tvnz.co.nzview/tvnz_story_skin/2059893.

25.   U.S. Centers for Disease Control and Prevention, "More than Twenty Percent of Children Not Fully Protected against Vaccine-Preventable Disease," press release, April 24, 2008, http://www.cdc.gov/media/pressrel/2008/r080424.htm.

26. *America's Children in Brief, 2008*, 10.
27. University of Cincinnati, "Many U.S. Public Schools in Air Pollution Danger Zone," Health News, news release, August 18, 2008, http://healthnews.uc.edu/news/print.php?id=7358.
28. Alexandra S., Appatova, Patrick H. Ryan, Grace K. LeMasters, and Sergey A. Grinshpun, "Proximal Exposure of Public Schools and Students to Major Roadways: A Nationwide U.S. Survey," *Journal of Environmental Planning and Management* 51, Issue 5 (September 2008): 631-646, http://www.informaworld.com/smpp/search~db=all?field1=all&searchmode=advanced&searchtitle=71342 9786&ssubmit=true&term1=health+risks+schools&vaa=1.
29. *America's Children in Brief, 2008*, 17.
30. National Environmental Education Foundation, *Environmental Management of Pediatric Asthma: Guidelines for Health Care Providers,* (Washington, DC: August 2005): 6, http://www.neefusa.org/pdf/AsthmaDoc.pdf.
31. U.S. Centers for Disease Control and Prevention, "Children and Secondhand Smoke Exposure," Office of Smoking and Health, National Center for Health Marketing, September 18, 2007, www.cdc.gov/features/childrenandsmoke.
32. Ibid.
33. Mayo Clinic Staff, "Lead Poisoning," MayoClinic.com, March 15, 2007, http://www.mayoclinic.com/health/lead-poisoning/fl00068.
34. U.S. Centers for Disease Control and Prevention, "General Lead Information: Questions and Answers," The National Center for Environmental Health, Lead Program, undated, http://www.cdc.gov/nceh/lead/faq/about.htm (accessed March 13, 2009).
35. Robert L. Jones, David M. Homa, Pamela A. Meyer, Debra J. Brody, Kathleen L. Caldwell, James L. Pirkle, and Mary Jean Brown, "Trends in Blood Lead Levels and Blood Lead Testing among U.S. Children Aged 1 to 5 Years, 1988 to 2004," *Pediatrics* 123, no. 3 (March 2009): e376-e385, http://pediatrics.aappublications.org/cgi/content/full/123/3/e376?maxtoshow=&HITS=10&hits=10&RESULTFORMAT=&fulltext=trends+in+blood+lead+levels&searchid=1&FIRSTINDEX=0&sortspec=relevance&resourcetype=HWCIT (accessed March 13, 2009).
36. Ibid.
37. U.S. Environmental Protection Agency, "Drinking Water and Health: What You Need to Know," Office of Water (Washington, DC: October 1999): 1-11, http://www.epa.gov/safewater/dwh/dw-health.pdf.
38. U.S. Environmental Protection Agency, "National Ground Water Awareness Week, March 9-14, 2009," Safewater, 2009, http://www.epa.gov/safewater/groundwater-awareness/index.html.
39. *America's Children in Brief, 2008*, 11.
40. The National Center on Family Homelessness, *America's Youngest Outcasts: State Report Card on Child Homelessness* (Newton, MA: 2009): Executive Summary, i. http://www.homelesschildrenamerica.org/pdf/rc_full_report.pdf (accessed March 13, 2009).
41. Ibid., Ten of those states are: Nevada, New Mexico, Texas, Arkansas, Louisiana, Mississippi, Georgia, Florida, North Carolina, and Kentucky.
42. Ibid., *America's Youngest Outcasts.*
43. Ibid.
44. James Cosgrove, "Medicaid: Concerns Remain about Sufficiency of Data for Oversight of Children's Dental Services," testimony before the Subcommittee on Domestic Policy, Committee on Oversight and Government Reform, U.S. House of Representatives, U.S. Government Accountability Office, Report#GAO-07-826T, May 2, 2007, http://www.gao.gov/htext/d07826t.html.

45. *America's Children in Brief, 2008*, 9.
46. U.S. Centers for Disease Control and Prevention, "Oral Health: Preventing Cavities, Gum Disease, and Tooth Loss," National Center for Chronic Disease Prevention and Health Promotion, modified March 3, 2009, under "Oral Health Problems are Common, Costly and Painful," http://www.cdc.gov/NCCDPHP/publications/AAG/doh.htm.
47. Ibid., under "Oral Health Problems are Costly."
48. Ibid., under "Oral Health Facts."
49. *America's Children in Brief, 2008*, 8.
50. Ibid.
51. U.S. Federal Interagency Forum on Child and Family Statistics, *America's Children in Brief: Key National Indicators of Well-Being, 2007,* (Washington, DC: GPO, July 2007): 23-24.
52. Ibid., 35.
53. Ibid.
54. *America's Children in Brief, 2008*, 13.
55. *America's Children in Brief, 2007*, 35.
56. Ibid., 36.
57. Ibid., 38.
58. Ibid.
59. Ibid, 37.
60. Ibid., 39.
61. National Alliance on Mental Illness, "Teenage Suicide," reviewed by Dr. David Shaffer and Dr. Rex Cowdry, November 1999, http://www.nami.org/Content/ContentGroups/Helpline1/Teenage_Suicide.htm.
62. Kevin Caruso, "Suicide Causes," Suicide.org, undated, http://www.suicide.org/suicide-causes.html.
63. Meenaz M. Munshi, "Facts about Teen Suicide: Causes of Teen Suicide," Buzzle.com, Mary 16, 2008, http://www.buzzle.com/articles/facts-about-teen-suicide-causes-of-teenage-suicide.html.
64. *America's Children in Brief, 2008*, 12.
65. Ibid.
66. Chyke A. Doubeni, Wenjun Li, Hassan Fouayzi, and Joseph R. DiFranza, "Perceived Accessibility of Cigarettes Among Youth: A Prospective Cohort Study," *American Journal of Preventive Medicine* 36, Issue 3 (March 2009): 239-242, http://www.ajpm-online.net/article/S0749-3797(08)00951-3/abstract.
67. *America's Children in Brief, 2007*, 43.
68. *America's Children in Brief, 2008*, 12.
69. Ibid., 13.
70. "Politically Divergent Groups Call for Dialogue about Sex," *The Washington Times,* May 18, 2006 (updated May 19, 2006), http://www.washingtontimes.com/news/2006/may/18/20060518-114121-4341r/print/.
71. *America's Children in Brief, 2007*, 44.
72. Janice Shaw Crouse, "Reducing Teen Pregnancies and Abortions," *Townhall.com,* September 8, 2008, http://townhall.com/columnists/JaniceShawCrouse/2008/09/08/reducing_teen_pregnancies_and_abortions.
73. U.S. Centers for Disease Control and Prevention, National Center for Health Statistics, *Health, United States, 2007,* (Washington, DC: GPO, November 2007): 477, http://www.cdc.gov/nchs/data/hus/hus07.pdf (accessed March 13, 2009).
74. *America's Children in Brief, 2007*, 45.
75. *America's Children in Brief, 2008*, 13.

76.   Joyce A. Martin, Brady E. Hamilton, Paul D. Sutton, Stephanie J. Ventura, Fay Menacker, Sharon Kirmeyer, and T.J. Matthews, "Births: Final Data for 2006," *National Vital Statistics Reports*, 57, no. 7 (January 7, 2009): 33, Table 4, http:// www.cdc.gov/nchs/data/nvsr/nvsr57/nvsr57_07.pdf (accessed March 13, 2009).

77.   Ibid.

78.   *America's Children in Brief, 2007*, 44.

·79.   Paula Fomby and Andrew Cherlin, "Family Instability and Child Well-Being," *American Sociological Review* 72, (April 2007): 181-204.

80.   Meg Jalsevac, "Study Shows Family Instability has bad Effect on Children's Behavior," LifeSiteNews.com, April 2, 2007, http://www.lifesite.net/Idn/2007/ apr/07040202.html.

81.   Fomby and Cherlin, "Family Instability."

I must study politics and war that my sons may have liberty to study mathematics and philosophy. My sons ought to study mathematics and philosophy, geography, natural history, naval architecture, navigation, commerce and agriculture in order to give their children a right to study painting, poetry, music, architecture, statuary, tapestry and porcelain.
—John Adams

12

Education

Today's technological society requires well-trained, highly skilled workers; the complexity of the modern world demands clear thinkers, highly developed logical ability, wide knowledge, discernment, and good judgment. Yet it is acknowledged—and very obvious—that our public schools are failing too many of the nation's children by not preparing them to meet even the most basic standards for being well educated or to compete for good paying jobs requiring skilled workers.

The cause of this deficiency is not a lack of money devoted to the task. In 2006, America spent $599 billion, or 7.4 percent of GDP, to educate the nation's children (about $10,800 per child in public and private elementary and secondary schools).[1] Yet, the sad and unavoidable fact is that (despite a 33 percent increase in spending per student in constant dollars since 1990 and a 10 percent decrease in the number of students per teacher) student achievement has, at best, remained essentially the same.

Former President George W. Bush promoted education through his "No Child Left Behind" program. In his final State of the Union Address, given on January 28, 2008, the president reported good news regarding the education of the nation's children, "Fourth and eighth graders achieved the highest math scores on record." He also reported that reading scores were on the rise (turns out, for 4th graders, only very slightly) with African American and Hispanic students posting all time high achievement scores. He didn't report that the reading scores for 8th graders during the No-Child-Left-Behind period, 2002 to 2007, fell slightly behind previous scores.[2] The world's remaining superpower cannot be satisfied with such meager achievements.

A friend of mine arrived in Washington, DC and went with great expectations to his first day on the job at the United States Department of Education. He was chagrined to see on the door where he was to enter, a sign warning, "The door be broke." That sign is emblematic of what's wrong with education in America.

What happened in our nation's schools when two decades ago America's children were among the best in test results? Oprah Winfrey, who hosts the most popular daytime show on television, said—in a 2006 interview with Bill and Melinda Gates that focused on education—that American schools are in "crisis." She cited a report from the Organization for Economic Cooperation and Development that American children now place 24th in math behind such diverse nations as Canada, Germany, France, Korea, Poland, Hungary, and Slovakia.[3] Just how difficult is the testing by which this ranking was established? Just look at this example of a 4th-grade mathematics test question used by The International Association for the Evaluation of Educational Achievement.

Al wanted to find how much his cat weighed. He weighed himself and noted that the scale read 57 kg. He then stepped back on the scale holding his cat and found that it read 62 kg. What was the weight of the cat in kilograms?

Only 60 percent of American students received full credit on their answers, which placed them in a tie with the Slovak Republic for the rank of 24th. The students from eleven countries had correct answers of 80 percent or better.[4]

Bill Gates, the founder of Microsoft and one of the world's richest men, describes American schools as obsolete, designed for 1956, and built for the industrial age—not the digital age. He and his wife, Melinda, lament that about one-third of students drop out of school (about half among minorities), and about 40 percent of those who go on to college have to do remedial work in order to compete successfully.[5] Since the average school has only one computer per five students, perhaps Mr. Gates could begin his reform efforts by providing the nation's schools with enough cutting-edge computers that all students could have access to the Internet and computing technology.

In a world economy, our graduates are too often ill-prepared to compete with those whose education is more rigorous; our graduates are too often not ready to contribute to their own or the nation's prosperity. Limited educational attainment produces a significant gap in earnings potential.

The Bureau of Labor Statistics reported that median weekly earnings in 2007 of someone with less than a high school degree was only 71 percent of that of a high school graduate; that median weekly earnings of a person with an associates degree was nearly 23 percent higher than that of a person with just a high school diploma; and that a person with a bachelor's degree earned 63 percent more than one with only a high school education.[6] These earnings differentials make huge differences in the long run. Analysts at the Census Bureau estimate that a high school graduate's career earnings would total $1.2 million (in 1999 dollars), compared with an associate degree graduate's earnings that would be about $1.6 million and a person with a bachelor's degree, who would likely earn $2.1 million.[7]

Further, poor education produces uninvolved citizens and a society without the manpower necessary for smooth and effective functioning. Also, the fault lines in the nation's schools are producing wide gaps in educational attainment between those whose school district is top quality and those whose schools are not performing to acceptable levels.

Better progress is necessary for American children to reach their full potential and for the economic and social advancement of the nation. But, the public schools face enormous challenges, with two primary ones being how to address both unmotivated and unmanageable students and the increasing diversity of the school population. According to the Department of Education's National Center for Education Statistics (NCES), there were some 3.7 million teachers engaged in classroom instruction of nearly 49.6 million children enrolled in public schools and 6.2 million in private schools in 2007.[8] This works out to an average of just over fifteen students per teacher—which is cause for doubting the perennial complaint that quality education is not possible because there are not enough teachers.

Based on data from the Parent Survey of the 1999 National Household Education Surveys Program (NHES) and the Parent and Family Involvement in Education Survey of the 2003 and 2007 NHES, analysts at the Department of Education estimate that the number of home-schooled children has increased by 77 percent from 1999 to 2007. Such rapid growth clearly speaks to a high level of parental dissatisfaction with the conditions in American schools.[9] Estimates of the total number being home schooled vary between the NCES's estimate 1.5 million in 2007 and the National Home Education Research Institute's estimate of as many as 2 million.

In 2006, ethnic and racial minorities constituted 43 percent of public school enrollment (compared to only 22 percent in 1972).[10] Nearly 20 percent of the teachers handling these sensitive situations are new-hire teachers.[11] One of the reasons for the high percentage of new hires, of course, is the frequent turnover in teachers; the average teacher earns about $50,000 per year, which in constant dollars has remained essentially unchanged over the last fifteen years.[12]

The dramatic increase in diversity in the nation's public schools leads some critics to declare that the increasing segregation of schools creates, in effect, "apartheid schools" where at least 99 percent of the students are minorities.[13] According to Jonathan Kozol, author of *The Shame of the Nation,* "The average African-American and Latino 12th grader currently reads at the same level as the average white seventh grader."[14]

The segregated schools tend to be in the cities of the Northeast and Midwest while the suburbs of those cities are more racially balanced. The *Christian Science Monitor* points out that segregated schools tend to be "highly correlated with such things as school performance and the ability to attract teachers."[15] These students fall victim to what former President Bush called, "The soft bigotry of low expectations."

Two schools in the Chicago area switched classrooms as an experiment.[16] Harper High School (in a low-income area of Chicago) graduates 40 percent of its students; Neuqua Valley (in high-income suburban Naperville) graduates 99 percent of its students. Harper's students score dramatically and appallingly poorer on standardized tests. In reading, Neuqua students score 78 percent to Harper's 16 percent; in science, Neuqua students score 76 percent to Harper's 1.5 percent; in math, Neuqua students score 77 percent to Harper's .5 percent. In addition, Neuqua "offered an Olympic-sized pool, gym and fitness center, an award winning music department, a huge computer lab, and a rigorous course curriculum." The students from both schools were shocked at the disparities between the two schools.

Finding similar disparities in school facilities, the Washington, DC, City Council designated over a billion dollars to modernize school buildings over the next decade. Not everyone is convinced that the money will ever actually get to the school repairs. The District of Columbia already spends more per pupil than almost any other school district in the nation—close to $25,000 per child[17]—on a par with tuition at the exclusive Sidwell Friends, the private school Chelsea Clinton attended and where the Obama girls now go to school. Yet, the DC schools consistently rank among the poorest in the nation with run-down facilities and bloated central management. The range in education spending is huge: New York and New Jersey spend $13,780 annually per pupil compared to Utah, which spends the least per pupil annually at $5,516.[18]

The Fordham Foundation report summarized the nation's education situation in a November 2006 press release: "Half of American states 'miss the bus' on vital education goals." The Fordham report found that only eight states had achieved what they called "even moderate success" over the past fifteen years in improving poor and minority students' scores on reading, mathematics, and science. Fordham officials noted that non-needy white students scored a "not-so-shabby B" on the same rating scales.[19] However, only 7 to 8 percent of African-American 8th graders are at or above the proficient level in science and math whereas 38 to 39 percent of white students are at those levels.[20] What is their conclusion? "Tough-minded education reforms tend to get results. Strong curricular content, real accountability and expanded parental choice can help raise the achievement of our neediest students."[21]

But education begins in the home, and basic language skills and literacy development depend upon parents reading to their children. The rate at which parents read to pre-school children in America fluctuates: in 1993 over half (53 percent) of the nation's children were read to on a daily basis by a family member, 54 percent in 1999, and 60 percent in 2005.[22] No one will be surprised by the fact that the higher the mother's education, the more likely she is to read to her children (72 percent of college-educated mothers read to their children, compared to only 41 percent of mothers with less than a high school diploma). White and Asian parents are more likely than black or Hispanic parents to read to their children (white, 68 percent; Asian, 66 percent, black, 50 percent, and Hispanic, 45 percent). Likewise, parents who are better-off financially read to their children more than poorer parents (parents at 200 percent over poverty, 65 percent; below poverty level, 50 percent). Again, it comes as no surprise that children are read to more often in two-parent families than in a single-parent home (62 percent in two-parent homes compared to 53 percent in single-parent homes). Parents in the Northeast (66 percent), Midwest (62 percent), and West (61 percent) are more likely to read to their children than parents in the South (56 percent). [23]

American children's progress in mathematics and reading is assessed at grades 4, 8, and 12 by the National Assessment of Educational Progress (NAEP). The NAEP assessment indicates students' skills in the specific subject areas as well as the national trends in these important educational skills. The mathematics achievements in 2005 for grades 4 and 8 showed improvement in academic achievement (from 1996 to 2007 the percentage of 4th graders at or above the basic level rose from 63 percent to 82 percent and the percentage of 8th graders at or above the basic level rose from 61 percent to 71 percent); the change in 12th-grade assessment could not be calculated because of changes in curriculum and standards. Sadly, children's reading scores from 1998 to 2007 showed only very slight improvement (for 4th graders) or a slight decline (for 8th graders). [24]

The Department of Education's standard graduation measure is derived from the status completion rate (i.e., the percentage of persons sixteen through twenty-four not enrolled in high school who do not have a high school credential) and this metric indicates school drop-out rates to be in a range of 12 to 15 percent; this result, however, is challenged as being far too low by a number of independent researchers. Christopher B. Swanson, in a 2008 report for the Education Research Center, estimated the graduation rate to be slightly less than 70 percent in 2003-2004. He estimated the graduation rates of African American students to be 53 percent and the rate for Hispanic students to be 58 percent. Even more depressing are his estimates of the graduation rates for the fifty major cities of the United States, seventeen of which are below 50 percent.[25] Paul E. Barton, in a 2005 report published by the Educational Testing Service, reports estimates of graduation rates in the range of 66 to 71 percent. Worse still is the fact his data indicate that the graduation rates fell in forty-four states from 1990 to 2000. [26]

While it is a cliché to state that education is vitally important to a child's future, the facts confirm that truth. A report by Princeton University and the Brookings Institution estimates that a high school dropout in the United States "will earn nearly a quarter of a million dollars less over his lifetime than a high school graduate that completes no further education." Further, they report that the aggregated losses from eighteen-year-old dropouts totals up to $200 billion.[27]

The publication, in 1983, of *A Nation at Risk* informed the nation that our children are not learning enough in school, and our schools are not effective enough in educating our children. Subsequently, high schools have instituted school reforms emphasizing increased academic rigor. As a result, in 2004 more than half of high school graduates have taken an advanced science course; over one-third, an honors-level English course; and over one-third, a foreign language course. In spite of this improvement in rigor, the NAEP scores for high school graduates show no improvement since the early 1980s.[28]

Years later, there was an attempt to evaluate the changes in education prompted by that controversial report. The public needed information about the return they received from the money invested in the recommended reforms. *A Nation Accountable: Twenty-Five Years after a Nation at Risk*, a report issued in April 2008, summed up the outcome of their efforts. "The Commission [National Commission on Excellence in Education] was disturbed by the easy courses and 'curricular smorgasbord' available to high school students. Unfortunately, this has not changed greatly. Both easy courses and this smorgasbord still remain, with diluted content now hiding behind inflated course names."[29]

Since the early 1980s, as the premium in earnings paid to college graduates as compared with high school graduates began rising, the percentage of the nation's high school graduates who go on to college has been on an upward trend with two-thirds enrolling in college in 2005 within twelve months of graduating as compared with only about one-half in 1980—with greater female enrollment beginning in about 1996.[30] However, in light of the inadequate preparation that many students have received in high school, it is not all that surprising that only about 25-30 percent of American citizens have ultimately earned a college degree or higher.[31]

In some measurements of student achievement, schools are flunking out. The national average awarded by the Fordham Foundation is a D, and no state earned a grade higher than a D+.[32] States appear to be working hard to merely keep up with the federal requirements. Specifically, as already mentioned, schools are doing better in teaching math, but progress in reading and science remains static.

School districts are trying numerous ways to address the problems in the nation's schools. One successful attempt to provide quality education is Charter Schools—publicly funded schools that are run like private schools with accountability and performance standards. There are now over four thousand charter schools across the nation. One of the most successful charter school efforts is the Harlem Children's Zone schools in New York City where students enter via a lottery. The schools operate under a strict philosophy of *in loco parentis* which they implement by "creating a disciplined, orderly and demanding counterculture to inculcate middle-class values." They also "pay meticulous attention to behavior and attitudes" and are "rigorous and college-focused." The typical student enters in the sixth grade with math and verbal ability scores in the 39th percentile among New York City students. By eighth grade the typical student was in the 74th percentile in math and 53rd percentile in verbal ability. These improvements are unprecedented and they eliminated the black-white achievement gap. Some educators are calling the success "the equivalent of curing cancer."[33]

Discouraged over mediocre schools, ill-equipped teachers pushing radical ideologies—more concerned with condoms, abortion, and sexual orientation than on reading, writing, and arithmetic—that create an increasingly hostile environment for those holding traditional values, many parents are taking over their children's education. About one-third of the nations' students who have left the public schools report having done so because of the negative "environment" and because of parental desire to "provide religious or moral instruction."[34]

Virtual education and distance learning are becoming popular options. Over one-third of the nation's schools offer the option of students enrolling in distance-learning courses. As a result, about 9 percent of all schools offer some form of distance learning and about 15 percent of rural schools provide distance-education options.[35]

Many parents are turning to educational savings accounts as a way to enrich their child's public-school education. Federal law, under the Coverdell Education Savings Account Program, enables parents to save for their children's education with their after-tax dollars earning interest if they are applied to specific educational opportunities including tutoring, summer school, and enrichment programs, as well as traditional K-12 schooling and higher education.

More and more education and policy experts are recommending school choice as a way to improve the education of the nation's children. While rare just decades ago, millions of parents today can benefit from public policies that allow them to choose their children's schools. While nearly 75 percent of the nation's children attend government-assigned schools, Dan Lips, Education Analyst at the Heritage Foundation, said, "Approximately 150,000 children are using publicly funded scholarships to attend private schools."[36] The private school choice option is open to students in only thirteen states and, during the Bush administration, the District of Columbia, but other states are currently considering such programs. Expanding the school choice option is only a beginning to education reform in the United States, but it is a major step forward in motivating all schools to provide high-performing educational environments for the nation's children.

When I was a public school teacher, my colleagues and I used to laugh at the new jargon introduced periodically as a "reform" of the public schools. In the intervening years, little has changed except for regular infusions of new jargon. Reform is not complicated; in fact, it is very simple. First, parents need to be able to choose the best schools for their children. Second, high standards of achievement need to be set and the school held accountable for reaching those standards. Third, a solid, rich curriculum taught by well-trained, interesting, and knowledgeable teachers is necessary. Fourth, education needs to focus on children's well-documented educational needs rather than the whims of educators or the demands of the teacher's unions.[37]

It is long past time, however, for everyone to realize that schools cannot do it all. We continue to pour money into programs and policies that focus on the "four walls of the classroom," yet we know that money, computers, and standards of learning will inevitably fail unless we restore the "essential ingredient"—parents. We established the Head Start program in the 1960s in recognition of the fact that some children were lagging behind at school because they were not getting what they needed at home before entering school.[38] Now there are advocates for year-round schools and pre-kindergarten programs as another way to make up for the lack of family involvement that keeps so many students from achieving academically and prevents them from reaching their potential in life.

Three decades ago, many of the "boat people" who escaped Vietnam after the war immigrated to the United States. Most lived in the worst parts of our cities and their children attended the worst schools. Nevertheless, so many of those children excelled in school that in 1992 *Scientific American* researched the reason and found that the families so value education that after school the parents supervised their homework before the children could play or watch television.[39] Often, too, it is not just the extra support of parents that make the difference. Much of the difference is the unspoken, but obvious, value that is placed upon education by the family and community. Children work to be good at what is valued by family.

Numerous reports and education experts point to the "disproportionate influence of factors beyond the control of educators in the performance of students."[40] In his book, *Sweating the Small Stuff: Inner-City Schools and the New Paternalism*,[41] David Whitman describes six inner-city secondary schools that are succeeding. The University Park Campus School (UPCS) in Worcester, one of Whitman's case-study schools, is the only public school in Massachusetts where every 10th grade student passed all the state tests in both English and math for two consecutive years.[42] What is their secret? They believe in self-discipline. They inculcate values like diligence, cleanliness, and manners, because they believe that those qualities are essential for future success in life. The school's founders stress the belief that it is primarily disorder, not violence or poverty, which prevents learning. Whitman's case-study schools operate *in loco parentis*; they take on part of the parental role in order to cultivate a work ethic and culture of achievement for the students. The school provides those things that too many students today lack: involved family, community support, cultural reinforcement, and accountability.

At some point, we will have to come to grips with the fact that a very large percentage of our students fail because they lack a father and mother who value, encourage, support, and reinforce their efforts to learn. A long-time teacher told me that the most discouraging factor for her is that too many parents expect very little from their children. Common sense tells us that there is no surer recipe for the child to lag behind in learning than having to contend with the strain and disruption of a broken, dysfunctional family where the parent or parents are so focused on themselves and their needs that they have little emotional energy to spare for the child's needs. Children have the best odds for success when somebody believes in them and expects the best from them. Good parenting provides the foundations for learning before children even begin their formal schooling. Before we can address the problems of American public education, those problems must be identified and "owned" by the public. Only then can we begin the massive overhaul of cultural values that will be necessary to close the educational gaps in America.

Notes

1.   Thomas D. Snyder, Sally A. Dillow, and Charlene M. Hoffman, U.S. Department of Education, National Center for Education Statistics, *Digest of Education Statistics, 2007,* (Washington, DC, 2008): 14, Table 3, and 44, Table 26, http://nces.ed.gov/pubsearch/pubsinfo.asp?pubid=2008022 (accessed February 15, 2009); spending per child and percentage change calculated by the author.
2.   Michael Planty, William Hussar, Thomas Snyder, Stephen Provasnik, Grace Kena, Rachel Dinkes, Angelina KewalRamani, and Jana Kemp, U.S. Department of Education, National Center for Education Statistics, *The Condition of Education, 2008,* (Washington, DC, 2008): 103, Table 12-1, http://nces.ed.gov/Pubsearch/pubsinfo.asp?pubid=2008031 (accessed February 15, 2009).

3.   "The Oprah Winfrey Show," "Failing Grade," April 11, 2006, Screen 1, http://www. oprah.com/slideshow/oprahshow/oprahshow1_ss_20060411/10 (accessed February 1, 2008).

4.   Patrick Gonzales, Trevor Williams, Leslie Jocelyn, Stephen Roey, David Kastberg, and Summer Brenwald, U.S. Department of Education, National Center for Education Statistics, *Highlights From TIMSS 2007: Mathematics and Science Achievement of U.S. Fourth-and Eight-Grade Students in an International Context,* (Washington, DC, 2008): B-2, Appendix B, http://nces.ed.gov/Pubsearch/pubsinfo. asp?pubid=2009001 (accessed February 15, 2009).

5.   "Winfrey," "Failing Grade," Screen 2.

6.   U.S. Bureau of Labor Statistics, Current Population Survey, "Education pays... Education pays in higher earnings and lower unemployment rates," Employment Projection Program (last modified April 15, 2008), http://www.bls.gov/emp/ emptab7.htm. Percentages computed by the author.

7.   Jennifer Cheeseman Day and Eric C. Newburger, "The Big Payoff: Educational Attainment and Synthetic Estimates of Work-Life Earnings," Current Population Reports, Series P-23, no. 210 (Washington, DC: U.S. Bureau of the Census, July 2002): 4, http://www.census.gov/prod/2002pubs/p23-210.pdf (accessed February 15, 2009).

8.   *Digest of Education Statistics, 2007,* 13, Table 2.

9.   U.S. Department of Education, National Center for Education Statistics, "1.5 Million Homeschooled Students in the United States in 2007," *Issue Brief,* NCES 2009-030 (December 2008): 1, http://nces.ed.gov/pubs2009/2009030.pdf (accessed February 16, 2009).

10.   *The Condition of Education, 2008,* 85, Table 5-1.

11.   U.S. Department of Education, "Annual Report on American Schools Shows Growth, Diversity," press release, June 1, 2005, http://www.ed.gov/news/press-releases/2005/06/06012005.html (accessed February 1, 2009).

12.   *Digest of Education Statistics, 2007,* 109, Table 75.

13.   Adam Doster, "Resegregation of American schools is deepening," *The Raw Story,* January 26, 2008, http://rawstory.com/news/2007/Resegregation_of_American_schools_deepening_0126.html (accessed February 1, 2008).

14.   "Winfrey," "Failing Grade," Screens 3-4.

15.   As quoted in Doster, "Resegregation of American schools."

16.   "Winfrey," "Failing Grade," Screen 12.

17.   Andrew J. Coulson, "The Real Cost of Public Schools," editorial, *The Washington Post,* April 6, 2008.

18.   U.S. Department of Education, National Center for Education Statistics, National Assessment of Educational Progress State Assessment, updated October 18, 2006, http://nces.ed.gov/nationsreportcard/states/ (accessed January 19, 2009).

19.   Jennifer Leischer, "Many Kids Still Left Behind—States Show Weak Gains for Needy Students," The Thomas B. Fordham Foundation, press release, November 1, 2006, http://www.edexcellence.net/detail/news.cfm?news_id=417 (accessed January 20, 2009).

20.   *The Fordham Report 2006: How Well Are States Educating Our Neediest Children?* The Thomas B. Fordham Foundation, November 1, 2006: 3, http://www. edexcellence.net/doc/TFR06FULLREPORT.PDF (accessed January 20, 2009).

21.   Leischer, "Many Kids Still Left Behind."

22.   U.S. Federal Interagency Forum on Child and Family Statistics, *America's Children in Brief: Key National Indicators of Well-Being, 2008,* (Washington, DC: GPO, July 2008): 14, http://www.childstats.gov/pubs/index.asp (accessed February 15, 2009).

23. Ibid.
24. *The Condition of Education, 2008*, 103, Table 12-1 and 108, Table 13-1.
25. Christopher B. Swanson, "Cities in Crisis: A Special Analytic Report on High School Graduation," Editorial Projects in Education Research Center (April 1, 2008): 1 and 9.
26. Paul E. Barton, "One-Third of a Nation: Rising Dropout Rates and Declining Opportunities," Policy Information Center, Educational Testing Service (February 2005): 9 and 11, http://www.ets.org/Media/Research/pdf/PICONETHIRD.pdf.
27. Susanna Loeb, Cecilia Elena Rouse and Anthony Shorris, "Introducing the Issue," *The Future of Children* 17, no.1 (2007): 3.
28. U.S. Federal Interagency Forum on Child and Family Statistics, *America's Children in Brief: Key National Indicators of Well-Being, 2007,* (Washington, DC: GPO, July 2007): 54, http://www.childstats.gov/pdf/ac2007/ac_07.pdf (accessed February 15, 2009).
29. U.S. Department of Education, "A Nation Accountable: Twenty-five Years after a Nation at Risk," (Washington, DC, 2008): 4, *www.ed.gov/rschstat/research/pubs/risk25.html* (accessed February 15, 2009).
30. *Digest of Education Statistics, 2007*, 284-285, Table 192.
31. Day and Newburger, "The Big Payoff," 2.
32. *Fordham Report 2006*, 13.
33. David Brooks, "The Harlem Miracle," *The New York Times*, May 8, 2009. http://www.nytimes.com/2009/05/08/opinion/08brooks.html
34. Dan Lips, "School Choice: Policy Development and National Participation Estimates in 2007-2008," Heritage Foundation, *Backgrounder Report,* No. 2102 (January 31, 2008): 7, http://www.heritage.org/Research/education/bg2125.cfm (accessed February 15, 2009).
35. J. Carl Setzer and Laurie Lewis, U.S. Department of Education. National Center for Education Statistics, *Distance Education Courses for Public Elementary and Secondary School Students: 2002–03,* (Washington, DC, 2005): 4-8, http://nces.ed.gov/pubs2005/2005010.pdf (accessed February 16, 2009).
36. Lips, "School Choice," Executive Summary.
37. These are an adaptation of the goals found in the *Fordham Report 2006*, 9-10.
38. W.D. Clarkson, "Schools can't do it all," *Roanoke Times & World News*, January 11, 2009, found at *HighBeam Research,* http://www.highbeam.com (accessed February 8, 2009).
39. Ibid.
40. Walt Gardner, "Schools alone can't close achievement gap," *The Record* (Bergen County, NJ) July 19, 2008, found at *HighBeam Research,* http://www.highbeam.com (accessed February 8, 2009).
41. David Whitman, *Sweating the Small Stuff: Inner-City Schools and the New Paternalism,* (Washington, DC: Thomas B. Fordham Institute Press, 2008).
42. Joel Schwartz, "Pater Knows Best: The quest for success in inner-city schools," *The Weekly Standard*, February 2, 2009, 38.

If our American Way of Life Fails the Child, It Fails Us All.
—Pearl S. Buck

Conclusion

The Moral Dimension of Children's Well-Being

Prominently displayed in the lobby of the Hubert Humphrey Building, which houses the U.S. Department of Health and Human Services, there is a large bronze sculpture of a woman playing with her three children entitled, "Happy Mother." No father required. Nothing is more illustrative of the problems addressed in this book than that sculpture. The false values embodied in it—that a woman alone with her children comprises the archetype of happy motherhood—are at the root of forty years of failure by the research communities and the federal government to honestly report on the problems that are undermining the foundations of the American family and devastating to American children's well-being.

The preceding chapters have stressed a child's need for a married mother and father; his or her need for the protection and nurturing of a family to instill those qualities that will enable the child to become an ethical and productive citizen; and the need for society to support, rather than thwart, the family's efforts to provide a strong moral and spiritual foundation for children. Public opinion polls reveal that most Americans believe that the disintegration of our nation's moral standards and quality of life have contributed to the breakdown of marriage and the family. Americans also believe that the negative effects of that downward spiral particularly influence children's well-being.

Some commentators argue that those who focus on the breakdown of the family as the source of societal and children's problems are missing the point; they argue that our individual and corporate problems stem from a breakdown in morality. How can the two be separated? It's a chicken and egg argument. Since morality is molded at home, the breakdown of the family inevitably leads to a breakdown in morality, and vice versa. This book examines the many ways that values, beliefs, and attitudes are important in shaping perspectives about family structure and summarizes the research findings— which are consistent with the lessons and wisdom of the ages—as to what constitutes the best environment for children's growth and "well-being." In this final chapter, we look specifically at how the moral and religious underpinnings of American culture impact the other influences on children. We take the perspective of the late Father Richard John Neuhaus, who argued, "the great majority of Americans believe that morality is derived from religious faith and religious tradition."[1]

First, let us briefly review the impact that the changes in family structure and cultural disintegration have had on various aspects of children's well-being, and why it is necessary for society to promote healthy, traditional marriages. Millions of Americans are troubled by the dismissal of marriage as an outdated and dying institution. One cultural critic said it well, "Broken families mean broken societies, broken individuals and broken children. The research on this is as overwhelming as it is alarming."[2] The family is the glue that holds our communities, our society, our world together. Because that glue is weakening, the moral foundation necessary for a humane, civilized, functional society is crumbling all around us. When the inviolable family becomes, not a sacred spiritual unit, but nothing more than "any group of people living together," there is no moral source to establish the household rules or to be the final authority in terms of standards of behavior. The children, then, are left to find their own way—ill-prepared to cope on their own—and drifting aimlessly in an "anything goes" culture, often with crippling consequences.

Many Americans see the breakdown of the family for what it is: a national crisis that endangers children by making them vulnerable to a lifetime of negative consequences.[3]

As Bill Bennett wrote, "Most of our social pathologies—crime, imprisonment rates, welfare, alcohol and drug abuse, sexually transmitted diseases—all are manifestations, direct and indirect, of the crack-up of the modern American family."[4] Parents and other citizens are concerned about the "huge price" that all of us are paying for the decline in marriage and the breakdown of the family. We are paying that price "in higher taxes, in costly government programs, in more crime and juvenile delinquency, in declining cities and schools, and in countless immeasurable ways—from losing a sense of personal safety and happiness to watching our society become defined by 'rejection.'"[5] There is yet an additional price we pay that goes to a far more intimate level: the broken personal relationships and all the anger and bitterness that accompany a betrayal of trust, the emptiness when the priceless sense of connectedness is ripped to shreds.

The family is a child's training ground for becoming an ethical, moral, and empathic person who will become a contributor to a good and prosperous society. Most moral qualities—such as a sense of responsibility and self-control, caring and respect for others, delayed gratification, compassion, sense of fairness, generosity, empathy, and honesty, among others—are not just learned rationally through instruction. For the most part, they are absorbed—inculcated, if you will—through seeing them modeled in everyday family life. In order to learn those moral qualities, children need to see those characteristics acted out with consistency in the interactions, reactions, and relationships of the adults around them. Yet, too many children are growing up without ever seeing moral authority in an adult. How can they learn to trust or treat others fairly when they have little opportunity to see adults exhibit those qualities? Children too often miss out on critical moral development because they do not have the benefit of seeing essential moral qualities lived out in the efforts of a mother and father doing the hard work required to keep their commitments to each other and to their children.

The family is a child's first society; the family needs to be whole and healthy, because it is where children learn, for good or for ill, how to respect other people and how to live their lives. And that is how most parents want it to be. In hundreds of interviews with parents, Dana Mack, an affiliate scholar with the Institute for American Values, asked parents who, for example, should teach their children about sex. The parents overwhelmingly thought that was the parents' responsibility because they would put the information in a "moral context" that the schools cannot and will not do.[6] Nevertheless, as Dr. Mack points out:

> Parental autonomy has been supplanted by the tyranny of so-called experts in psychology, education, law and social science. Under their sway, the very institutions that could help parents to shore up their embattled authority—schools, courts, social service agencies, even religious institutions—actively thwart them instead.[7]

When the family disintegrates and marriage declines, the inevitable result is erosion in the quality of community life and a corresponding breakdown in social cohesion and institutional morality. The long-term British study, mentioned earlier in this book, noted the disturbing results of the loss of traditional marriage and family in that nation. Children are suffering because parents are "too self-absorbed; too focused on their own self-fulfillment; and too self-centered." As a result, Britain has "lost its moral compass" wrote *The Daily Mail*. The British people "no longer share a set of common values" and that lack of moral unity "cost the nation its sense of community."[8]

Those who care about the future of America and the well-being of our children should carefully consider the implications of this analysis of the British experience. A casual look at the world that our children inhabit reveals that the values vacuum has been filled by those who disparage traditional morality, virtue, and good manners with an end result of moral decay and worse, as vulgarity spirals downward into viciousness and base immorality. Nowhere is this showcased more blatantly than in "The Jerry Springer Show" and its imitators; though in a less crude form, we also have talk shows and political discourse where opponents go beyond disagreement to show contempt and mockery. The participants often dehumanize opponents and cruelly call anyone who disagrees with their position vulgar and demeaning names;[9] some of the comments posted on the Internet by supposedly rational people use vile gutter language to attack those who argue for traditional values and morality. Most parents prefer to shield their children from that kind of crudity and vulgarity as much as is feasible; but, according to a CNN/USAToday/Gallup Poll, nearly 80 percent of the American public believe that "the negative influences of today's culture are nearly impossible to avoid." Anyone who has contact with television programming, the movies, or the Internet is well aware of the extent to which Americans live on a "steady diet of hedonism and amorality."[10]

Contemporary entertainment enjoyed by children, teens, and young adults gives us a glimpse into what has thrived in the values vacuum. The late Steve Allen accused television and pop culture of exposing our children "to a barrage of images and words that threaten not only to rob them of normal innocence, but also to distort their view of reality and even undermine their character growth."[11]

Rock music and pop stars are notorious for pushing the envelope with a hedonistic lifestyle and songs with misogynistic, crude, coarse, and often shockingly gross and vile lyrics. Cartoons, popular movies, and television programs portray parents as out-of-touch, old-fashioned, and prudish; defiant and rebellious children talk back to teachers and parents; patriotism, family traditions, and religion are treated with disdain. Children are regularly bombarded by derogatory media images of adults who respect or exemplify traditional moral values; such adults are typically held in contempt, subtly mocked, or openly ridiculed as old-fashioned, prudish, and out-of-touch. Adults in positions of authority are often portrayed as buffoons that no one respects or admires. A favorite tactic of television situation comedies is to poke fun at bumbling, inept, and out-of-touch fathers.

This frequent portrayal of disrespect for the family is especially harmful for children's well-being because it calls into question their innocent faith that their parents know what is good and are able to keep them safe. By weakening children's respect for their parents and other adult authority figures these messages encourage covert or overt rebellion, create a false sense of freedom and tempt inexperienced youths to make far-reaching decisions or take huge risks with potentially costly consequences. When their bad choices create troubled or broken relationships, anger and alienation, they begin to taste, at too young an age, what it means to be isolated, unconnected and alone in facing the perplexities of life.

One of the most tragic aspects of our lack of positive adult male role models in our increasingly fatherless culture is that "children without fathers of their own seek ersatz fathers. Their search for parental authority and affirmation often leads to participation in gangs or in adolescent sexual experimentation. Children looking for love in all the wrong places take out their frustrations and anger by wreaking havoc on society."[12] That sounds remarkably like a fulfillment of the warning that came from Lenin, "The best revolutionary is a youth devoid of morals." Many cultural critics would argue that our father-absent homes are producing a generation devoid of both morals and human decency, many of whom become predators that threaten the safety of communities and neighborhoods.

A remarkable, astute wake-up call decrying America's cultural decline was sounded with Judge Robert H. Bork's publication of *Slouching towards Gomorrah*. He declared, "A nation's moral life is the foundation of its culture."[13] Judge Bork described the 1960s as a time when radical students, characterized by Harold Rosenberg as a "herd of independent minds,"[14] trampled America's "bourgeois morality" to do "serious, lasting, and perhaps permanent damage to valuable institutions, socially stabilizing attitudes, and essential standards."[15] Father Neuhaus described the influence of the 1960s:

> A number of things happened back in the 1960s with the war on poverty and related efforts that contributed to the truly alarming state of alienation of the urban underclass today. Charles Murray and others pointed to the system of incentives and disincentives that discouraged work or seeking work among a sector of the poverty population in America as one factor in this alienation.

Another often overlooked factor is the role of the elite culture of the 1960s, seventies, and eighties that threw itself into a spasm of myriad liberationisms: sexual liberations, liberation from the family as an oppressive institution, gender liberation, etc. These liberationisms, which may indeed have been experienced as liberating by economically secure and socially stable Americans, were absolutely devastating for the very poor whose lives were in no way stable or secure.[16]

Prior to World War II, a consensus on moral values served as a brake on non-traditional family structures and non-marital sexual behavior. Certainly, there were some people who flaunted those restraints and others who discretely did as they pleased without regard to the prevailing moral boundaries that shaped social norms. Nevertheless, the socially acceptable attitudes and behaviors were consistent with Judeo-Christian principles and values, and they were adhered to and respected or at least given lip service by the majority of citizens.

During the post-WWII period, there was a substantial weakening of the old consensus on moral values that formerly shaped social norms and censured nontraditional living arrangements (e.g., cohabitation) and other instances of non-marital sexual behavior.[17] The increasing impotence of moral restraints, particularly in the anonymity of the big city life, generated growing problems in all of the areas that we focus on in this book. As a consequence, there was ever increasing pressure by some to institute government policies to "solve the problems."

Policymakers and social service personnel sought to fill the vacuum resulting from the withering of social institutions that had traditionally shaped and supported men in their role of father. They were concerned about the damage resulting from the impaired relationships between fathers and their children; thus, they looked for ways for the government to provide programs and policies to supply the needs of single mother households. One initiative was the effort to determine paternity. That initiative was coupled with a substantial effort to ensure that noncustodial parents (primarily fathers) pay child support. It is worth noting that, following the decline in marriage, the original means by which the community provided legal rights and protections to the child, it became necessary to create alternative legal mechanisms to accomplish these ends, namely, certificates acknowledging paternity and court orders to pay child support.

A well-placed mother in the 1990s famously declared, "It takes a village to raise a child." This book presents the data needed to answer Dr. Phil's essential question, "How's that working for you?"

With the decline of marriage has come the gradual destruction of the social standards that emanate from a community populated by strong families; their preservation in the culture and community has, consequently, suffered substantially as the percentage of families headed by a married coupled has steadily declined. Dozens of the problems plaguing our nation are rooted in the disappearance from everyday life of essential moral codes. Their absence has been ruinous to vulnerable children who are the ones most devastated by the social engineers and "the armies of bureaucrats and theory-wielding experts" who "wreaked havoc on society."[18]

The national media's misleading portrayal of broken families and its obsession with the promotion of vogue lifestyles has led to a weakened understanding of what family is all about. For centuries, we have understood that "family" consists of related individuals bound together by marriage, birth, blood, and/or adoption. Family is a unique relationship characterized by love and commitment, rather than by mere convenience and-experimentation. Is anyone surprised that as the nation has changed its definition of family, the number of vulnerable children has also increased?

Since 1996, the amount of detailed information on marriage and divorce has been greatly curtailed making it more difficult to assess the effects of family structure on children. The National Center for Health Statistics (NCHS) no longer compiles and publishes detailed annual data on marriages and divorces. In the short form of the Year 2000 Census questionnaire, which went to 80 percent of the population, the government did not ask about marital status. Without information on the basic and fundamental characteristics of family formation and dissolution, perspectives on trends will be hard to gain, and researchers will be less able to analyze the impact of family breakdown on the nation's culture and society.

We know that the failure to raise children in healthy families costs society a very high price. When an unmarried woman gives birth to a child, the state makes every effort to persuade her to sign a document declaring the paternity of the child. If she does not co-operate with the government's efforts to establish the paternity of her child, she cannot qualify for financial assistance should the need arise. Of course, the expense of raising children is such that there is a very high probability that the need for assistance will arise for unmarried mothers. If paternity is disputed, genetic testing is required to resolve the question. Also, without legally establishing paternity, the courts cannot issue a child-support award to the mother. The federal government spends more than $31 million annually on paternity tests. If necessary, a woman is required to obtain a court order to enforce child support. The government spends over $4 *billion* annually administering an increasingly intrusive system of child-support enforcement. What a gross alternative we've engineered as a substitute for marriage. If this is progress, who needs it?

What are the possibilities for a regeneration of traditional values? A few years back, Wendy Shalit published a defense of sexual restraint, *A Return to Modesty*, which was well received among college students and became a popular subject of media talk shows. Danielle Crittenden's *What Our Mothers Didn't Tell Us* launched a frontal attack on the assumptions made by the last generation of feminists about women's roles in the workplace versus their very important roles as wives and mothers. This book had similar popularity.

In addition to publications like the Shalit and Crittenden books, there are powerful national organizations working at the public policy level. Concerned Women for America, the nation's largest public policy women's organization founded thirty years ago by Beverly LaHaye, works alongside the Family Research Council, the American Family Association and others, to restore Judeo-Christian values and strengthen the family in America. CWA provides social science based research and commentary through its think tank, The Beverly LaHaye Institute. Likewise, Promise Keepers and the fatherhood movement challenge men to take responsibility for their families.

But the fate of marriage still hangs in the balance. If the clear pro-marriage message of these organizations fails to reach the culture in a transforming manner, then our discoveries and even belief in the positive benefits of marriage will be for naught. In a survey of the attitudes of high school seniors about marriage, the National Marriage Survey discovered that although a vast majority of students said that having a good marriage is "extremely important," fewer expressed confidence that *their* marriage would last a lifetime. If marriage is seen as merely one of many viable family structures, or as an unattainable ideal, the inherent aspiration for a good marriage will not have a revitalizing effect on the next generation.

Since cohabitation is more and more prevalent as the first "living together" experience for couples seeking to establish a bond, we must understand the misinformation that has created this tendency as well as understand the repercussions of this trend. The fact that young people persist in longing for marriage even in the face of all that we have noted is encouraging; even so, it is absolutely necessary to equip young people to act responsibly on this wish for marriage in order to make the goal become reality. Since many young people grow up with very poor examples of marriage, or the good examples seem elusive in their own circumstances, we need to increase young peoples' understanding of commitment, provide couples as examples in how to build a marriage, encourage marriage counseling at the grassroots level (particularly through faith-based initiatives) and continue to erase the idea that divorce is a good choice for struggling couples.

Since the Welfare Reform Movement of 1996, there has been a growing realization that public policy has a significant effect on the marital choices of the populace. It is important that we not only encourage a more positive attitude toward marriage, but also provide political and economic policies that favor marriage and create strong incentives for it. Also we must revive those values in our society that discourage sexual promiscuity, single parenthood, cohabitation, and other lifestyles that threaten traditional marriage.

Democracy as a form of government depends on the moral character of its people. When we cease to be a moral people, the freedoms that are afforded by democracy will not long survive, nor will democracy itself. Already, our children cannot play outside without supervision. Most of them cannot walk to and from school alone. They cannot run down the street to play with a friend after dark. The freedoms that were commonplace for children short decades ago, when the more moral national climate made such freedoms safe, are increasingly rare.

The late Russell Kirk called our national cultural decay a "bent time"[19] and made a persuasive case for reestablishing the "permanent things" as the foundation for people's lives and interactions with others. Dr. Tim LaHaye, co-author of the popular *Left Behind* novels, reasoned that those permanent things are invisible in today's culture because the public is "not exposed to the biblical alternative."[20] In the absence of attractive and persuasive alternatives, the forces of corruption prevail; like a fire that burns itself out if no effort is made to add fuel, the moral standards of one generation will expire if they are not vigorously taught to the children of the next. Society's moral force will subside if we do not teach the values that keep it strong and vital.

Without the compass of truth and faith, there is nothing to protect our children from deception. James Russell Lowell (1819-1891) a poet of the Romantic period used his poetry for reform and was a leader in the slavery abolitionist movement. His assessment of his era could easily apply to those in our bent time where people want to make their own rules rather than "bend the knee" in recognition of God. Lowell wrote that it is important to know not merely "what things exist, but what they mean; it is not memory but judgment." Rather than be one of those who move with the herd of independent minds, Lowell made our challenge clear and stark:

> Once to every man and nation
> Comes the moment to decide
> In the strife of Truth with Falsehood
> For the good or evil side...
> Then it is the brave man who chooses
> While the coward stands aside...
> Though the cause of evil prosper
> Yet the truth alone is strong.

This book presents both the challenges we face in protecting our children and the strength of truth in facing those challenges.

On a recent airplane flight I sat beside a college student named Jason who initiated a conversation. When he found out that I tracked data about marriage, he said to me, "I don't believe in true love anymore." I said, "Oh, Jason, that makes me really sad. Why would you say that?" He replied that his sister had lived with her boyfriend about five years, got married, and was divorced about a year later. He said, "I was so shocked." "You know, Jason," I responded, "that doesn't shock me at all because the data bears this out. Most cohabiting relationships do lead to divorce. They don't lead to a happy marriage." He said, "Well, I can tell you this. I am not ever going to get married. My parents are divorced, now my sister is, and I don't know anybody who is happily married."

Jason is like so many young people; they've never seen a happy marriage as a model for their future.

We caught a brief glimpse of how family breakdown played out in one young woman's life recently at a restaurant. Our waitress was an almost-surly teen who, at first, appeared to have a speech impediment. It turned out to be simply the challenge of trying to talk with a large metal stud in her tongue. Toward the end of the meal, after establishing rapport. I asked her why she had the stud. She replied, surprisingly with a smile, that she got it when she was fifteen to make a statement to the effect that she was a "semi-bad" girl. I didn't press for an explanation of what constituted semi-bad. Instead, I asked what her mother had to say about the stud. Her reply was, "Oh, she's cool with it." And her dad? He's "irrelevant." But then she quickly and rather fiercely added, "Oh, he is around."

She most definitely wanted us to understand that, even though her parents were not together, she was not fatherless, that she did indeed have a father, and that they did make contact from time to time. But then as she amplified the details a bit, it became clear that, for the most part, the contact—when it occurred—was because she initiated it. "I call him sometimes," but, "he doesn't matter; my mom is the one that counts."

She is not a statistic; she is a lovely young woman who, sadly, can be described as emotionally malnourished. It is written all over her, especially in the way that she interacts with others. She is a living example of how our personhood is formed in our earliest childhood by those with whom we are connected or by those with whom no connection is possible. Life cannot be perfect, but life's hurts should not start where love ought to begin, and children should not be the ones most damaged by adult failures.

And, finally, we recently saw the kind of family model that should be commonplace, but is all too rare. On a recent Sunday morning, we arrived with our weekend guests at the Washington National Cathedral just as the service was beginning. We quickly found seats and almost immediately noticed the attractive family in the row directly in front of us. Despite their typical tourist attire, it gradually became apparent that this was not your average family visiting Washington to see the sights. After the service, when we were complimenting the parents on their well-mannered children, we learned that the family had journeyed to Washington for the burial of the wife's father in Arlington National Cemetery earlier in the week. Her father was a Vietnam veteran, and she proudly related the fact that he had won the Silver Star for valor in combat.

Seeing the couple with their three children formed a lasting image for our minds and hearts on that Sunday morning. For one thing, though they were not in a familiar setting and had no children's books or toys to keep them occupied, the two older children's quiet and respectful behavior spoke volumes about what they had been taught; they clearly had more than a little experience with being calm and orderly during Sunday worship. Snuggled in her carrier on the seat between the mother and father, the youngest child, an infant, slept undisturbed.

Anyone not watching closely would have missed the moment, but during an opening hymn, in a move as smooth as any quarterback's handoff to his running back, the father shifted the baby's carrier to his own seat and moved to stand by his wife. He handled the baby carrier with such deftness that it was clear the role of protector was ingrained; he was anything but inexperienced and awkward. Later on when the infant opened its incredibly bright eyes, the father, with sure hand, nudged the pacifier back into her mouth so gently that she fell back asleep almost immediately. It was wonderful to see a little one so obviously cherished that it was not discomforted in the least by all that was going on around her.

As the man moved alongside his wife, her hand moved to rest lightly on his forearm. Seeing the contact, I recognized it as yet another visible expression of the emotional bond that linked that family together. Such touches are simple expressions of love, but somehow they always warm our hearts and comfort our spirits.

Later, as the congregation stood to sing a hymn, the mother leaned toward the daughter, who appeared to be about six or seven years of age, and with her finger traced the location of the words to assist the daughter's fledgling efforts. When we sat back down, the father's arm came to rest lightly on the mother's back—not in showy ostentation or possession, but in an expression of the deep-seated human need to feel directly connected to those we love, something as natural and necessary as breathing.

Like a screensaver on a computer etching out an image, little by little as they worshipped, the separate signs merged together to form a clear picture of the relationship of this couple and their children. By the time the Eucharist was celebrated near the end of the service, I was not the least surprised—and inwardly applauded—when the father demurred at the usher's assurance that the baby would be all right if she were left sleeping in her seat while the parents took communion with the older children. Instead, with one strong hand, the dad lifted the carrier and held it by his side as the family moved forward to receive the elements. The infant was still fast asleep when they returned to their seats.

I remember very little about the sermon that morning, but the image of that family is still sharply focused in my memory. To my mind, the message of the morning was embodied in the strength and functionality of a grieving family who had come that day to worship despite their loss.

The love that the family obviously shared illustrates the ways in which a healthy, loving marriage protects the innocence of the family's children and ensures their well-being.

Notes

1. Richard John Neuhaus, "Religion's Role in Public Life," *The Acton Institute for the Study of Religion and Liberty*, 3, no. 5, (September/October, 1993), http://www. acton.org/publications/randl/rl_interview_92.php.
2. Bill Muehlenberg, "The Tragic Results of Marriage Breakdown and Family Fragmentation," *Culture Watch*, April 29, 2008, http://www.billmuehlenberg. com/2008/04/29/the-tragic-results-of-marriage-breakdown-and-family-fragmentation.
3. Ibid.
4. William J. Bennett, *The Broken Hearth: Reversing the Moral Collapse of the American Family*, (New York: Doubleday, 2001): Front Matter.
5. "Consequences of the Breakdown of Marriage," The Marriage and Family Foundation, 2009, http://www.marriagefamilyfoundation.org/consequences-of-the-breakdown-of-marriage.
6. Dana Mack, *The Assault on Parenthood: How our Culture Undermines the Family*, (New York, Simon and Shuster, 1997): p. 152.
7. Dana Mack, "The Assault on Parenthood," Front Flap.
8. David Wilkes, "Selfishness, Greed and Family Breakdown: Study's Damning Verdict on Modern Britain," *The Daily Mail*, April 20, 2008, http://www.dailymail. co.uk/news/article-560867/Selfishness-greed-family-breakdown-studys-damning-verdict-modern-Britain.
9. Michael Gerson, "Vulgarian at the Gate," *The Washington Post*, June 18, 2008, http://www.washingtonpost.com/wp-dyn/content/article/2008/06/17/ AR2008061702006.html.
10. Jerold Aust, "How Can You Help Restore the Disappearing Family?" *The Good News: A Magazine of Understanding,* July/August, 2008, http://www.gnmagazine. org/issues/gn77/help-restore-disappearing-family.htm.
11. Steve Allen, *Vulgarians at the Gate: Trash TV and Raunch Radio: Raising Standards of Popular Culture,* (New York: Prometheus Books, 2001): p. 18.
12. D. James Kennedy, Ph.D., "Breakdown of the Family," *Issues Tearing Our Nation's Fabric*, (Ft. Lauderdale, Florida, Coral Ridge Ministries, Updated July 13, 2002), http://www.leaderu.com/issues/fabric/chap03.html.
13. Robert H. Bork, *Slouching Towards Gomorrah*, (New York, Regan Books/HarperCollins, 1996): Back Cover.
14. Ibid., p. 30.
15. Ibid., p. 32.
16. Neuhaus, "Religion's Role in Public Life."
17. For an excellent historical summary, see Allan C. Carlson, *Conjugal America*, (Piscataway, N.J., Transaction Publishers, 2006): pp. 98-106.
18. Kennedy, "Breakdown of the Family."
19. James M. Kushiner, Editor, *Creed and Culture,* The Fellowship of St. James, (Wilmington, Delaware, ISI Books, Intercollegiate Studies Institute, 2003): p. xi.
20. David A. Noebel, *The Battle for Truth: Defending the Christian Worldview in the Marketplace of Ideas,* (Eugene, Oregon, Harvest House Publishers, 2001): Back Cover.

Index